FROM HELL *by Robert Bloch*

My name is Jack. **WITHDRAWN**
At least that's what I called myself in a letter and
a card to the Central News Agency. When I wrote
to the Whitechapel Vigilance Committee the address
I gave was "From Hell." I sent along half of a kidney
torn out of a victim and told them I fried and ate the
other half. No need for a signature because all London
knew it, all the world knew my name.

Between August 31st and November 9th, 1888,
I cut the throats of five women — and that wasn't all I cut.
Four died quickly on the streets, two of them within an hour on
the same night. The fifth one's life was knifed in her room and
there I took my own sweet time.

Mind you, the police were everywhere, and hundreds of
detectives on assignment from Scotland Yard. The whole city was
on the lookout, four million pairs of eyes searching the shadows.

But after that fifth murder I disappeared into those shadows
and they never found me. All they had was the nickname I'd given
them when I nicked the ladies.

Some said I was a doctor, a medical student, a slaughterhouse
worker, perhaps a boot-maker skillful with a knife. They were
suspicious of midwives who traveled the slum streets without
attracting attention; for the same reason they suspected the police.
Others thought I was a barrister named Druitt, a Russian
secret agent, a Yankee whose letters used American slang,
a murderer named Dr. Neill Cream, or even Queen Victoria's
own physician, Sir William Gull. The Queen herself had theories
about foreign sailors.

Wrong. Dead wrong. I fooled all London. And I could
fool them anywhere, even in Gotham City, if that's where I chose
to appear.

Batman?

Yes, I know the name. And perhaps he'll soon have reason
to remember yours truly,

JACK THE RIPPER

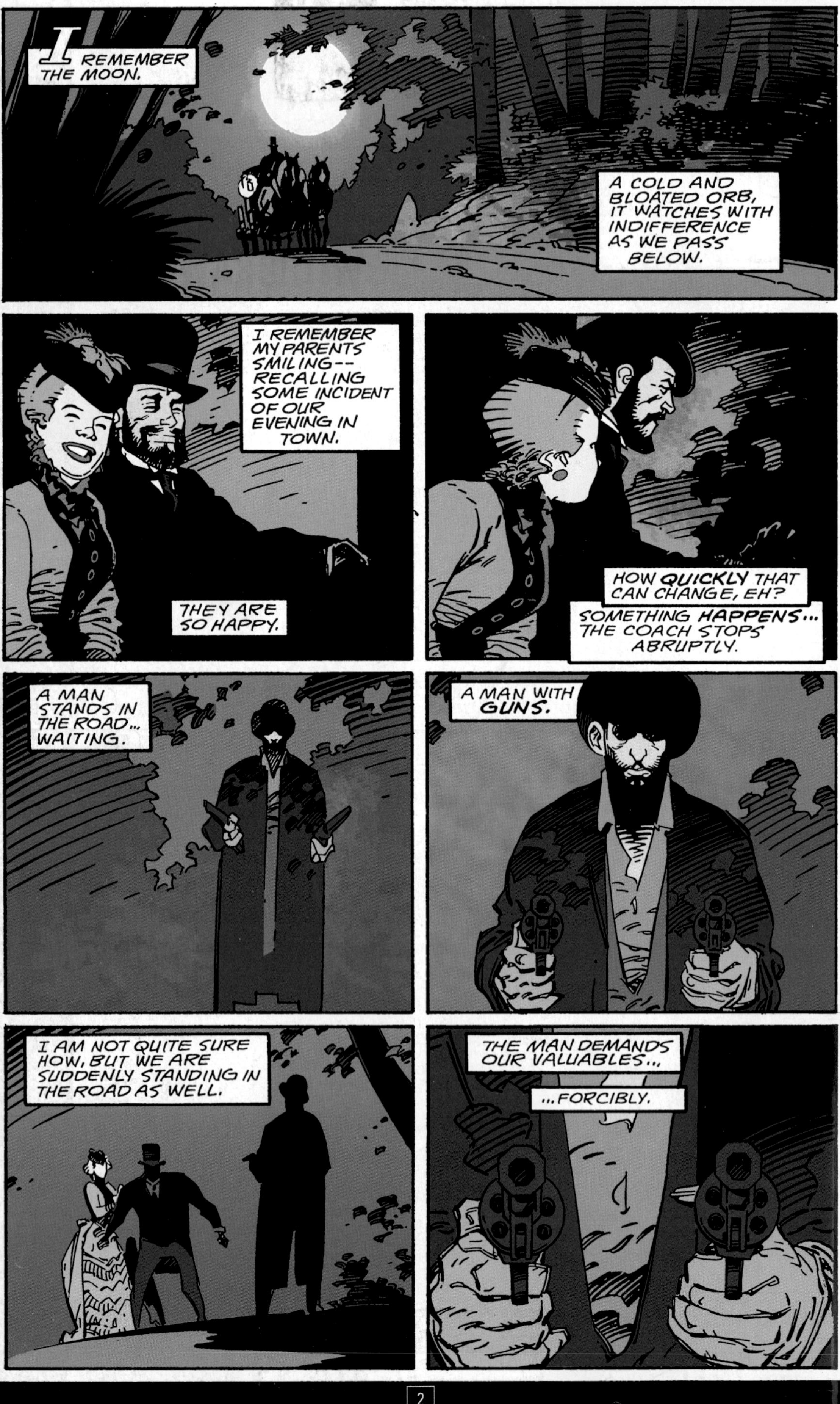
I REMEMBER THE MOON.
A COLD AND BLOATED ORB, IT WATCHES WITH INDIFFERENCE AS WE PASS BELOW.
I REMEMBER MY PARENTS SMILING-- RECALLING SOME INCIDENT OF OUR EVENING IN TOWN.
THEY ARE SO HAPPY.
HOW QUICKLY THAT CAN CHANGE, EH?
SOMETHING HAPPENS... THE COACH STOPS ABRUPTLY.
A MAN STANDS IN THE ROAD... WAITING.
A MAN WITH GUNS.
I AM NOT QUITE SURE HOW, BUT WE ARE SUDDENLY STANDING IN THE ROAD AS WELL.
THE MAN DEMANDS OUR VALUABLES...
...FORCIBLY.

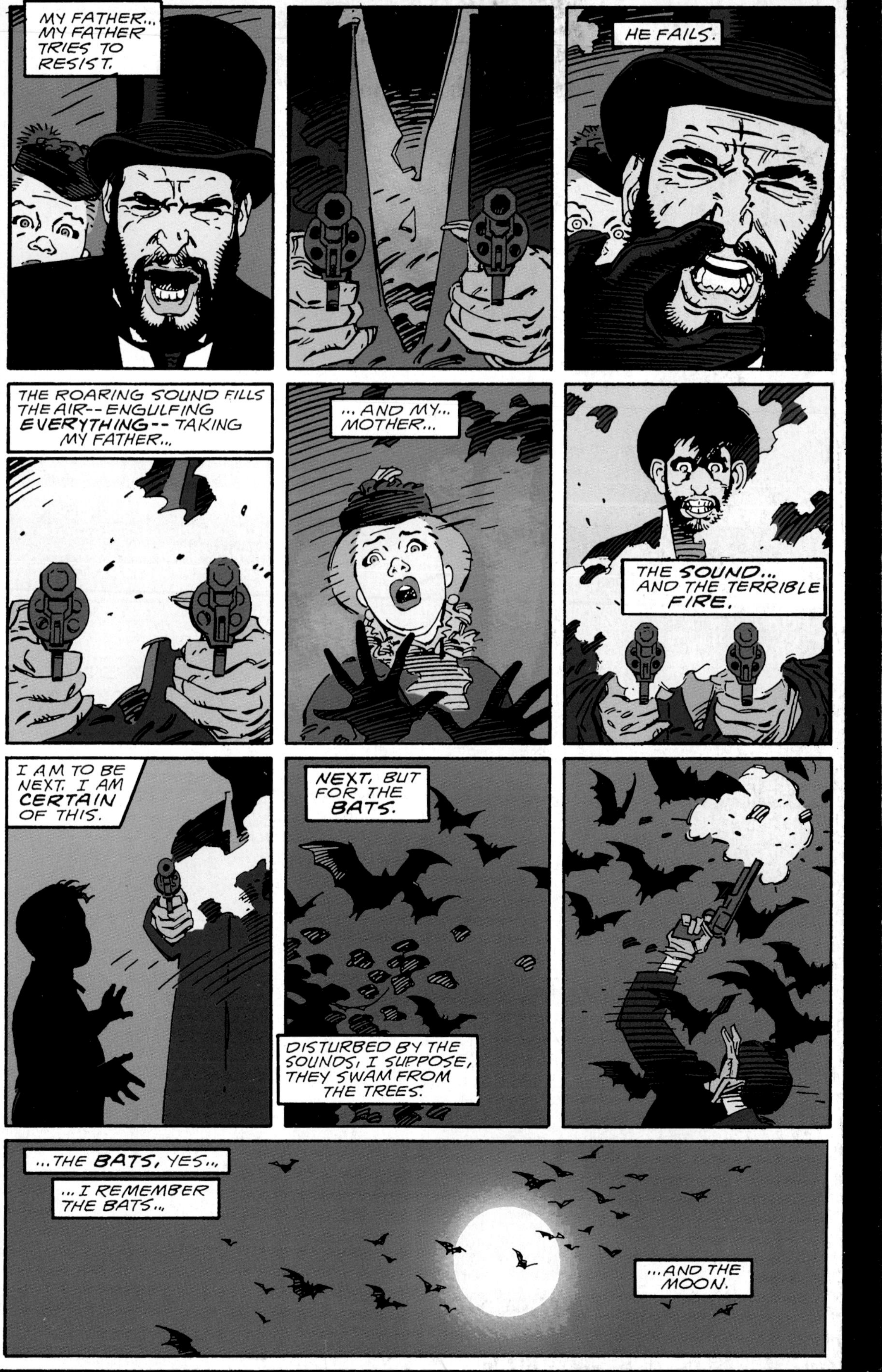
MY FATHER... MY FATHER TRIES TO RESIST.
HE FAILS.
THE ROARING SOUND FILLS THE AIR-- ENGULFING EVERYTHING-- TAKING MY FATHER...
...AND MY... MOTHER...
THE SOUND... AND THE TERRIBLE FIRE.
I AM TO BE NEXT. I AM CERTAIN OF THIS.
NEXT, BUT FOR THE BATS.
DISTURBED BY THE SOUNDS, I SUPPOSE, THEY SWAM FROM THE TREES.
...THE BATS, YES...
...I REMEMBER THE BATS...
...AND THE MOON.

VIENNA, 1889.

THAT IS MY *DREAM*, DOCTOR. IT IS ALWAYS THE SAME.

AND A MOST INTERESTING DREAM. A *SIGNIFICANT* DREAM, TOO, I THINK... YES?

I AM PARTICULARLY... FOND OF THE *BAT* IMAGES. WHAT DO YOU SUPPOSE *THEY* SIGNIFY?

SIGNIFY? *NOTHING.* IT'S JUST A *DREAM.*

YES, PERHAPS, BUT DREAMS CAN TELL US SO MUCH, YOU KNOW. THEY HOLD MANY *SECRETS.*

THAT MAY BE TRUE OF YOUR *PATIENTS*, DR. FREUD...IT IS *NOT* TRUE OF ME, I ASSURE YOU.

MY DREAM IS NOT SOME SYMBOL-LADEN *PUZZLE.* IT IS A RATHER PROSAIC REPLAYING OF AN *ACTUAL* EVENT.

MY PARENTS AND I *WERE* WAYLAID BY A BRIGAND WHO... WHO MURDERED THEM.

ACH, SUCH A TRAGEDY! STRUCK DOWN LIKE THAT, IN FRONT OF YOUR SO-VERY-YOUNG EYES. IT MUST HAVE LEFT TERRIBLE SCARS...

WE *CAN* DISCUSS THIS... IF YOU WISH.

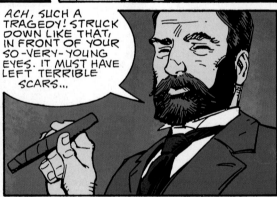

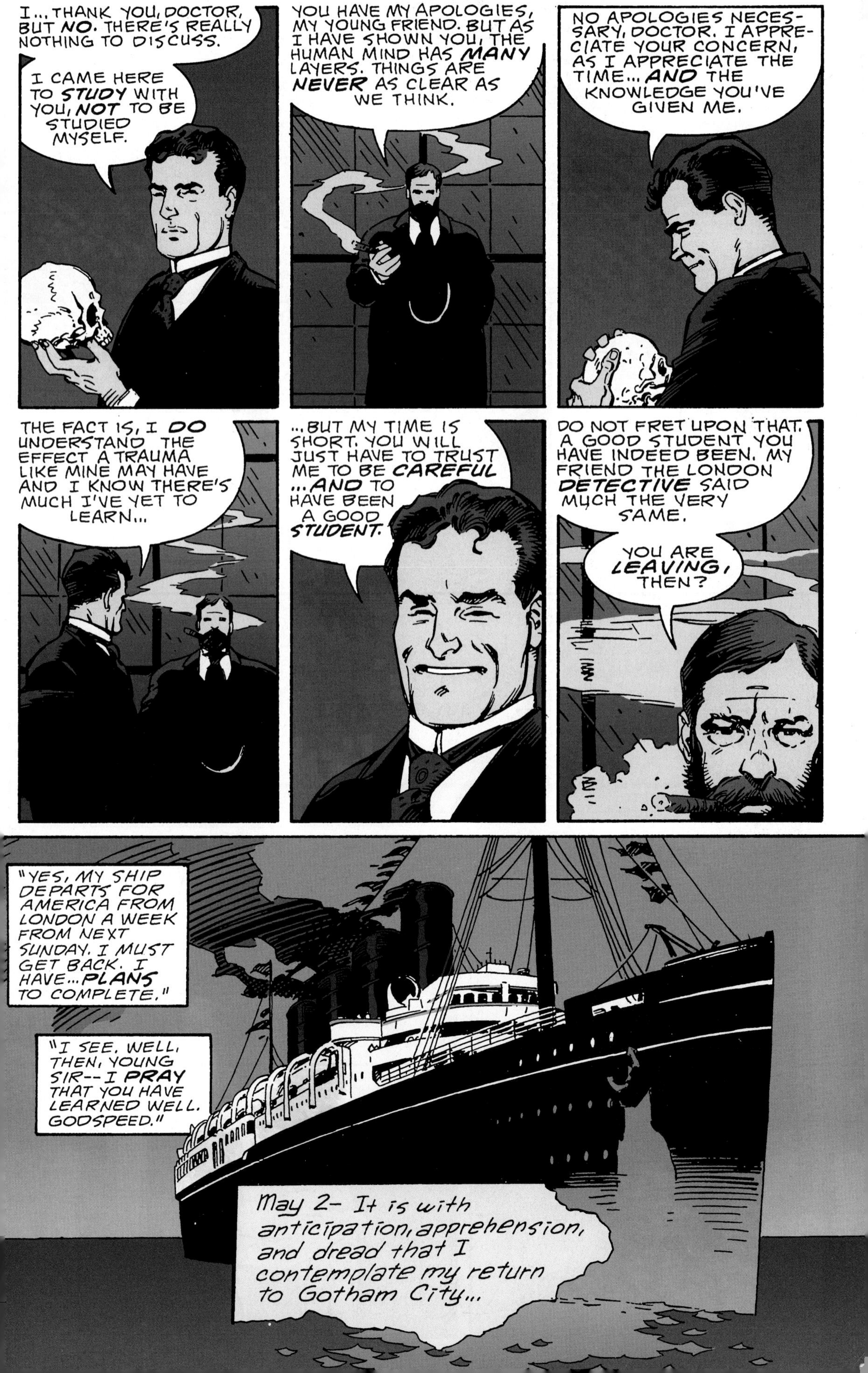
I... THANK YOU, DOCTOR, BUT NO. THERE'S REALLY NOTHING TO DISCUSS.
I CAME HERE TO STUDY WITH YOU, NOT TO BE STUDIED MYSELF.
YOU HAVE MY APOLOGIES, MY YOUNG FRIEND. BUT AS I HAVE SHOWN YOU, THE HUMAN MIND HAS MANY LAYERS. THINGS ARE NEVER AS CLEAR AS WE THINK.
NO APOLOGIES NECESSARY, DOCTOR. I APPRECIATE YOUR CONCERN, AS I APPRECIATE THE TIME... AND THE KNOWLEDGE YOU'VE GIVEN ME.
THE FACT IS, I DO UNDERSTAND THE EFFECT A TRAUMA LIKE MINE MAY HAVE AND I KNOW THERE'S MUCH I'VE YET TO LEARN...
...BUT MY TIME IS SHORT. YOU WILL JUST HAVE TO TRUST ME TO BE CAREFUL ...AND TO HAVE BEEN A GOOD STUDENT.
DO NOT FRET UPON THAT. A GOOD STUDENT YOU HAVE INDEED BEEN. MY FRIEND THE LONDON DETECTIVE SAID MUCH THE VERY SAME.
YOU ARE LEAVING, THEN?
"YES, MY SHIP DEPARTS FOR AMERICA FROM LONDON A WEEK FROM NEXT SUNDAY. I MUST GET BACK. I HAVE... PLANS TO COMPLETE."
"I SEE. WELL, THEN, YOUNG SIR-- I PRAY THAT YOU HAVE LEARNED WELL. GODSPEED."
May 2- It is with anticipation, apprehension, and dread that I contemplate my return to Gotham City...

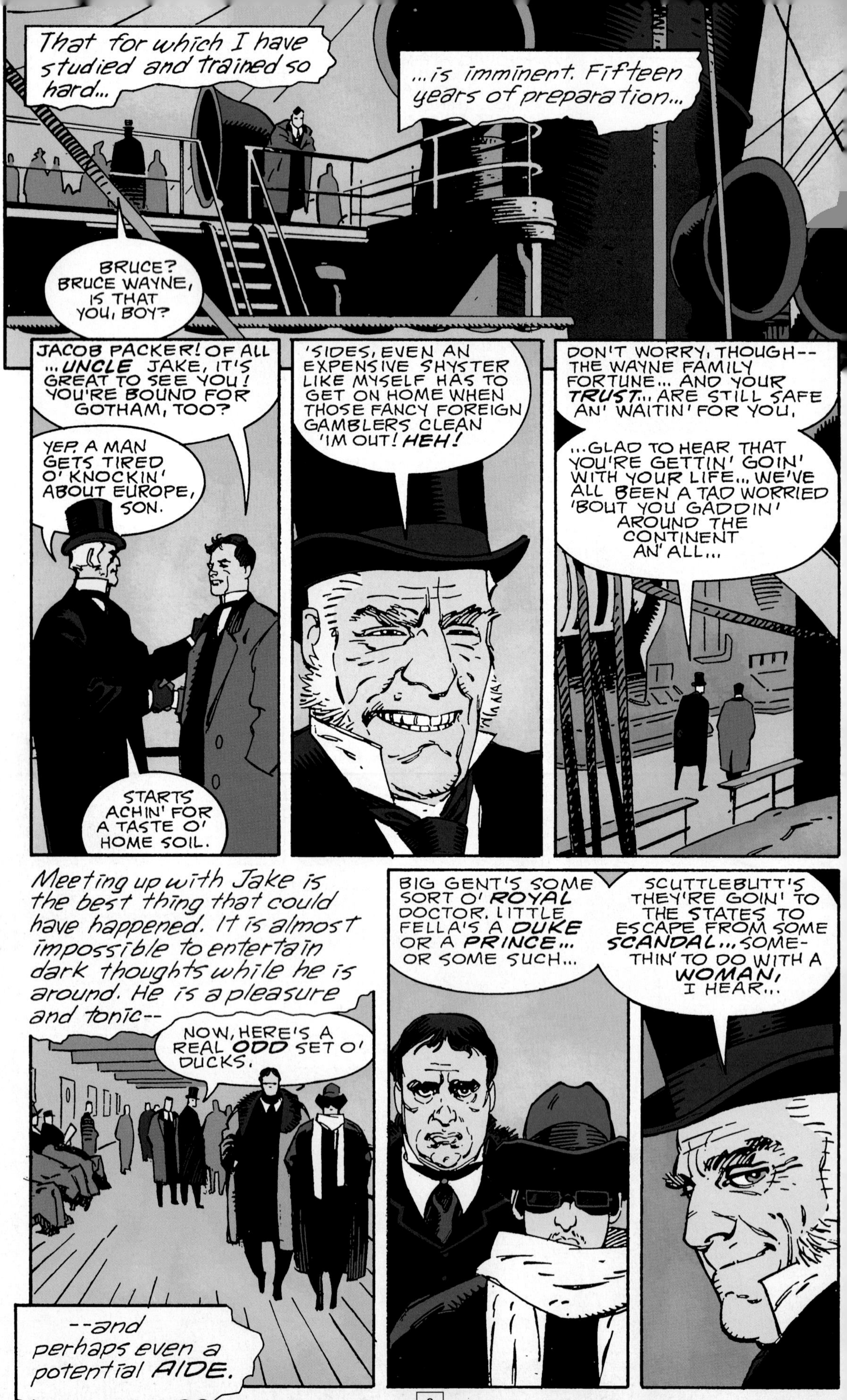

That for which I have studied and trained so hard...
...is imminent. Fifteen years of preparation...
BRUCE? BRUCE WAYNE, IS THAT YOU, BOY?
JACOB PACKER! OF ALL ...UNCLE JAKE, IT'S GREAT TO SEE YOU! YOU'RE BOUND FOR GOTHAM, TOO?
YEP. A MAN GETS TIRED O' KNOCKIN' ABOUT EUROPE, SON.
STARTS ACHIN' FOR A TASTE O' HOME SOIL.
'SIDES, EVEN AN EXPENSIVE SHYSTER LIKE MYSELF HAS TO GET ON HOME WHEN THOSE FANCY FOREIGN GAMBLERS CLEAN 'IM OUT! HEH!
DON'T WORRY, THOUGH-- THE WAYNE FAMILY FORTUNE... AND YOUR TRUST... ARE STILL SAFE AN' WAITIN' FOR YOU.
...GLAD TO HEAR THAT YOU'RE GETTIN' GOIN' WITH YOUR LIFE... WE'VE ALL BEEN A TAD WORRIED 'BOUT YOU GADDIN' AROUND THE CONTINENT AN' ALL...
Meeting up with Jake is the best thing that could have happened. It is almost impossible to entertain dark thoughts while he is around. He is a pleasure and tonic--
NOW, HERE'S A REAL ODD SET O' DUCKS.
--and perhaps even a potential AIDE.
BIG GENT'S SOME SORT O' ROYAL DOCTOR. LITTLE FELLA'S A DUKE OR A PRINCE... OR SOME SUCH...
SCUTTLEBUTT'S THEY'RE GOIN' TO THE STATES TO ESCAPE FROM SOME SCANDAL... SOME-THIN' TO DO WITH A WOMAN, I HEAR...

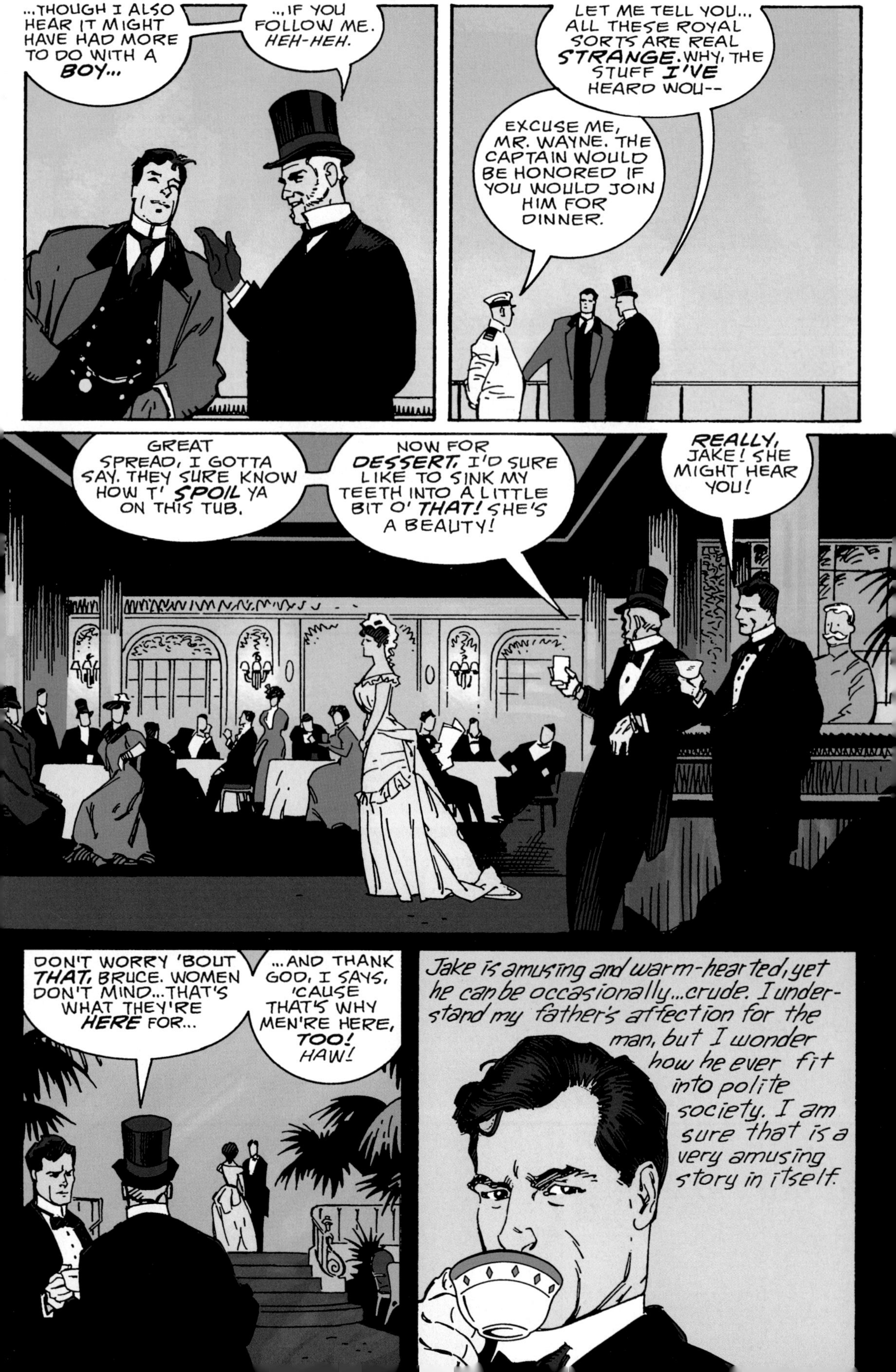
...THOUGH I ALSO HEAR IT MIGHT HAVE HAD MORE TO DO WITH A BOY...
...IF YOU FOLLOW ME. HEH-HEH.
LET ME TELL YOU... ALL THESE ROYAL SORTS ARE REAL STRANGE. WHY, THE STUFF I'VE HEARD WOU--
EXCUSE ME, MR. WAYNE. THE CAPTAIN WOULD BE HONORED IF YOU WOULD JOIN HIM FOR DINNER.
GREAT SPREAD, I GOTTA SAY. THEY SURE KNOW HOW T' SPOIL YA ON THIS TUB.
NOW FOR DESSERT. I'D SURE LIKE TO SINK MY TEETH INTO A LITTLE BIT O' THAT! SHE'S A BEAUTY!
REALLY, JAKE! SHE MIGHT HEAR YOU!
DON'T WORRY 'BOUT THAT, BRUCE. WOMEN DON'T MIND...THAT'S WHAT THEY'RE HERE FOR...
...AND THANK GOD, I SAYS, 'CAUSE THAT'S WHY MEN'RE HERE, TOO! HAW!
Jake is amusing and warm-hearted, yet he can be occasionally...crude. I understand my father's affection for the man, but I wonder how he ever fit into polite society. I am sure that is a very amusing story in itself.

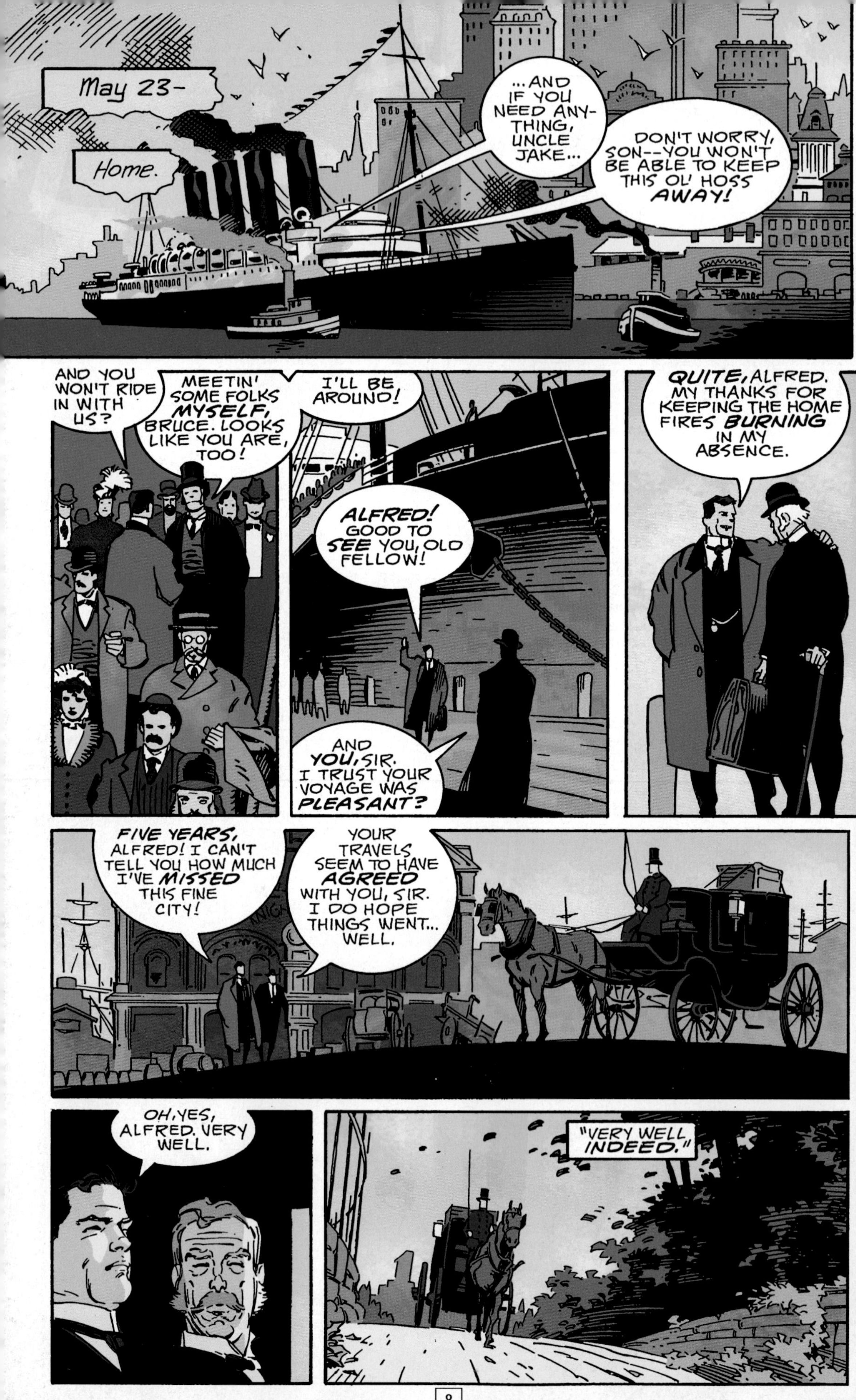
May 23-
Home.
...AND IF YOU NEED ANYTHING, UNCLE JAKE...
DON'T WORRY, SON--YOU WON'T BE ABLE TO KEEP THIS OL' HOSS AWAY!
AND YOU WON'T RIDE IN WITH US?
MEETIN' SOME FOLKS MYSELF, BRUCE. LOOKS LIKE YOU ARE, TOO!
I'LL BE AROUND!
ALFRED! GOOD TO SEE YOU, OLD FELLOW!
AND YOU, SIR. I TRUST YOUR VOYAGE WAS PLEASANT?
QUITE, ALFRED. MY THANKS FOR KEEPING THE HOME FIRES BURNING IN MY ABSENCE.
FIVE YEARS, ALFRED! I CAN'T TELL YOU HOW MUCH I'VE MISSED THIS FINE CITY!
YOUR TRAVELS SEEM TO HAVE AGREED WITH YOU, SIR. I DO HOPE THINGS WENT... WELL.
OH, YES, ALFRED. VERY WELL.
"VERY WELL INDEED."

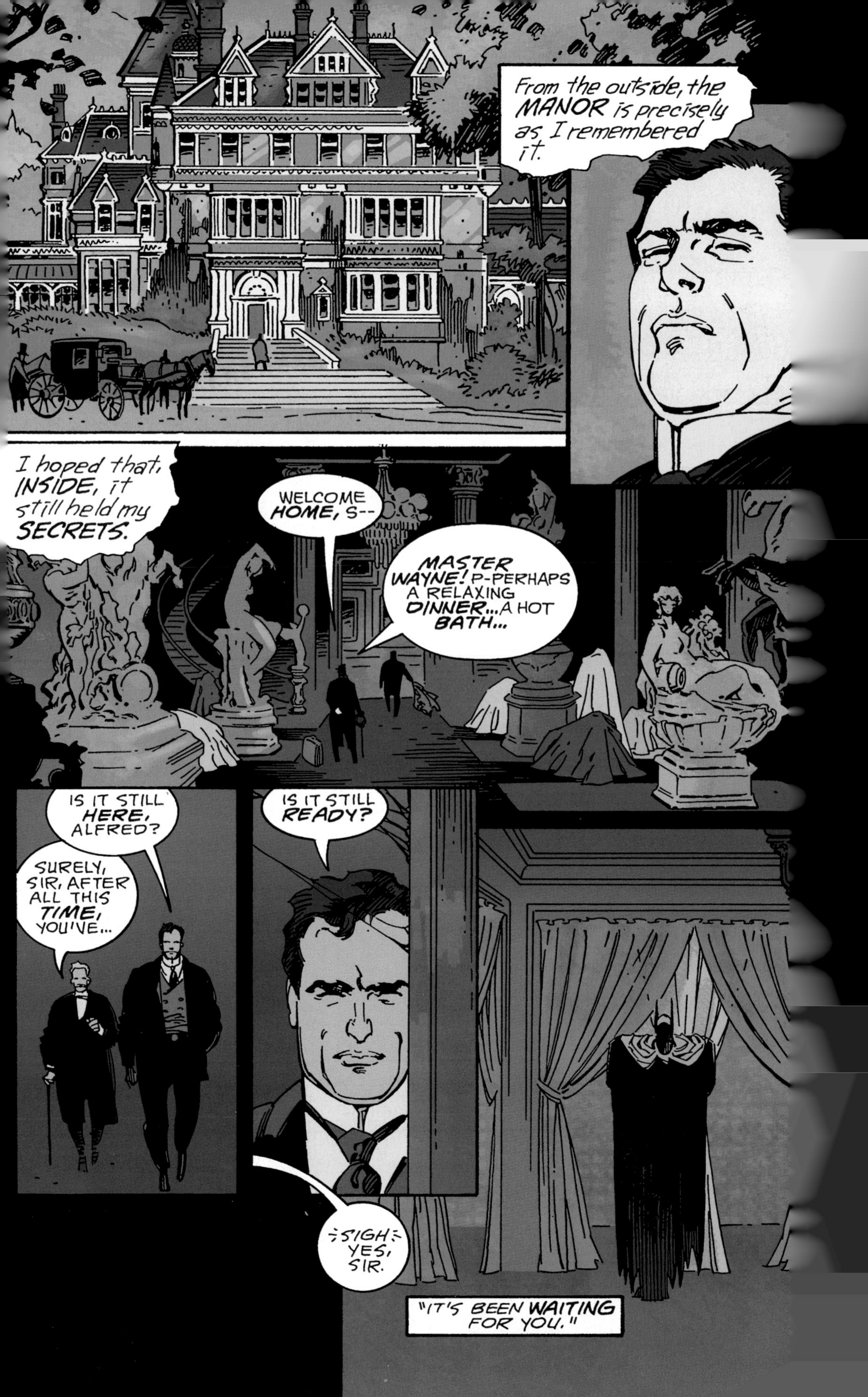
From the outside, the MANOR is precisely as I remembered it.
I hoped that, INSIDE, it still held my SECRETS.
WELCOME HOME, S--
MASTER WAYNE! P-PERHAPS A RELAXING DINNER...A HOT BATH...
IS IT STILL HERE, ALFRED?
SURELY, SIR, AFTER ALL THIS TIME, YOU'VE...
IS IT STILL READY?
:SIGH: YES, SIR.
"IT'S BEEN WAITING FOR YOU."

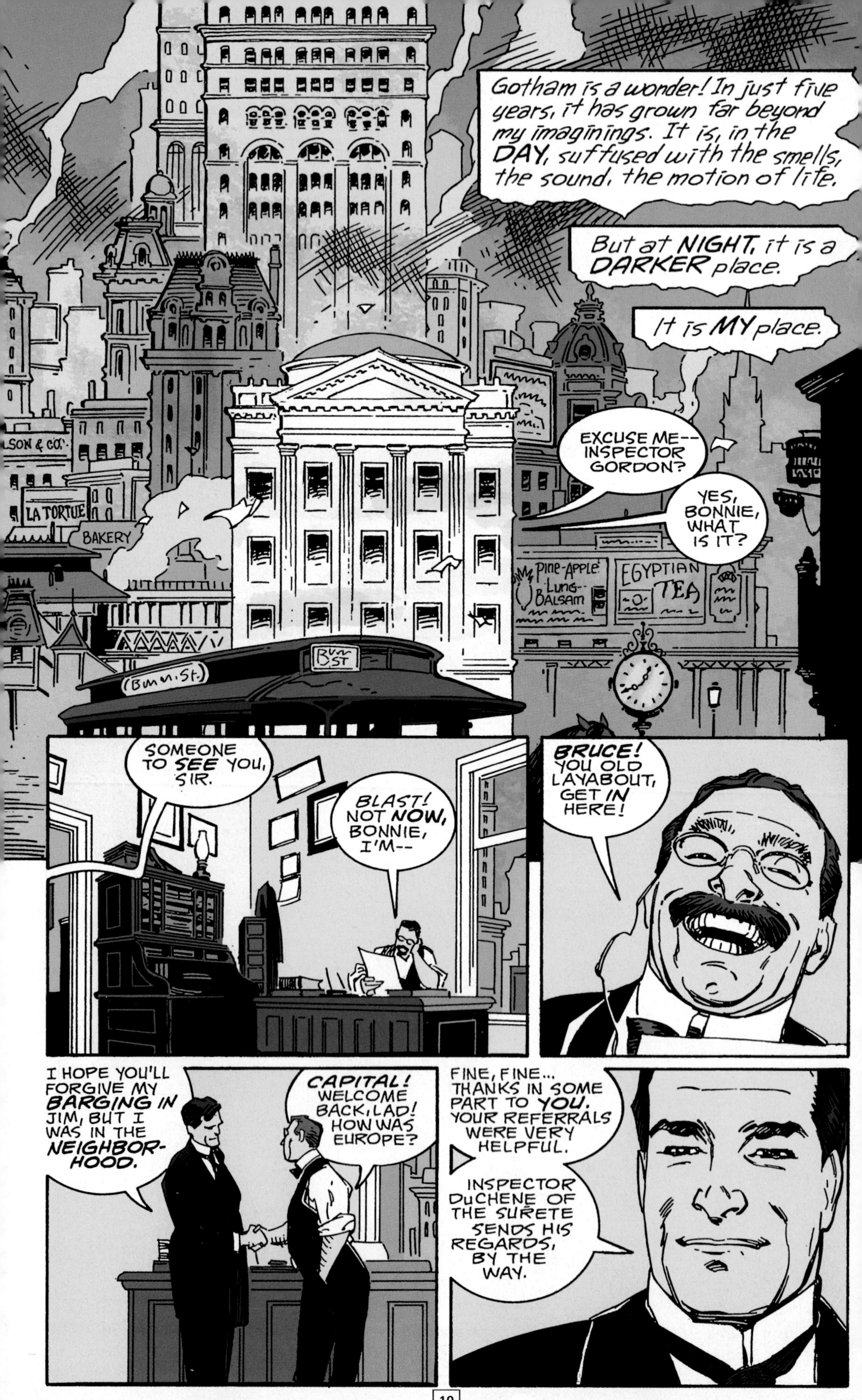

Gotham is a wonder! In just five years, it has grown far beyond my imaginings. It is, in the DAY, suffused with the smells, the sound, the motion of life.
But at NIGHT, it is a DARKER place.
It is MY place.
EXCUSE ME-- INSPECTOR GORDON?
YES, BONNIE, WHAT IS IT?
LA TORTUE
BAKERY
Pine-Apple Lung-Balsam
EGYPTIAN TEA
SOMEONE TO SEE YOU, SIR.
BLAST! NOT NOW, BONNIE, I'M--
BRUCE! YOU OLD LAYABOUT, GET IN HERE!
I HOPE YOU'LL FORGIVE MY BARGING IN JIM, BUT I WAS IN THE NEIGHBOR-HOOD.
CAPITAL! WELCOME BACK, LAD! HOW WAS EUROPE?
FINE, FINE... THANKS IN SOME PART TO YOU. YOUR REFERRALS WERE VERY HELPFUL.
INSPECTOR DUCHENE OF THE SURETE SENDS HIS REGARDS, BY THE WAY.

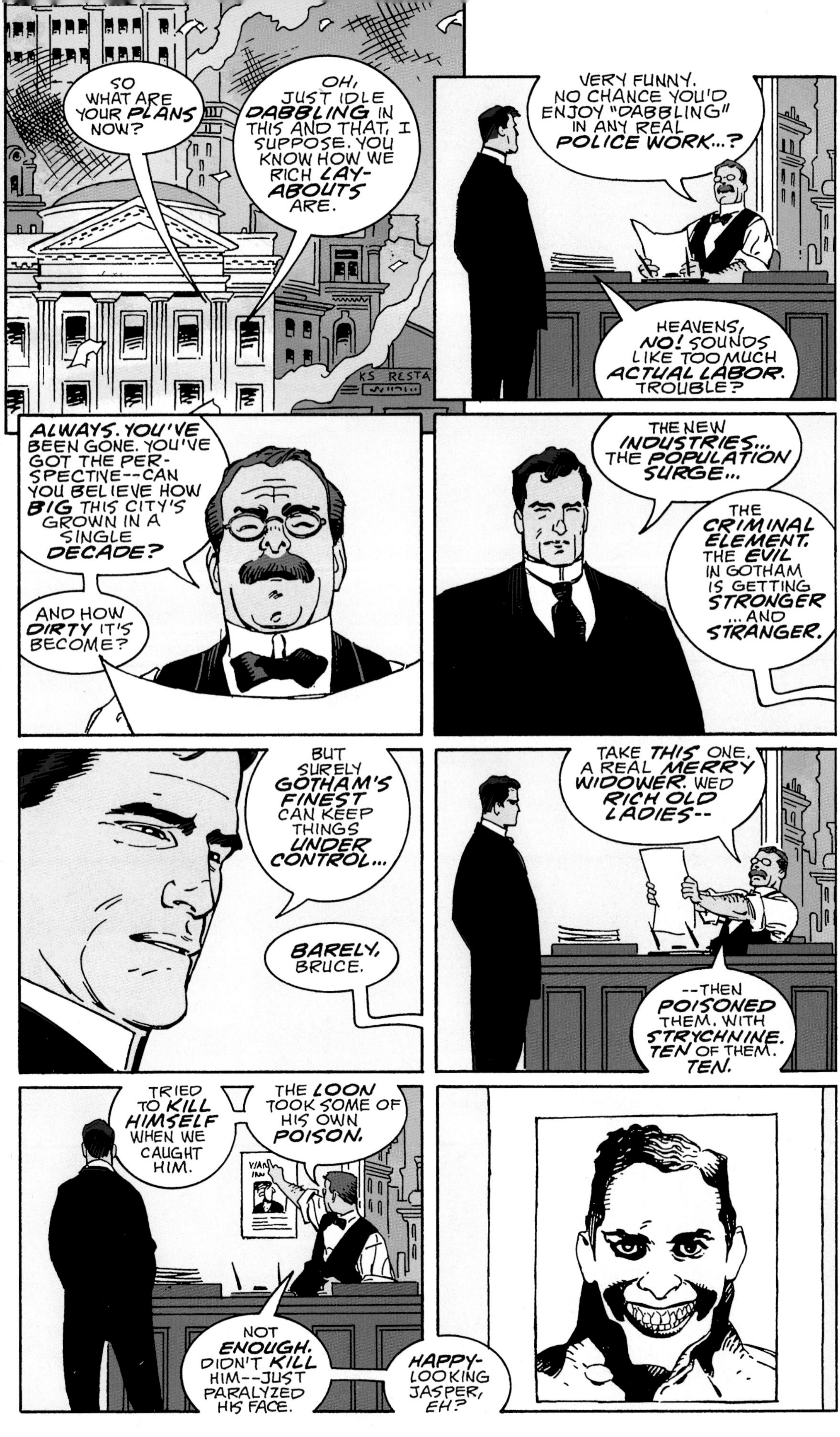
SO WHAT ARE YOUR PLANS NOW?
OH, JUST IDLE DABBLING IN THIS AND THAT, I SUPPOSE. YOU KNOW HOW WE RICH LAY-ABOUTS ARE.
KS RESTA
VERY FUNNY. NO CHANCE YOU'D ENJOY "DABBLING" IN ANY REAL POLICE WORK...?
HEAVENS, NO! SOUNDS LIKE TOO MUCH ACTUAL LABOR. TROUBLE?
ALWAYS. YOU'VE BEEN GONE. YOU'VE GOT THE PER-SPECTIVE--CAN YOU BELIEVE HOW BIG THIS CITY'S GROWN IN A SINGLE DECADE?
AND HOW DIRTY IT'S BECOME?
THE NEW INDUSTRIES... THE POPULATION SURGE...
THE CRIMINAL ELEMENT. THE EVIL IN GOTHAM IS GETTING STRONGER ...AND STRANGER.
BUT SURELY GOTHAM'S FINEST CAN KEEP THINGS UNDER CONTROL...
BARELY, BRUCE.
TAKE THIS ONE. A REAL MERRY WIDOWER. WED RICH OLD LADIES--
--THEN POISONED THEM. WITH STRYCHNINE. TEN OF THEM. TEN.
TRIED TO KILL HIMSELF WHEN WE CAUGHT HIM.
THE LOON TOOK SOME OF HIS OWN POISON.
NOT ENOUGH. DIDN'T KILL HIM--JUST PARALYZED HIS FACE.
HAPPY-LOOKING JASPER, EH?

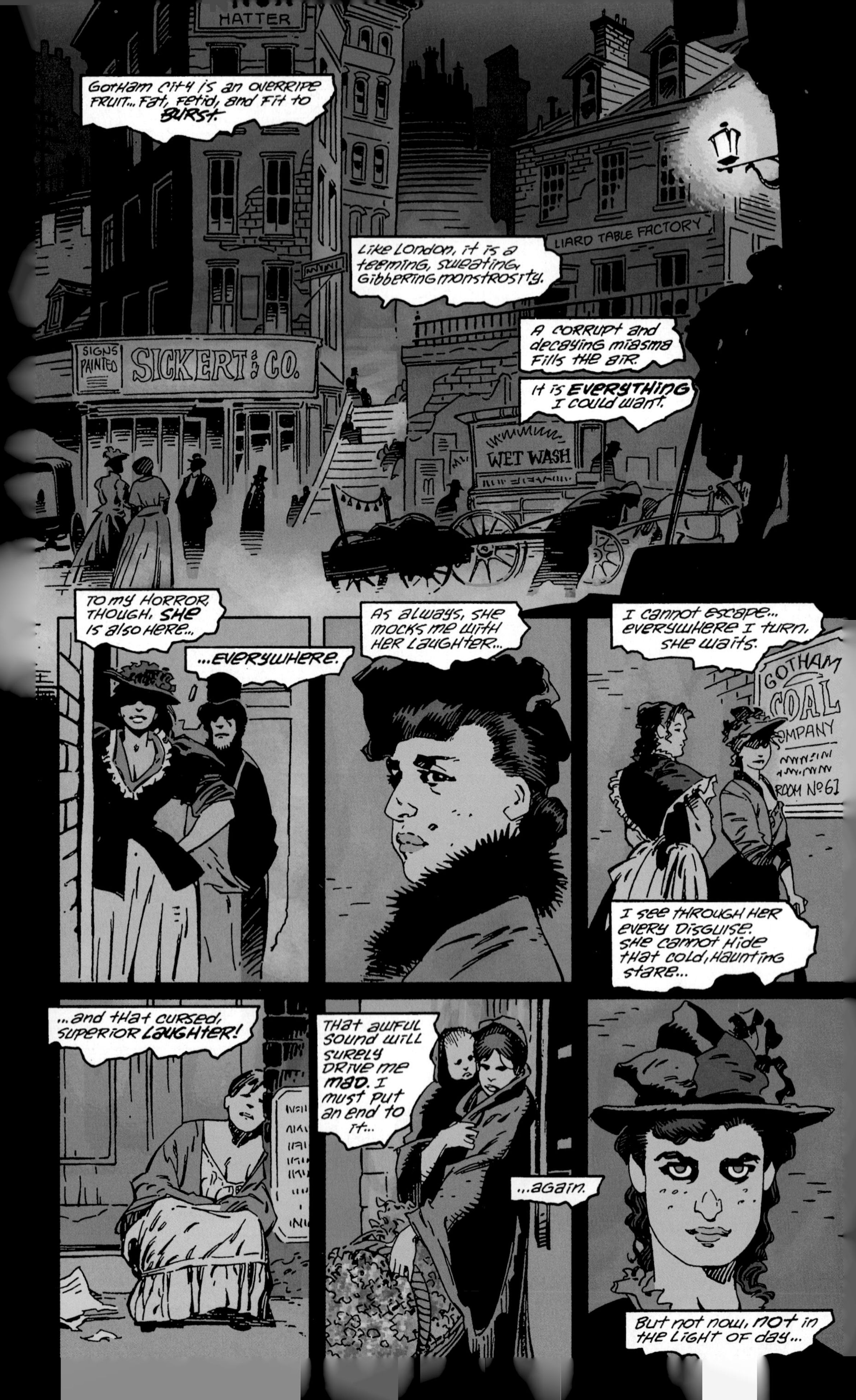
HATTER
Gotham City is an overripe fruit... fat, fetid, and fit to BURST.
Like London, it is a teeming, sweating, gibbering monstrosity.
LIARD TABLE FACTORY
SIGNS PAINTED
SICKERT & CO.
A corrupt and decaying miasma fills the air.
It is EVERYTHING I could want.
WET WASH
To my horror though, SHE is also here...
...EVERYWHERE.
As always, she mocks me with her laughter...
I cannot escape... everywhere I turn, she waits.
GOTHAM COAL COMPANY
ROOM No 61
I see through her every disguise. She cannot hide that cold, haunting stare...
...and that cursed, superior LAUGHTER!
That awful sound will surely drive me MAD. I must put an end to it...
...again.
But not now, NOT in the light of day...

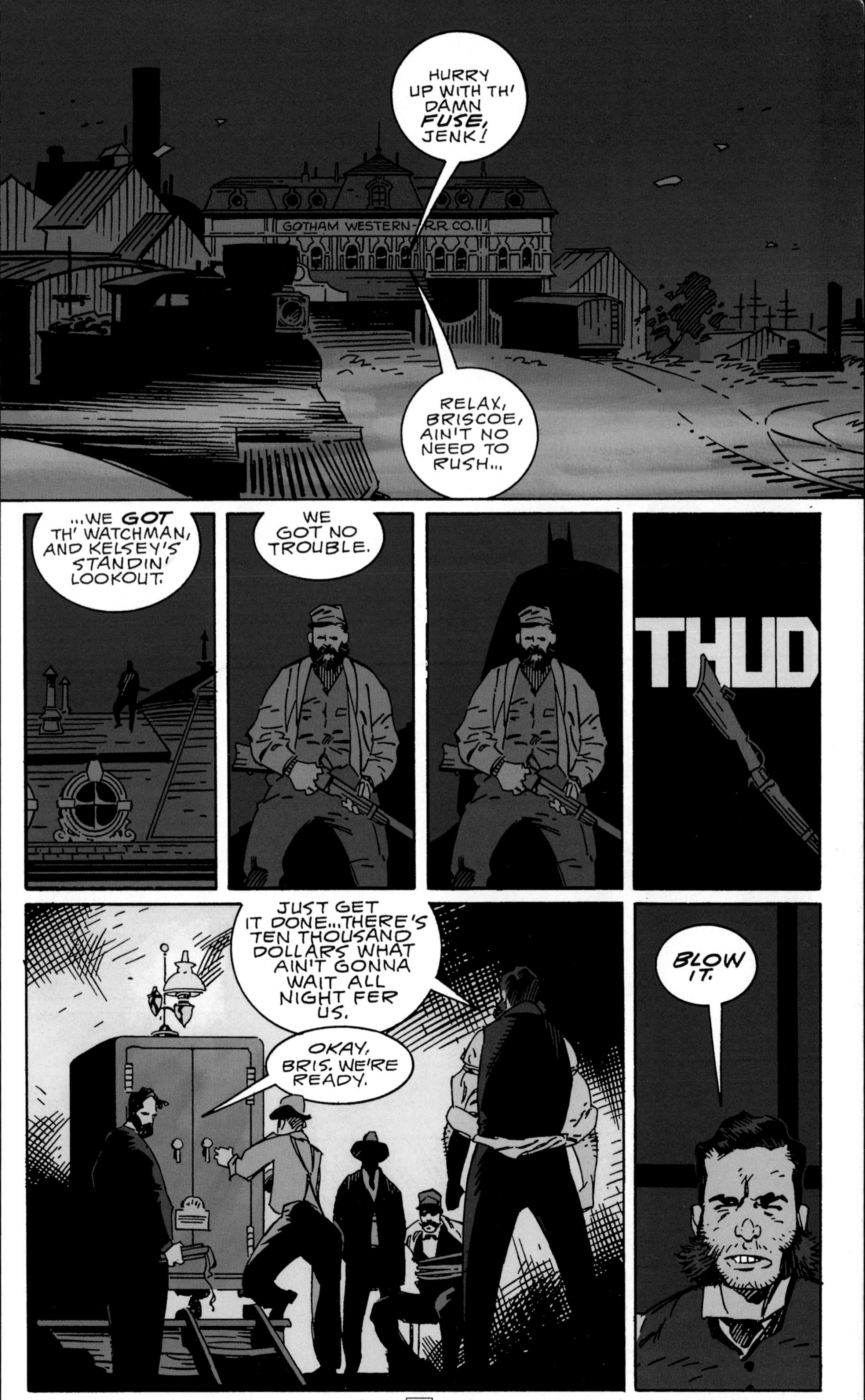
HURRY UP WITH TH' DAMN FUSE, JENK!
GOTHAM WESTERN RR. CO.
RELAX, BRISCOE, AIN'T NO NEED TO RUSH...
...WE GOT TH' WATCHMAN, AND KELSEY'S STANDIN' LOOKOUT.
WE GOT NO TROUBLE.
THUD
JUST GET IT DONE...THERE'S TEN THOUSAND DOLLARS WHAT AIN'T GONNA WAIT ALL NIGHT FER US.
OKAY, BRIS. WE'RE READY.
BLOW IT.

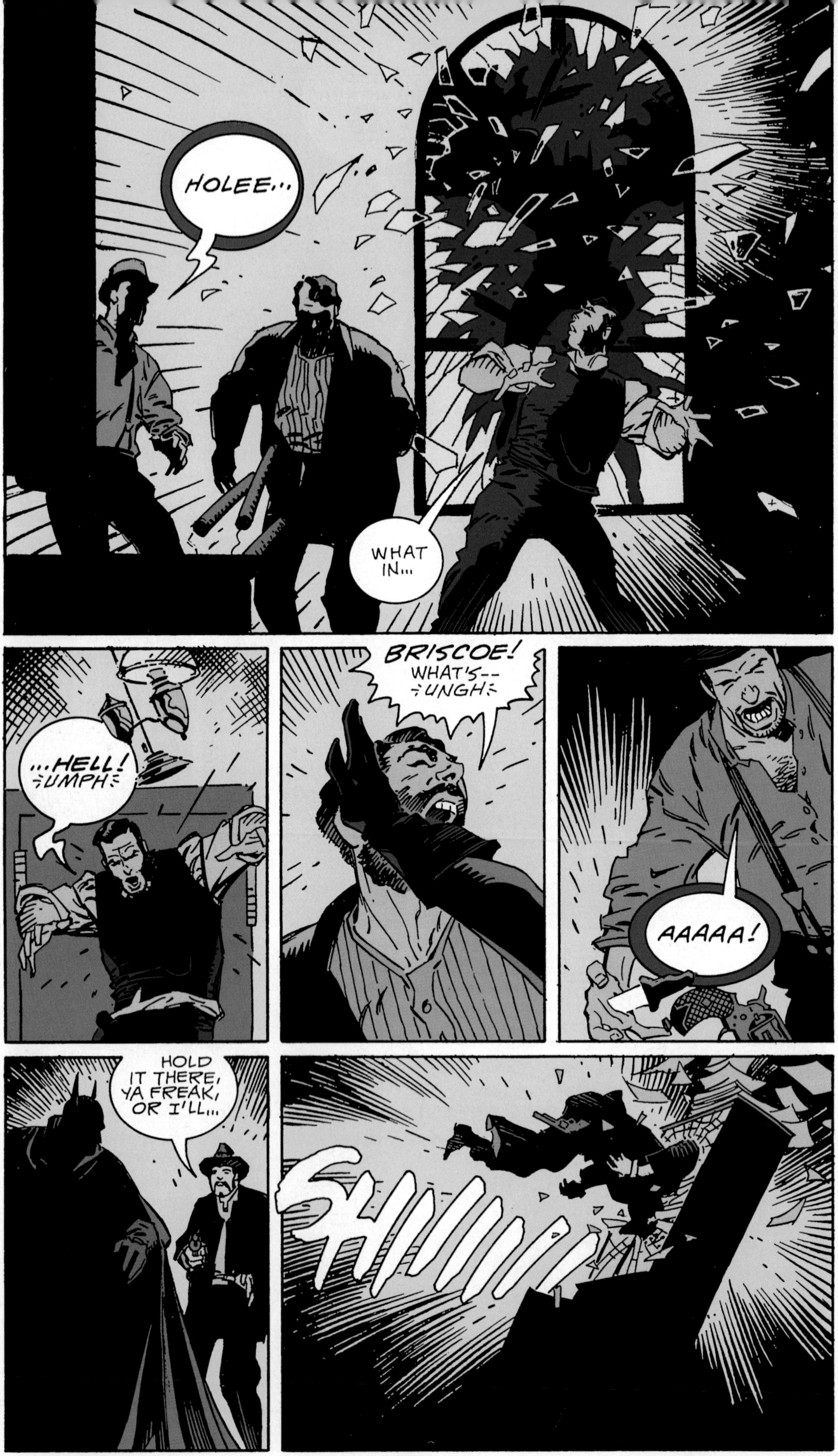
HOLEE...
WHAT IN...
...HELL! UMPH
BRISCOE! WHAT'S-- UNGH
AAAAA!
HOLD IT THERE, YA FREAK, OR I'LL...
SHHHHH

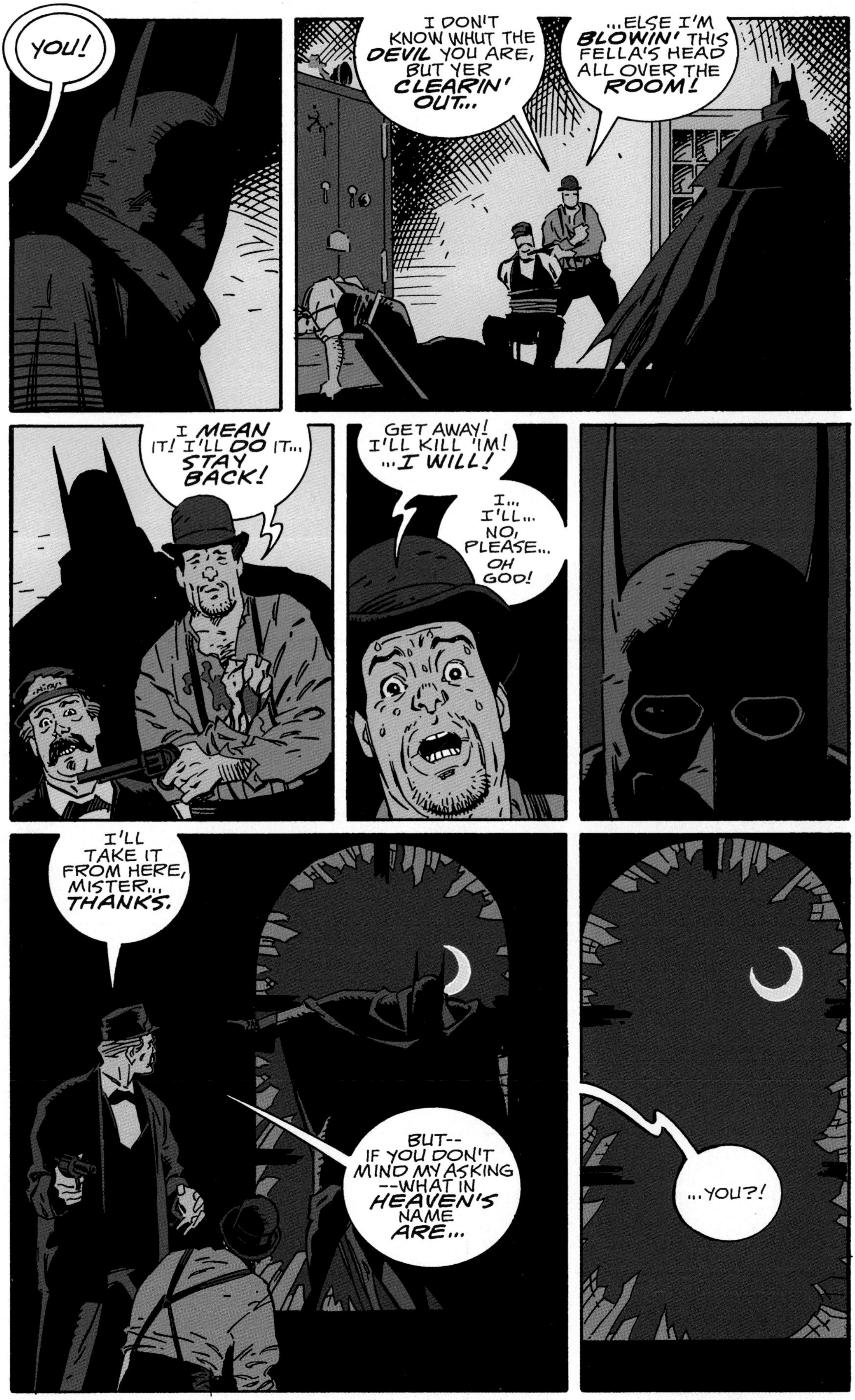
YOU!
I DON'T KNOW WHUT THE DEVIL YOU ARE, BUT YER CLEARIN' OUT...
...ELSE I'M BLOWIN' THIS FELLA'S HEAD ALL OVER THE ROOM!
I MEAN IT! I'LL DO IT... STAY BACK!
GET AWAY! I'LL KILL 'IM! ...I WILL!
I... I'LL... NO, PLEASE... OH GOD!
I'LL TAKE IT FROM HERE, MISTER... THANKS.
BUT-- IF YOU DON'T MIND MY ASKING --WHAT IN HEAVEN'S NAME ARE...
...YOU?!

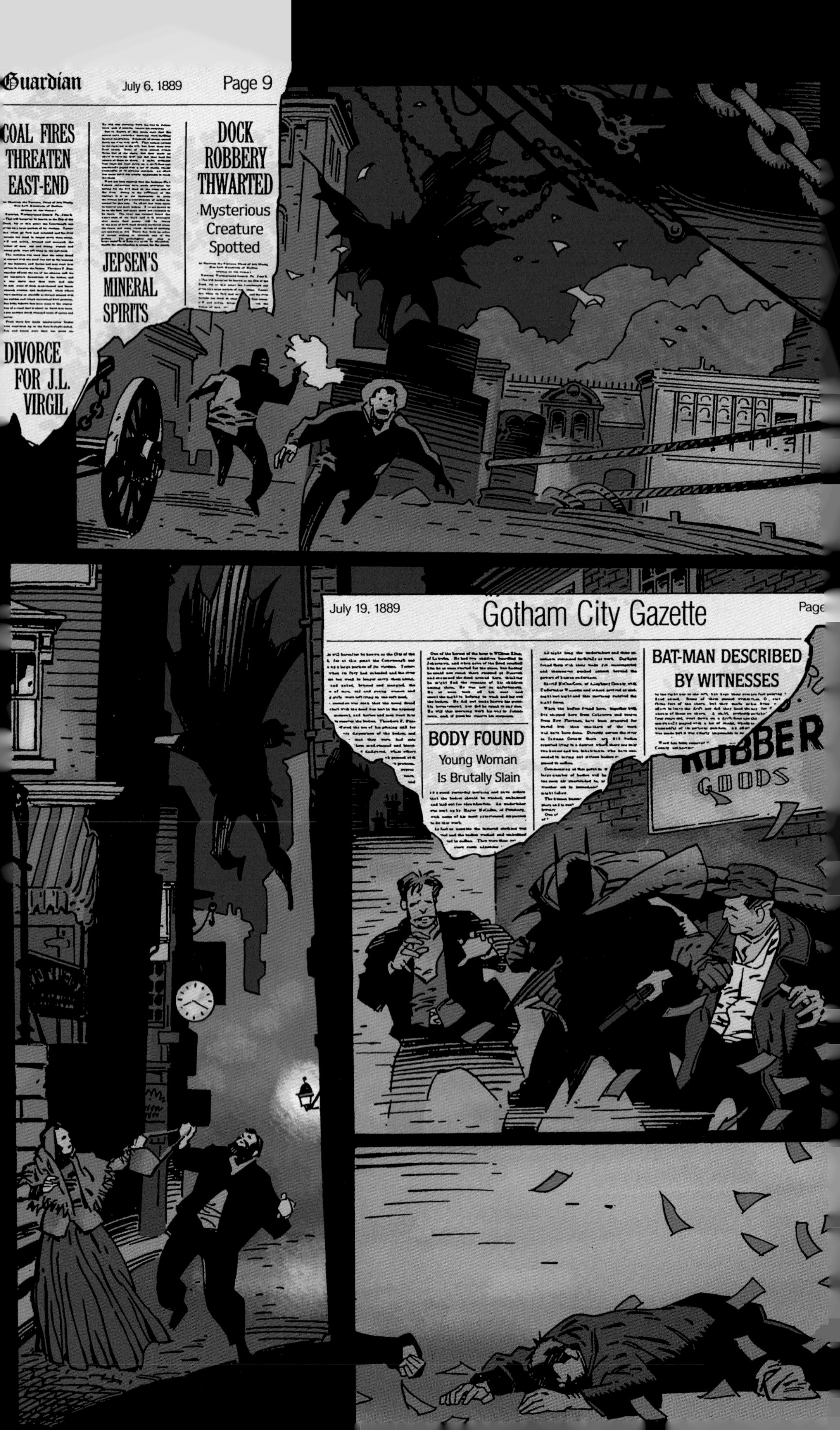

Guardian
July 6, 1889
Page 9
COAL FIRES THREATEN EAST-END
JEPSEN'S MINERAL SPIRITS
DOCK ROBBERY THWARTED
Mysterious Creature Spotted
DIVORCE FOR J.L. VIRGIL
July 19, 1889
Gotham City Gazette
Page
BODY FOUND
Young Woman Is Brutally Slain
BAT-MAN DESCRIBED BY WITNESSES
ROBBER
GOODS

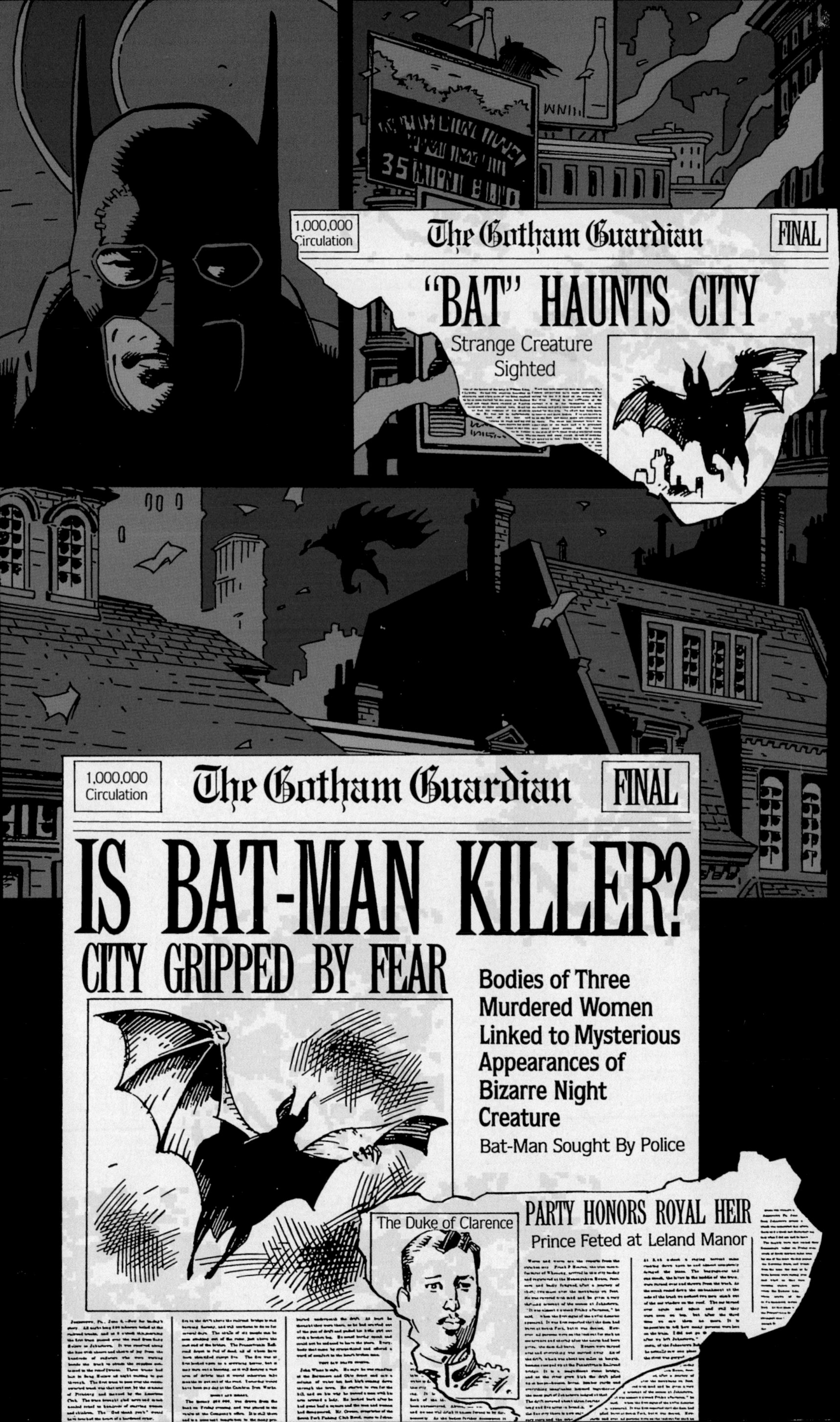

1,000,000 Circulation
The Gotham Guardian
FINAL
"BAT" HAUNTS CITY
Strange Creature Sighted
1,000,000 Circulation
The Gotham Guardian
FINAL
IS BAT-MAN KILLER?
CITY GRIPPED BY FEAR
Bodies of Three Murdered Women Linked to Mysterious Appearances of Bizarre Night Creature
Bat-Man Sought By Police
The Duke of Clarence
PARTY HONORS ROYAL HEIR
Prince Feted at Leland Manor

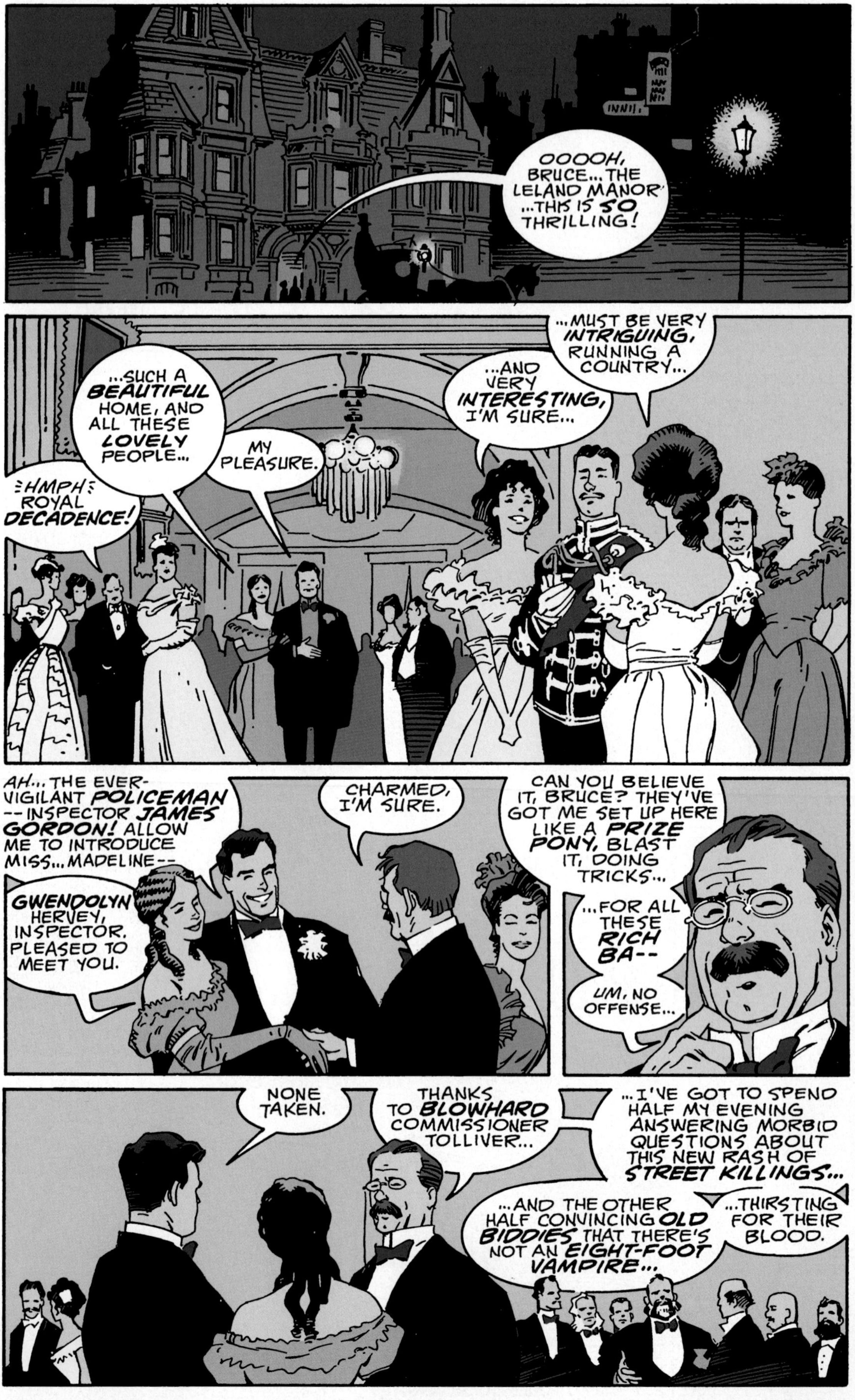

OOOOH, BRUCE... THE LELAND MANOR ...THIS IS SO THRILLING!
...SUCH A BEAUTIFUL HOME, AND ALL THESE LOVELY PEOPLE...
MY PLEASURE.
HMPH ROYAL DECADENCE!
...AND VERY INTERESTING, I'M SURE...
...MUST BE VERY INTRIGUING, RUNNING A COUNTRY...
AH... THE EVER-VIGILANT POLICEMAN -- INSPECTOR JAMES GORDON! ALLOW ME TO INTRODUCE MISS... MADELINE--
GWENDOLYN HERVEY, INSPECTOR. PLEASED TO MEET YOU.
CHARMED, I'M SURE.
CAN YOU BELIEVE IT, BRUCE? THEY'VE GOT ME SET UP HERE LIKE A PRIZE PONY, BLAST IT, DOING TRICKS...
...FOR ALL THESE RICH BA--
UM, NO OFFENSE...
NONE TAKEN.
THANKS TO BLOWHARD COMMISSIONER TOLLIVER...
...I'VE GOT TO SPEND HALF MY EVENING ANSWERING MORBID QUESTIONS ABOUT THIS NEW RASH OF STREET KILLINGS...
...AND THE OTHER HALF CONVINCING OLD BIDDIES THAT THERE'S NOT AN EIGHT-FOOT VAMPIRE...
...THIRSTING FOR THEIR BLOOD.

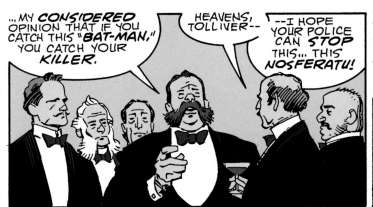

...MY CONSIDERED OPINION THAT IF YOU CATCH THIS "BAT-MAN," YOU CATCH YOUR KILLER.
HEAVENS, TOLLIVER--
--I HOPE YOUR POLICE CAN STOP THIS... THIS NOSFERATU!
TOLLIVER, SURELY THESE KILLINGS ARE THE WORK OF A SICK MAN, NOT SOME FANTASTIC CREATURE!
MADMAN OR MONSTER, WAYNE...
...THE "BAT-MAN" IS OUR KILLER... AND WE WILL CATCH HIM!
SIGH I FEEL SAFER ALREADY, COMMISSIONER.
AHEM ACTUALLY, WE'RE NOT CONVINCED THAT THERE'S ANY CONNEC--
NOW WHERE DID BRUCE GET OFF TO?
WHERE INDEED?
CHILDREN CRY FOR HELFER'S GASTORIA
MARK MY WORDS, GENTLEMEN, SO LONG AS I AM THE COMMISSIONER OF POLICE, LUNATICS WILL NOT WALK THE STREETS OF GOTHAM WITH IMPUNITY!
666
I have found her.
Again.

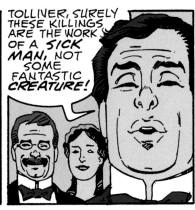

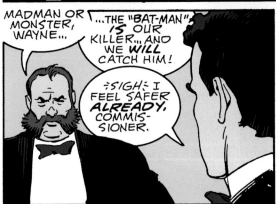

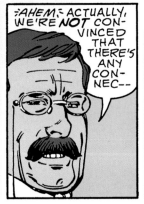

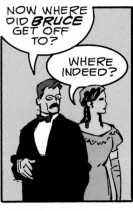

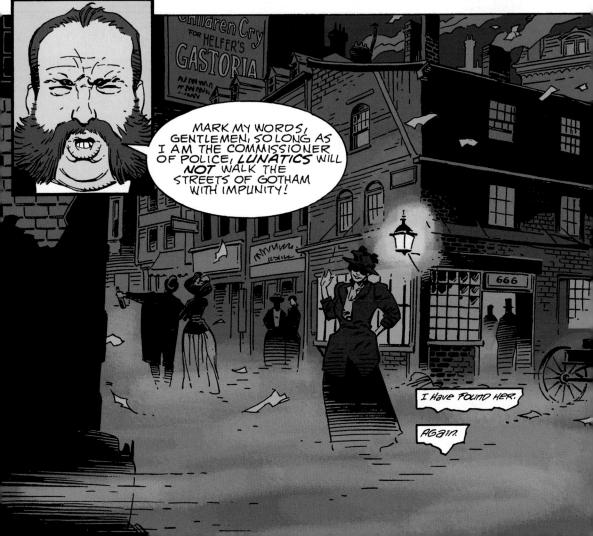

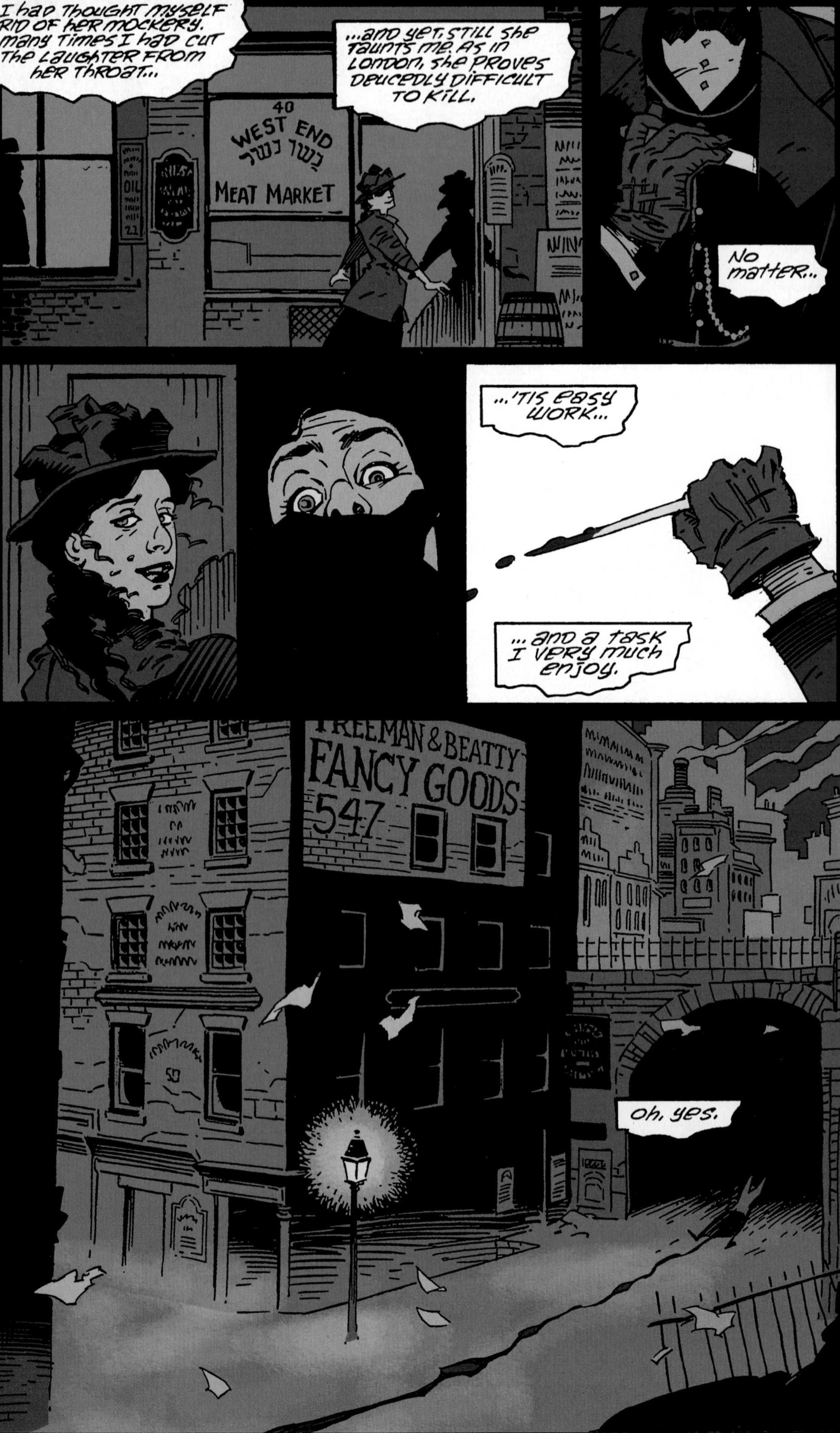
I HAD THOUGHT MYSELF RID OF HER MOCKERY. MANY TIMES I HAD CUT THE LAUGHTER FROM HER THROAT...
...AND YET, STILL SHE TAUNTS ME. AS IN LONDON, SHE PROVES DEUCEDLY DIFFICULT TO KILL.
40
WEST END
כשר
MEAT MARKET
OIL
No matter...
...'TIS EASY WORK...
...AND A TASK I VERY MUCH ENJOY.
FREEMAN & BEATTY
FANCY GOODS
547
Oh, yes.

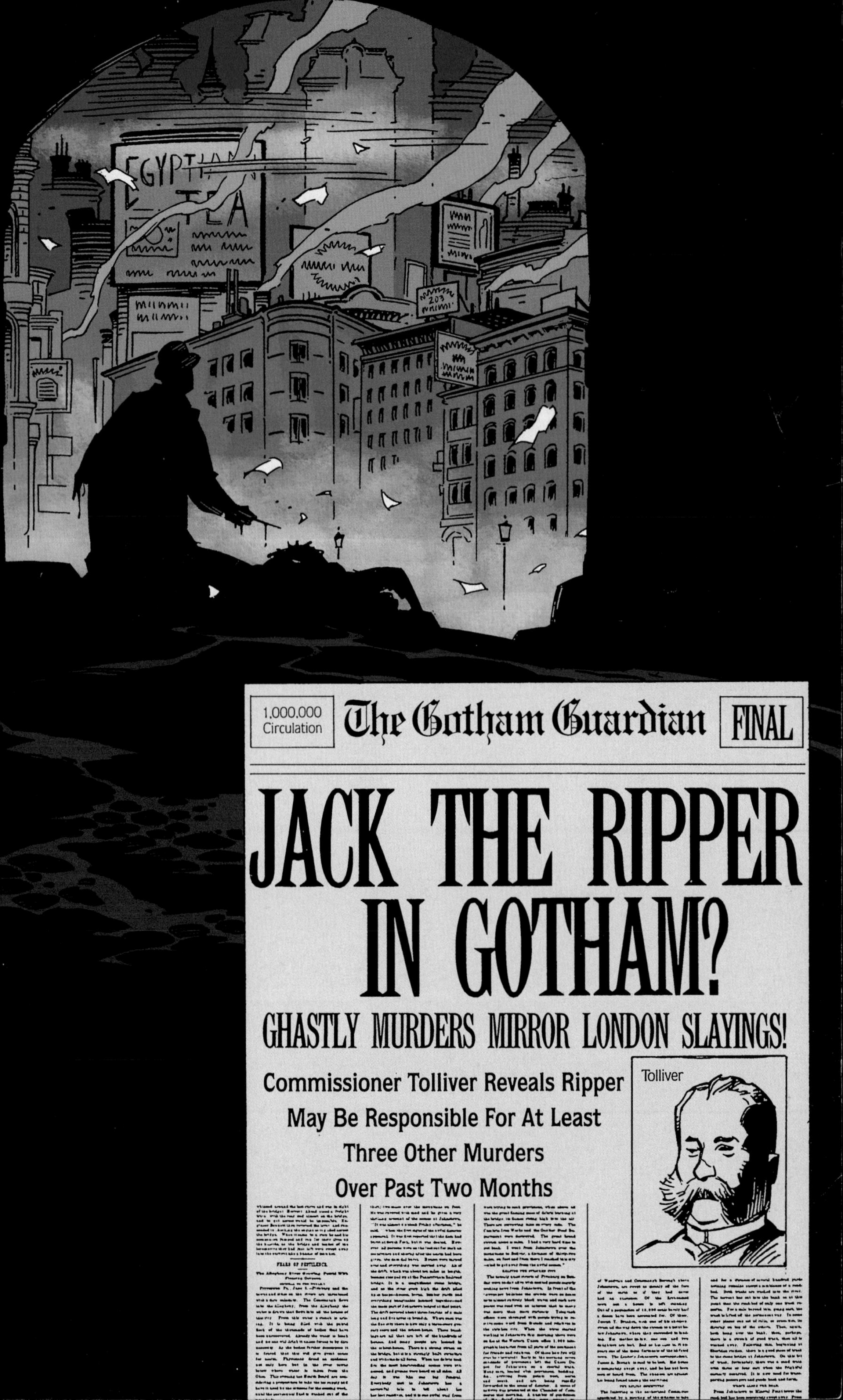
1,000,000 Circulation
The Gotham Guardian
FINAL
JACK THE RIPPER IN GOTHAM?
GHASTLY MURDERS MIRROR LONDON SLAYINGS!
Commissioner Tolliver Reveals Ripper May Be Responsible For At Least Three Other Murders Over Past Two Months
Tolliver

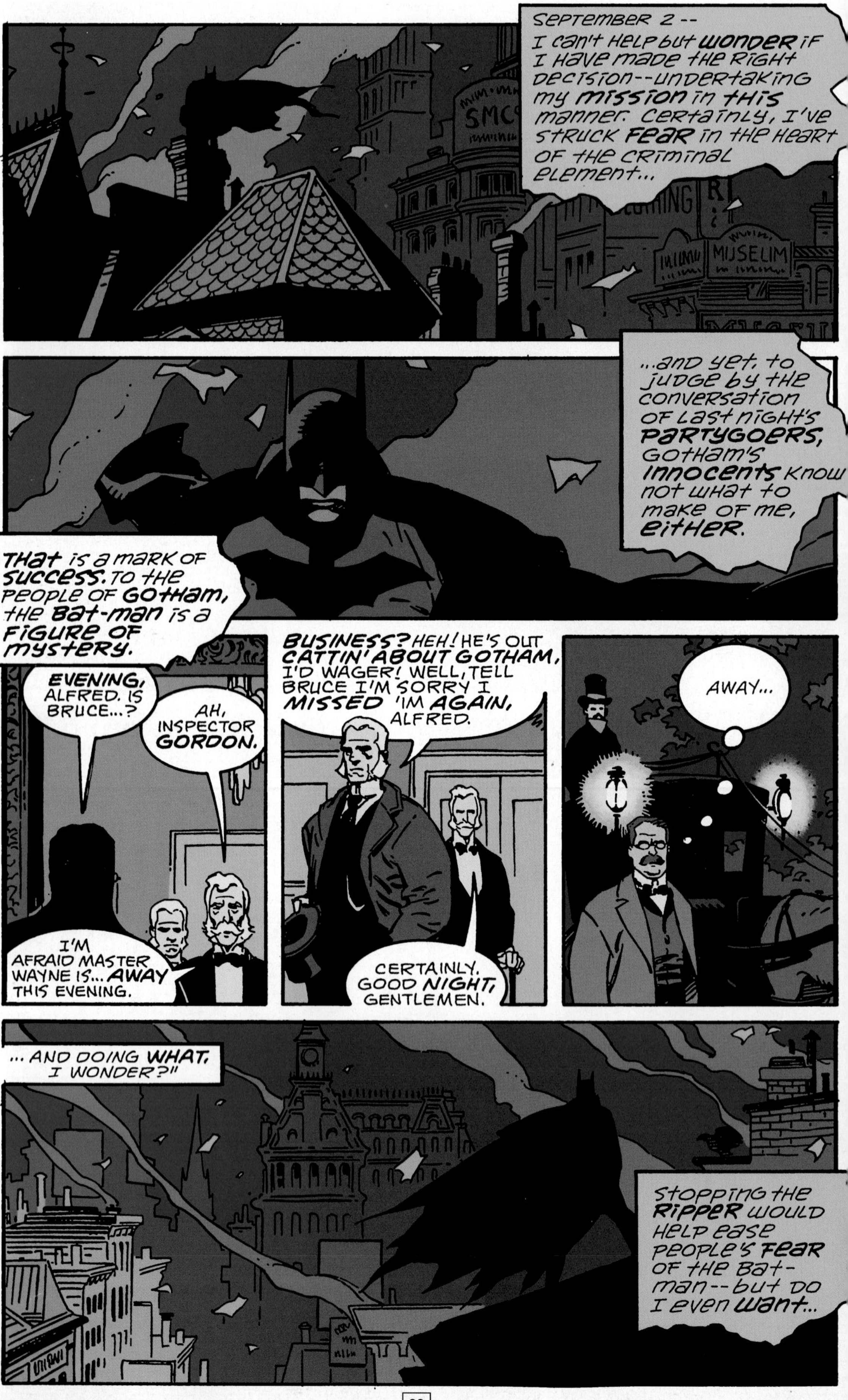
SEPTEMBER 2 --
I can't help but WONDER if I have made the right decision--undertaking my MISSION in THIS manner. Certainly, I've struck FEAR in the heart of the criminal element...
...and yet, to judge by the conversation of last night's PARTYGOERS, Gotham's INNOCENTS know not what to make of me, EITHER.
THAT is a mark of SUCCESS. To the people of GOTHAM, the BAT-MAN is a FIGURE OF MYSTERY.
EVENING, ALFRED. IS BRUCE...?
AH, INSPECTOR GORDON.
I'M AFRAID MASTER WAYNE IS... AWAY THIS EVENING.
BUSINESS? HEH! HE'S OUT CATTIN' ABOUT GOTHAM, I'D WAGER! WELL, TELL BRUCE I'M SORRY I MISSED 'IM AGAIN, ALFRED.
CERTAINLY. GOOD NIGHT, GENTLEMEN.
AWAY...
... AND DOING WHAT, I WONDER?"
Stopping the RIPPER would help ease people's FEAR of the Bat-man--but do I even WANT...

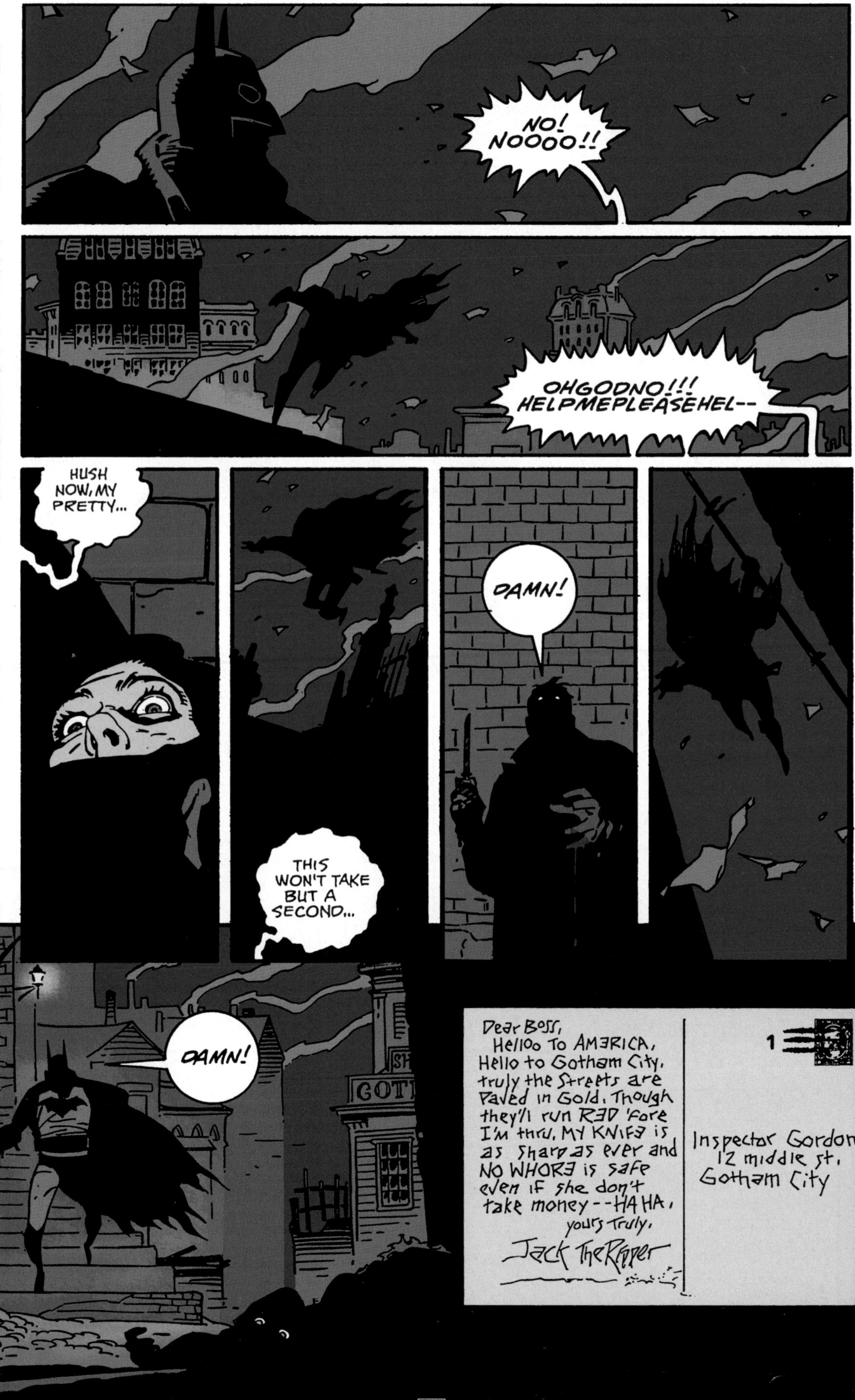
NO! NOOOO!!
OHGODNO!!! HELPMEPLEASEHEL--
HUSH NOW, MY PRETTY...
THIS WON'T TAKE BUT A SECOND...
DAMN!
DAMN!
Dear Boss,
Helloo to AMERICA,
Hello to Gotham City,
truly the Streets are
Paved in Gold. Though
they'll run RED 'fore
I'm thru. MY KNIFE is
as Sharp as ever and
NO WHORE is safe
even if she don't
take money --HA HA,
yours truly,
Jack The Ripper
1
Inspector Gordon
12 middle st.
Gotham City

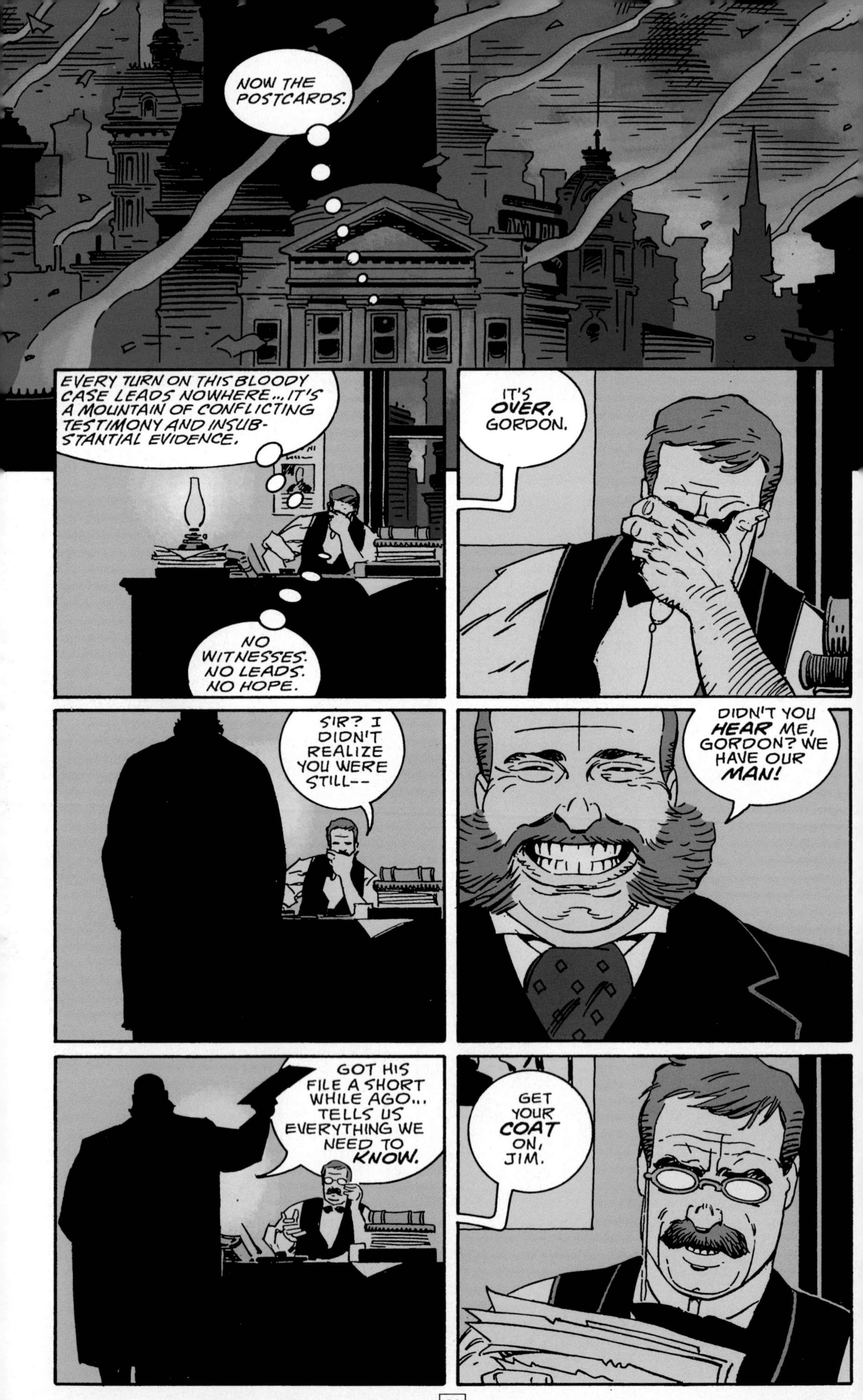
NOW THE POSTCARDS.
EVERY TURN ON THIS BLOODY CASE LEADS NOWHERE... IT'S A MOUNTAIN OF CONFLICTING TESTIMONY AND INSUB-STANTIAL EVIDENCE.
NO WITNESSES. NO LEADS. NO HOPE.
IT'S OVER, GORDON.
SIR? I DIDN'T REALIZE YOU WERE STILL--
DIDN'T YOU HEAR ME, GORDON? WE HAVE OUR MAN!
GOT HIS FILE A SHORT WHILE AGO... TELLS US EVERYTHING WE NEED TO KNOW.
GET YOUR COAT ON, JIM.

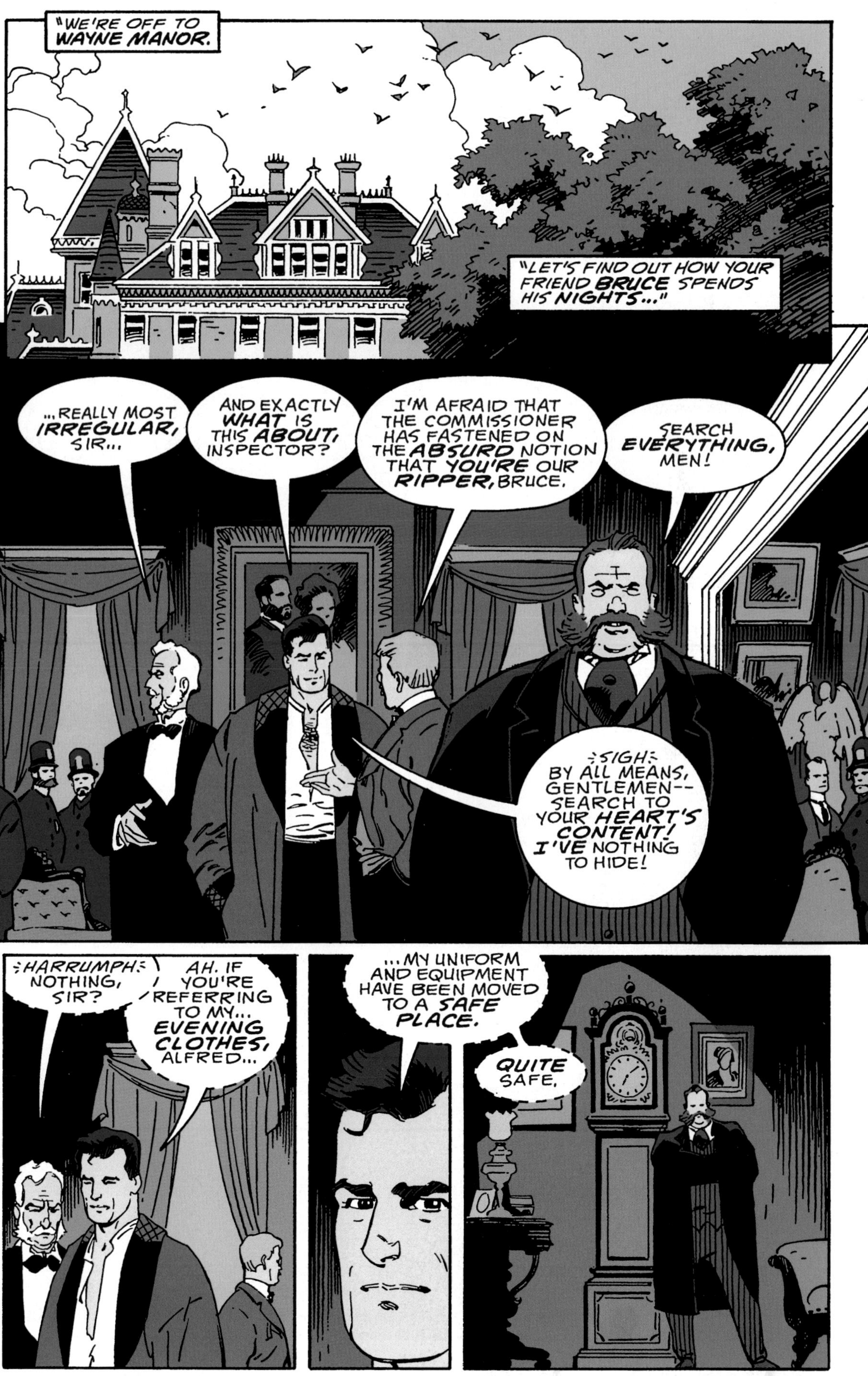
"WE'RE OFF TO WAYNE MANOR.
"LET'S FIND OUT HOW YOUR FRIEND BRUCE SPENDS HIS NIGHTS..."
...REALLY MOST IRREGULAR, SIR...
AND EXACTLY WHAT IS THIS ABOUT, INSPECTOR?
I'M AFRAID THAT THE COMMISSIONER HAS FASTENED ON THE ABSURD NOTION THAT YOU'RE OUR RIPPER, BRUCE.
SEARCH EVERYTHING, MEN!
SIGH BY ALL MEANS, GENTLEMEN-- SEARCH TO YOUR HEART'S CONTENT! I'VE NOTHING TO HIDE!
HARRUMPH NOTHING, SIR?
AH. IF YOU'RE REFERRING TO MY... EVENING CLOTHES, ALFRED...
...MY UNIFORM AND EQUIPMENT HAVE BEEN MOVED TO A SAFE PLACE.
QUITE SAFE.

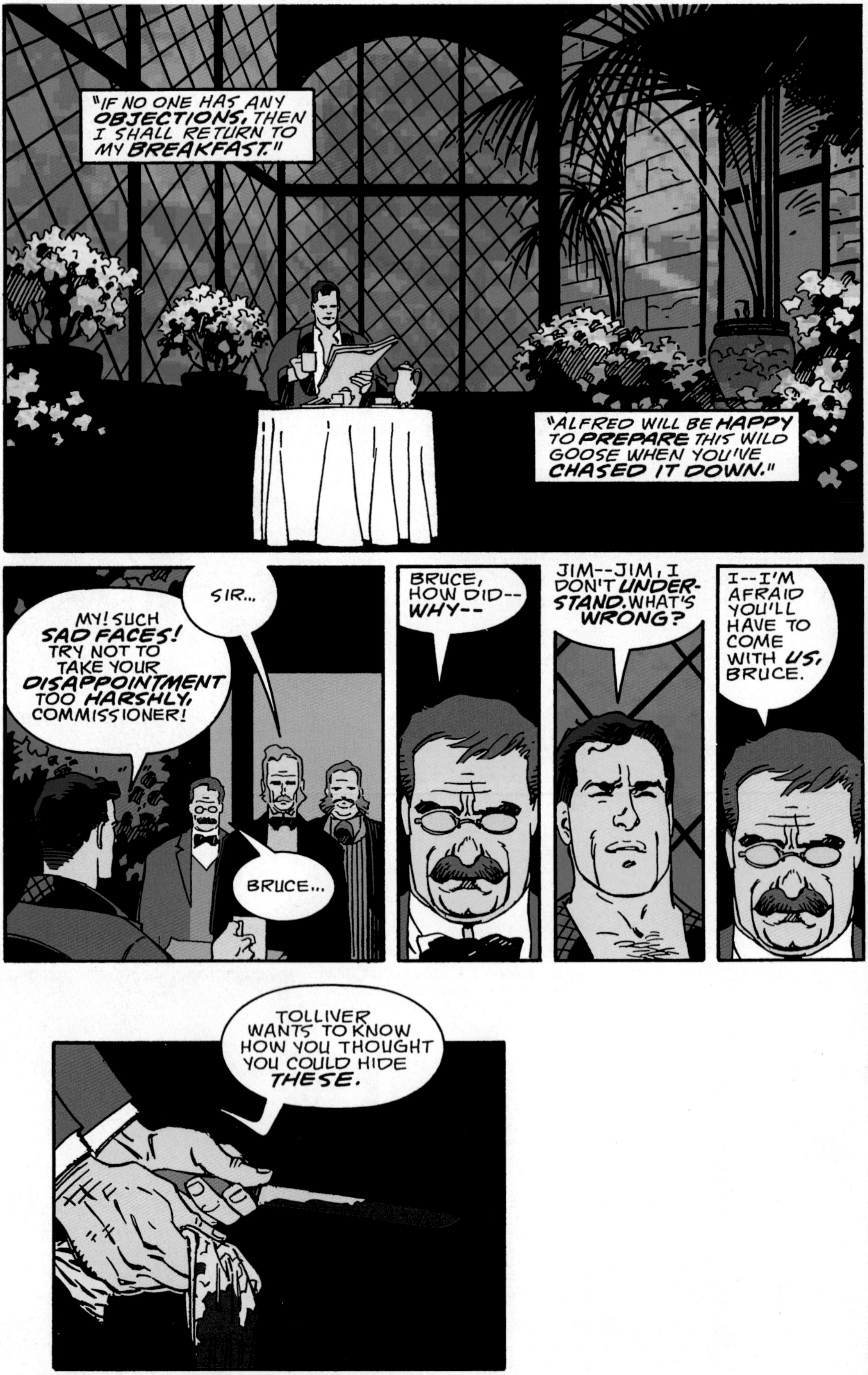
"IF NO ONE HAS ANY OBJECTIONS, THEN I SHALL RETURN TO MY BREAKFAST."
"ALFRED WILL BE HAPPY TO PREPARE THIS WILD GOOSE WHEN YOU'VE CHASED IT DOWN."
MY! SUCH SAD FACES! TRY NOT TO TAKE YOUR DISAPPOINTMENT TOO HARSHLY, COMMISSIONER!
SIR...
BRUCE...
BRUCE, HOW DID-- WHY--
JIM--JIM, I DON'T UNDERSTAND. WHAT'S WRONG?
I--I'M AFRAID YOU'LL HAVE TO COME WITH US, BRUCE.
TOLLIVER WANTS TO KNOW HOW YOU THOUGHT YOU COULD HIDE THESE.

OCTOBER 9--
MY TRIAL BEGAN TODAY. THE COURT-HOUSE WAS PACKED WITH THE CURIOUS MULTITUDE.

THE INDICTMENTS AGAINST ME FOR THE MURDERS OF THE WOMEN WERE READ. UNCLE JAKE, ACTING AS MY COUNSEL, ASSURES ME THAT THE STATE'S CASE IS WEAK AND GUARANTEES ME A SPEEDY ACQUITTAL.

WE HEARD THE OPENING REMARKS BY GOTHAM'S ESTEEMED DISTRICT ATTORNEY. WITHIN TEN MINUTES, I WAS CALLED A "MURDEROUS MONSTER" FOUR TIMES AND A "BLOOD-LUSTING MANIAC" TWICE. I HAD THOUGHT HARVEY AND I WERE **FRIENDS**.

OCTOBER 12--

THE PROSECUTION TROTTED OUT MORE OF THEIR "WITNESSES." ONE WOMAN EVEN CLAIMED TO HAVE **SEEN** ME, KNIFE IN HAND, RUNNING FROM THE SCENE OF A MURDER. IT IS OBVIOUS TO ALL THAT THE WOMAN DRINKS HEAVILY AND VIEWS EVERYTHING THROUGH A RUM-SOAKED HAZE. EVEN THE JURY MUST REALIZE THIS.

I AM BEGINNING TO BE CONCERNED WITH GOTHAM'S AND TOLLIVER'S DESPERATE HUNGER FOR A SCAPEGOAT. WHEN I AM ACQUITTED, I MUST FIND THE RIPPER **POSTHASTE**.

OCTOBER 15--

TOLLIVER TOOK THE STAND TO PRESENT THE POLICE DEPARTMENT'S CASE. HE OUTLINED THE LONDON RIPPER MURDERS AND POINTED UP THE SIMILARITIES. WHILE IT IS OBVIOUS EVEN TO A FATUOUS IDIOT LIKE TOLLIVER THAT THE KILLINGS **ARE** THE WORK OF THE SAME HAND, MY "GUILT" IS "ESTABLISHED" BY THE REVELATION THAT I WAS IN LONDON AT THE TIME OF THE ORIGINAL RIPPER SLAYINGS--AND THAT I HAVE TROUBLE ACCOUNTING FOR MY **NIGHTS**.

THE RIPPER IS SAID TO HAVE MEDICAL TRAINING --AND SO MY RELATIONSHIP WITH MY FATHER THE **DOCTOR** IS INVOKED.

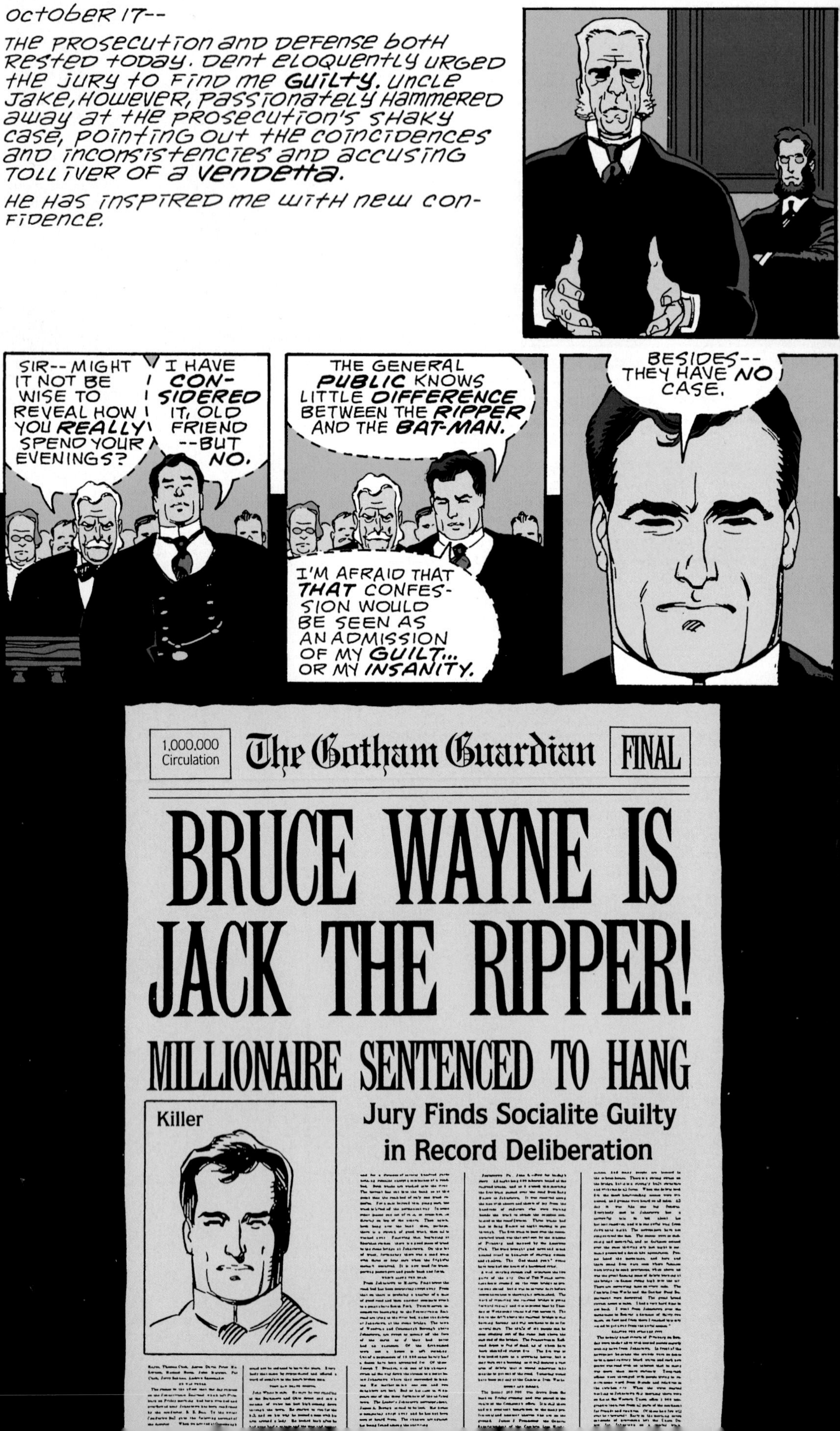

october 17--

the prosecution and defense both rested today. Dent eloquently urged the jury to find me GUILTY. Uncle Jake, however, passionately hammered away at the prosecution's shaky case, pointing out the coincidences and inconsistencies and accusing Tolliver of a VENDETTA.

He has inspired me with new confidence.

SIR-- MIGHT IT NOT BE WISE TO REVEAL HOW YOU *REALLY* SPEND YOUR EVENINGS?

I HAVE CONSIDERED IT, OLD FRIEND --BUT NO.

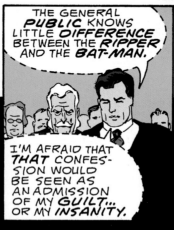

THE GENERAL *PUBLIC* KNOWS LITTLE *DIFFERENCE* BETWEEN THE *RIPPER* AND THE *BAT-MAN.*

I'M AFRAID THAT *THAT* CONFESSION WOULD BE SEEN AS AN ADMISSION OF MY *GUILT*... OR MY *INSANITY*.

BESIDES-- THEY HAVE *NO* CASE.

1,000,000 Circulation

The Gotham Guardian

FINAL

BRUCE WAYNE IS JACK THE RIPPER!

MILLIONAIRE SENTENCED TO HANG

Jury Finds Socialite Guilty in Record Deliberation

Killer

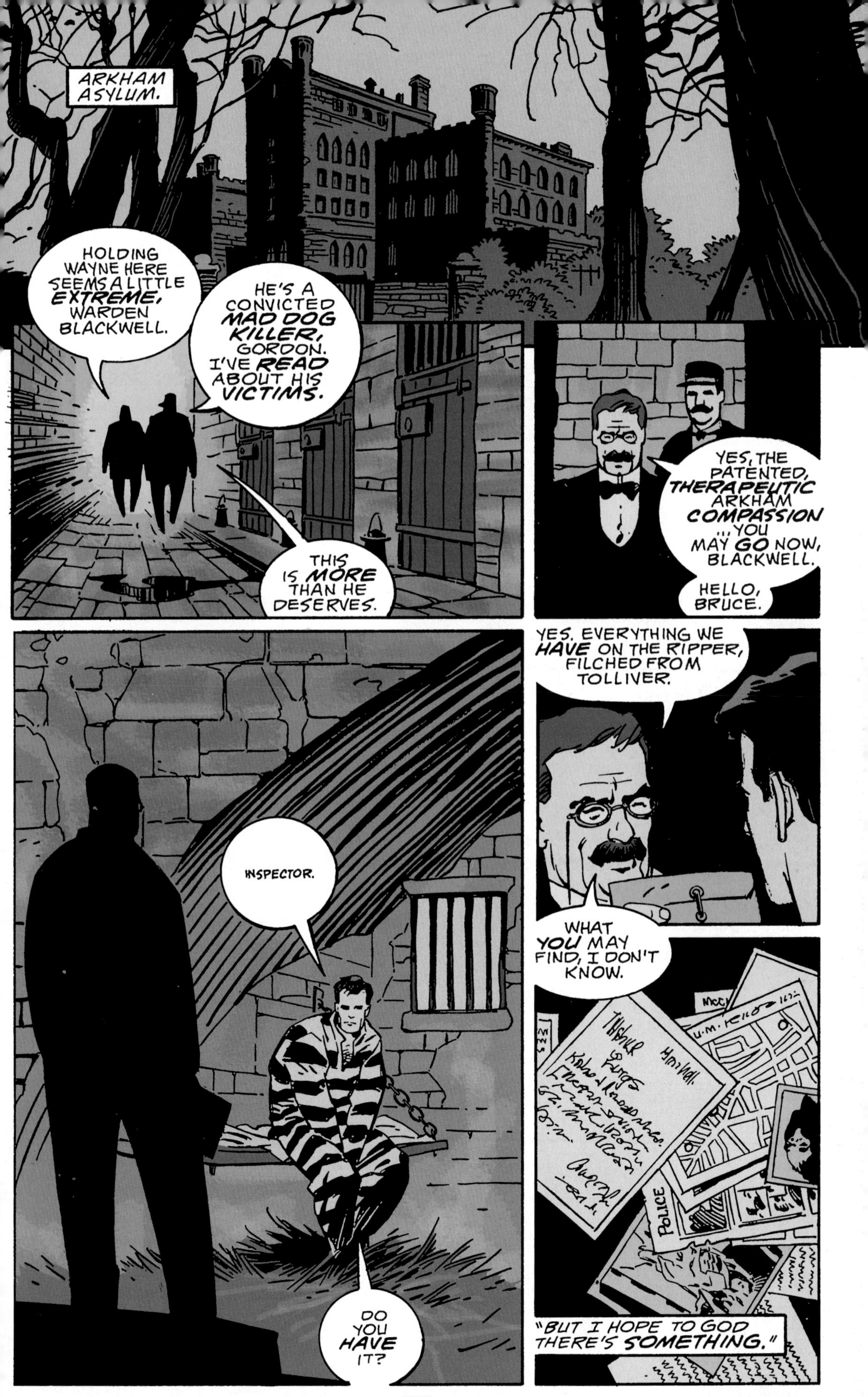
ARKHAM ASYLUM.
HOLDING WAYNE HERE SEEMS A LITTLE EXTREME, WARDEN BLACKWELL.
HE'S A CONVICTED MAD DOG KILLER, GORDON. I'VE READ ABOUT HIS VICTIMS.
THIS IS MORE THAN HE DESERVES.
YES, THE PATENTED, THERAPEUTIC ARKHAM COMPASSION ... YOU MAY GO NOW, BLACKWELL.
HELLO, BRUCE.
INSPECTOR.
DO YOU HAVE IT?
YES. EVERYTHING WE HAVE ON THE RIPPER, FILCHED FROM TOLLIVER.
WHAT YOU MAY FIND, I DON'T KNOW.
POLICE
"BUT I HOPE TO GOD THERE'S SOMETHING."

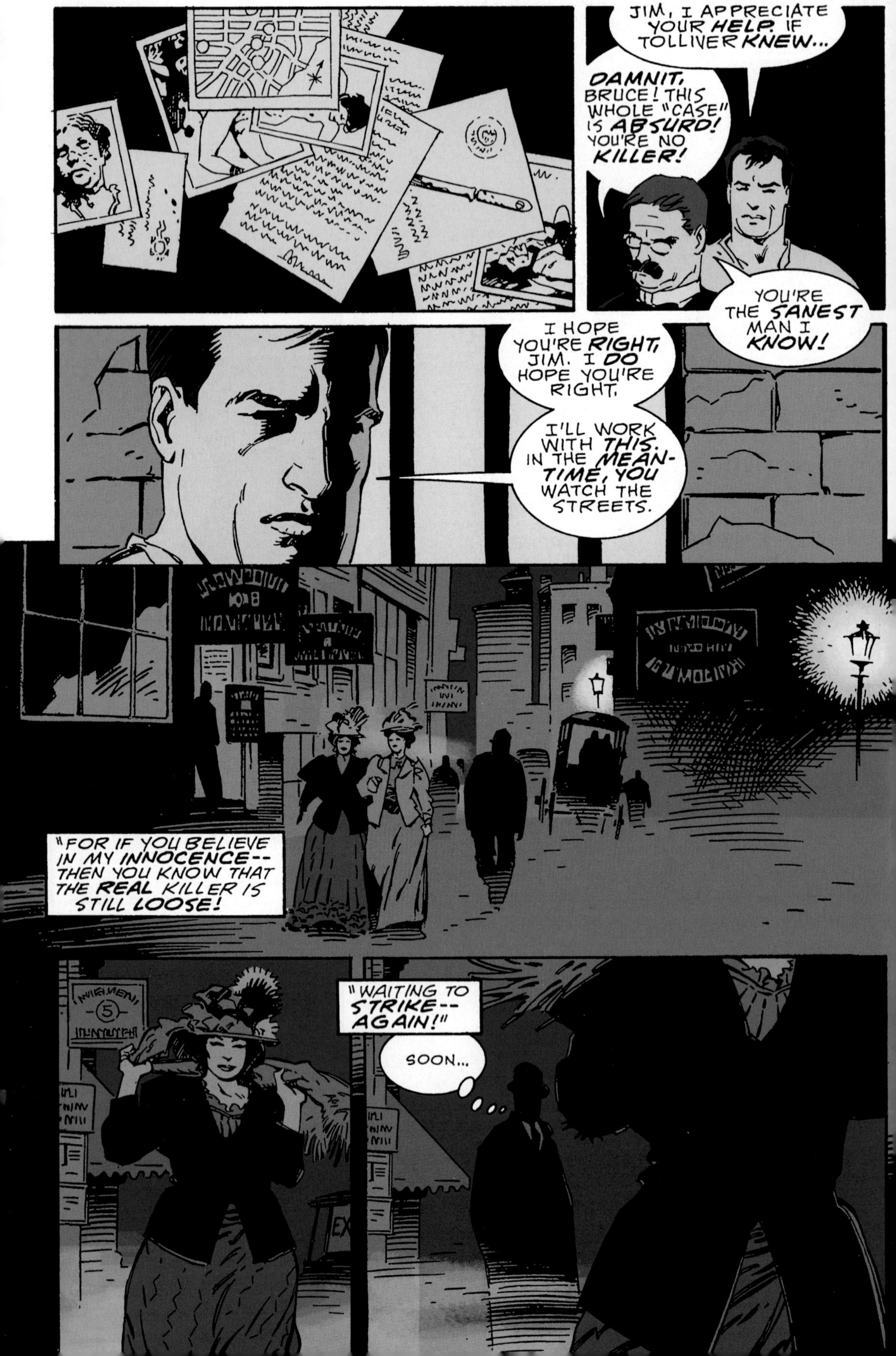
JIM, I APPRECIATE YOUR HELP. IF TOLLIVER KNEW...
DAMNIT, BRUCE! THIS WHOLE "CASE" IS ABSURD! YOU'RE NO KILLER!
YOU'RE THE SANEST MAN I KNOW!
I HOPE YOU'RE RIGHT, JIM. I DO HOPE YOU'RE RIGHT.
I'LL WORK WITH THIS. IN THE MEAN-TIME, YOU WATCH THE STREETS.
"FOR IF YOU BELIEVE IN MY INNOCENCE-- THEN YOU KNOW THAT THE REAL KILLER IS STILL LOOSE!
"WAITING TO STRIKE-- AGAIN!"
SOON...

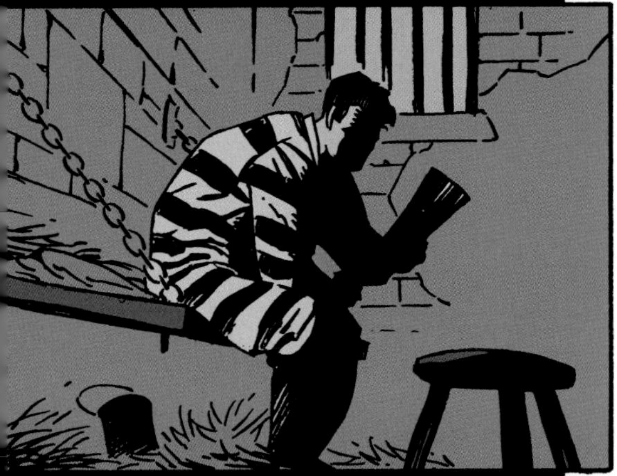

OCTOBER 21--

MY ONLY HOPE OF SURVIVAL LIES IN MY SOLVING CRIMES FROM MY **CELL**.... THAT TWO POLICE FORCES COULD **NOT**.

I HAVE SURROUNDED MYSELF WITH EVERY SCRAP OF EVIDENCE FROM TWO SIDES OF THE ATLANTIC, WITH NEWSPAPER REPORTS, AND EVEN WITH SOME OF MY FATHER'S OLD MEDICAL TEXTS SO AS TO BETTER UNDERSTAND THE RIPPER'S HANDIWORK.

I **MUST** FIND AN ANSWER.

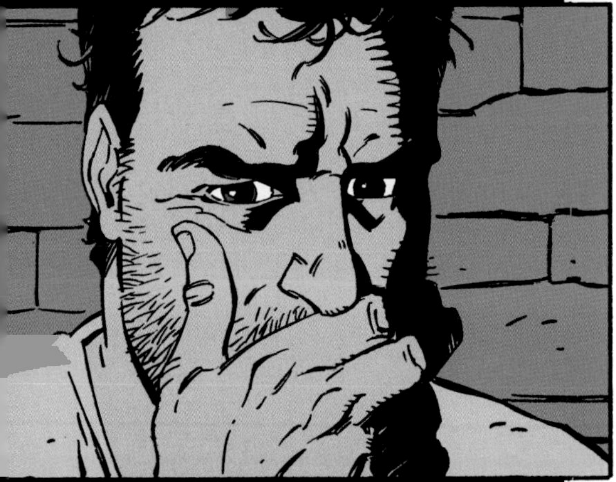

OCTOBER 23--

IT IS A PUZZLE WITH A MILLION PIECES AND NO CLUE TO THE FINISHED PICTURE. I CONSIDER MYSELF A TRAINED DETECTIVE-- I HAVE STUDIED WITH THE FINEST MINDS OF MY **TIME**-- AND NOW MUST APPLY ALL OF THAT LEARNED WISDOM TOWARDS A SOLUTION.

IT IS EITHER THAT...OR THE **GALLOWS**.

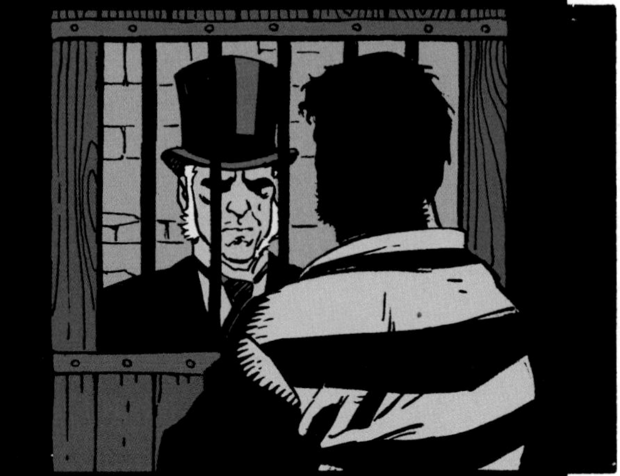

OCTOBER 26--

JAKE STOPPED BY WITH TERRIBLE NEWS. MY APPEAL WAS DENIED. THE POWERS THAT BE IN GOTHAM, ANXIOUS TO SET THIS WHOLE MESS BEHIND THEM, ARE CONTENT THAT THEY HAVE **FOUND** THEIR KILLER.

JAKE IS CRUSHED. HE HAS WORKED SO HARD ON MY BEHALF. I MUST REDOUBLE MY EFFORTS. I HANG IN FIVE DAYS.

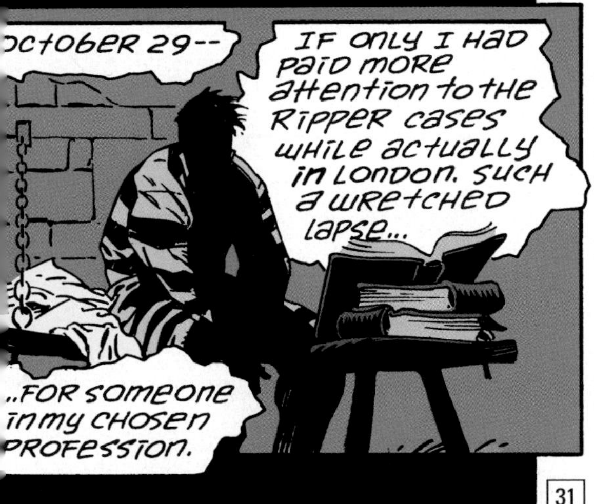
OCTOBER 29--
IF ONLY I HAD PAID MORE ATTENTION TO THE RIPPER CASES WHILE ACTUALLY IN LONDON. SUCH A WRETCHED LAPSE...
..FOR SOMEONE IN MY CHOSEN PROFESSION.

THE GOTHAM KILLINGS ARE A PERFECT MATCH FOR THE WHITECHAPEL MURDERS OF A YEAR AGO. THE METHODS OF ATTACK, DISSECTION, AND DISPOSAL ARE ALL IDENTICAL, EXECUTED WITH A SURGEON'S FINESSE. THE TAUNTING LETTERS SENT BY THE RIPPER TO THE BRITISH BOBBIES MATCH THOSE SENT TO GORDON RIGHT DOWN TO THE DOTS ON THE "I"S. IT IS CLEARLY THE WORK OF THE SAME MAN-- BUT **WHO?** AND WHY HAS HE FRAMED **ME** SO **PERFECTLY?** I DO NOT KNOW.

I DO NOT KNOW.

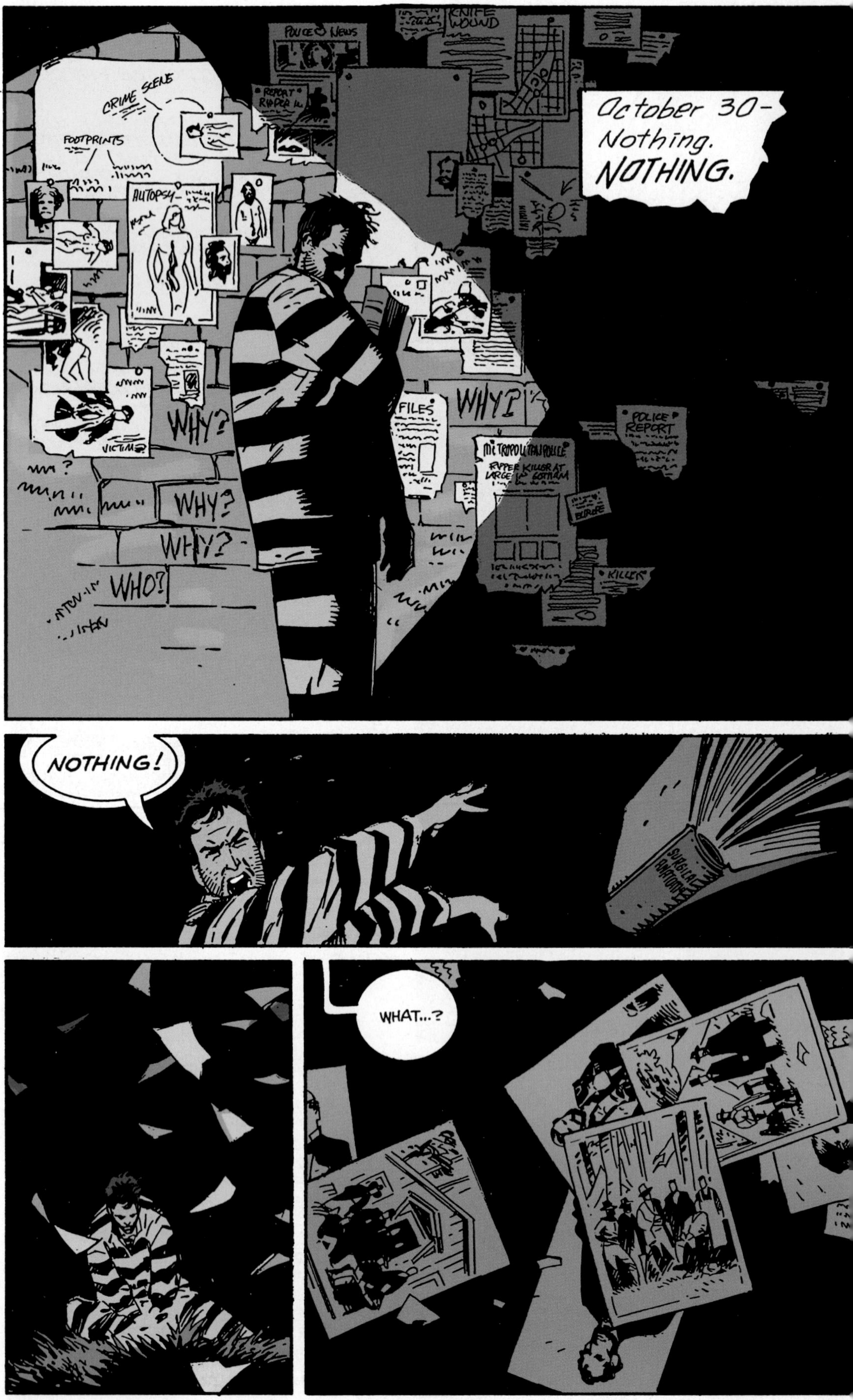
October 30-
Nothing.
NOTHING.
NOTHING!
WHAT...?

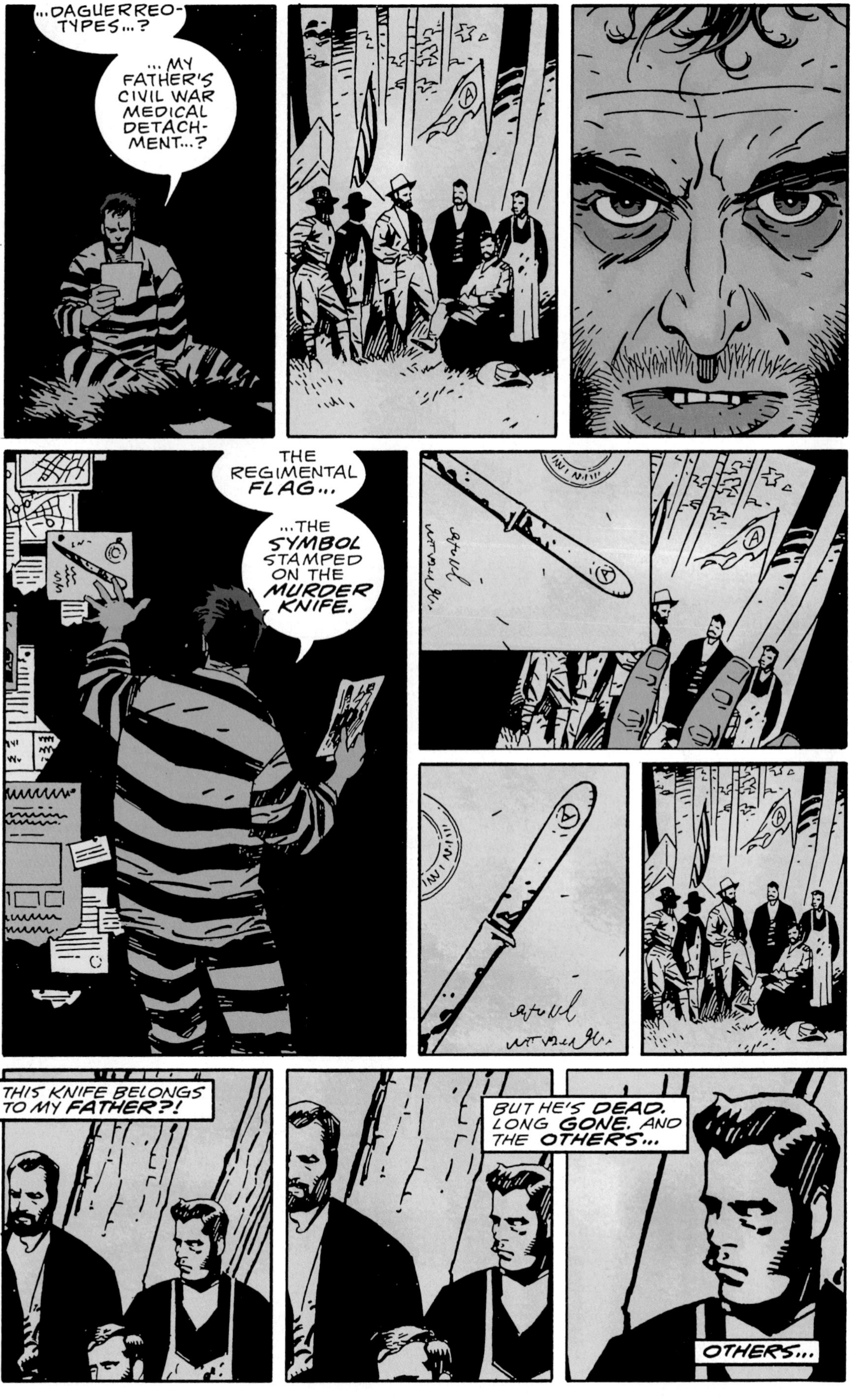
...DAGUERREO-TYPES...?
...MY FATHER'S CIVIL WAR MEDICAL DETACH-MENT...?
THE REGIMENTAL FLAG...
...THE SYMBOL STAMPED ON THE MURDER KNIFE.
THIS KNIFE BELONGS TO MY FATHER?!
BUT HE'S DEAD. LONG GONE. AND THE OTHERS...
OTHERS...

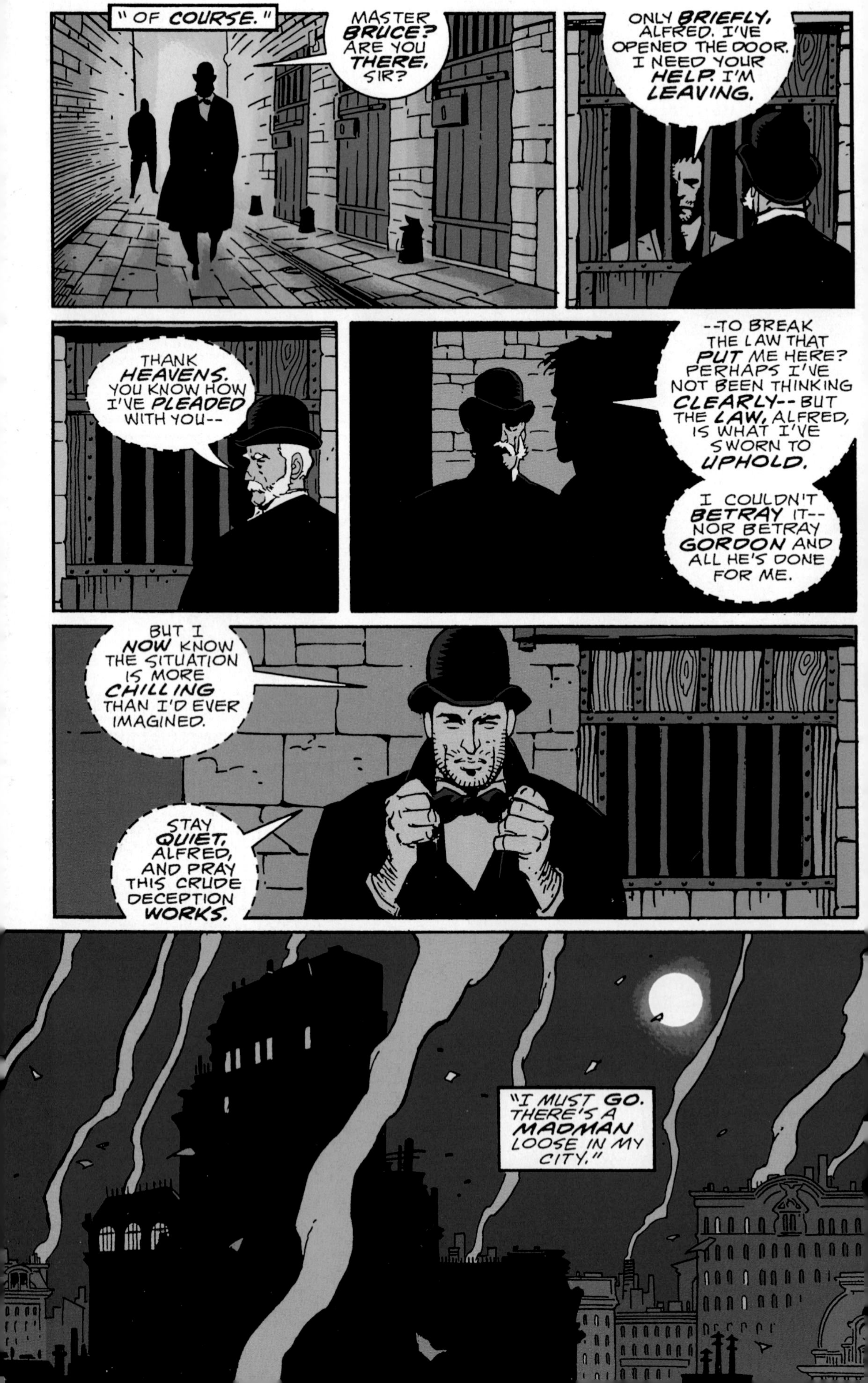
"OF COURSE."
MASTER BRUCE? ARE YOU THERE, SIR?
ONLY BRIEFLY, ALFRED. I'VE OPENED THE DOOR. I NEED YOUR HELP. I'M LEAVING.
THANK HEAVENS. YOU KNOW HOW I'VE PLEADED WITH YOU--
--TO BREAK THE LAW THAT PUT ME HERE? PERHAPS I'VE NOT BEEN THINKING CLEARLY-- BUT THE LAW, ALFRED, IS WHAT I'VE SWORN TO UPHOLD.
I COULDN'T BETRAY IT-- NOR BETRAY GORDON AND ALL HE'S DONE FOR ME.
BUT I NOW KNOW THE SITUATION IS MORE CHILLING THAN I'D EVER IMAGINED.
STAY QUIET, ALFRED, AND PRAY THIS CRUDE DECEPTION WORKS.
"I MUST GO. THERE'S A MADMAN LOOSE IN MY CITY."

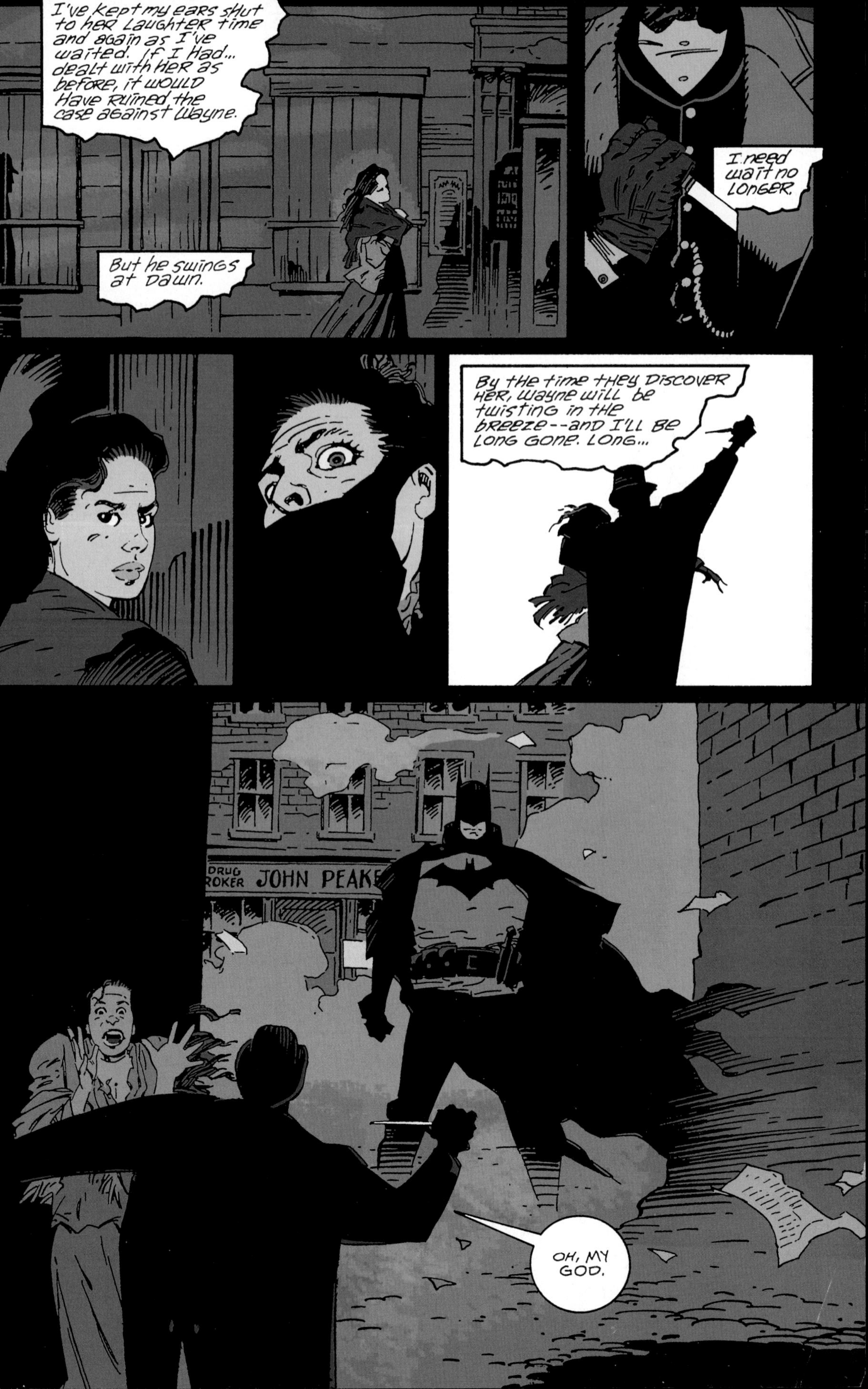
I've kept my ears shut to her laughter time and again as I've waited. If I had... dealt with her as before, it would have ruined the case against Wayne.
But he swings at dawn.
I need wait no longer.
By the time they discover her, Wayne will be twisting in the breeze--and I'll be long gone. Long...
DRUG ROKER JOHN PEAKE
OH, MY GOD.

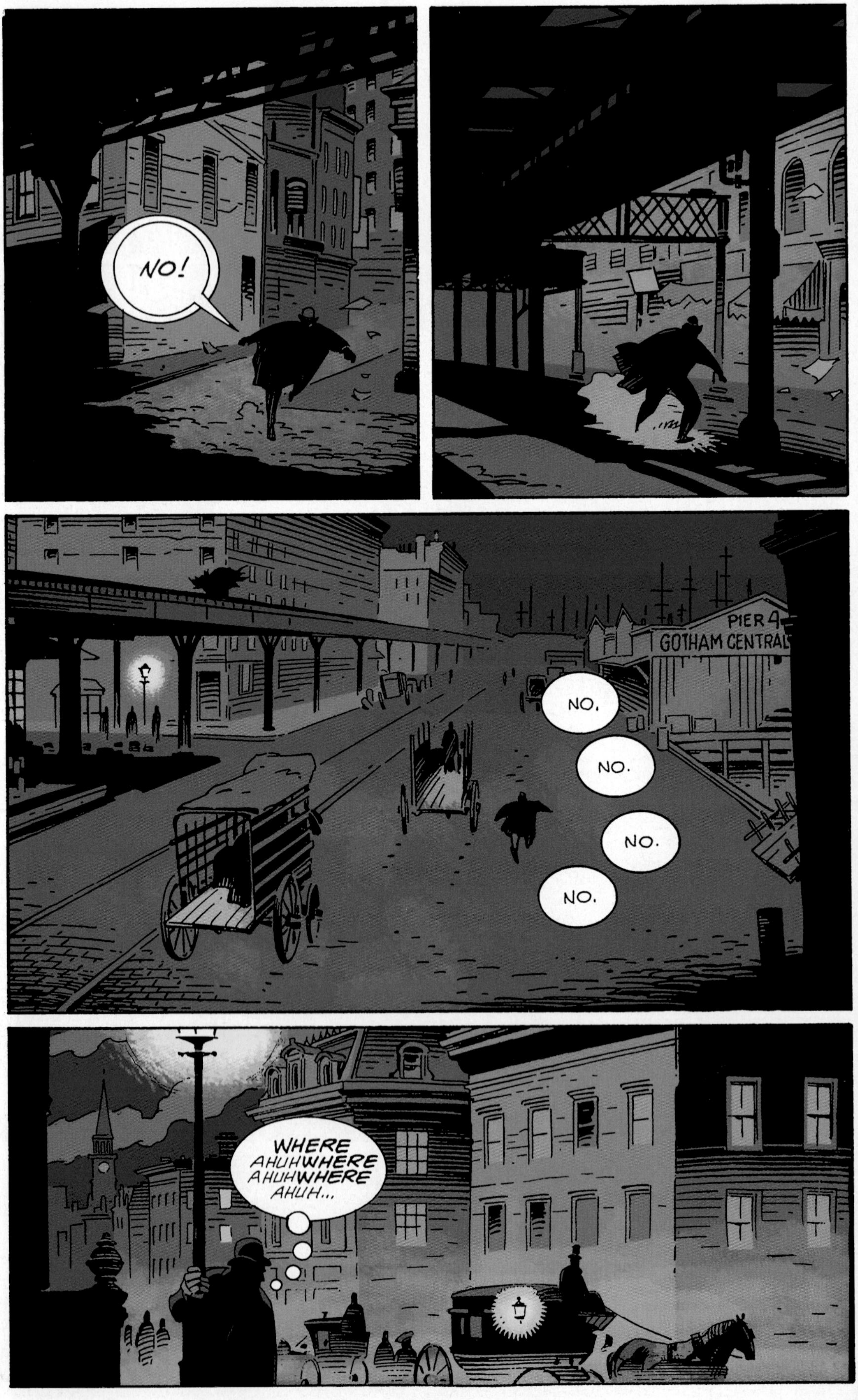
NO!
PIER 4
GOTHAM CENTRAL
NO.
NO.
NO.
NO.
WHERE
AHUHWHERE
AHUHWHERE
AHUH...

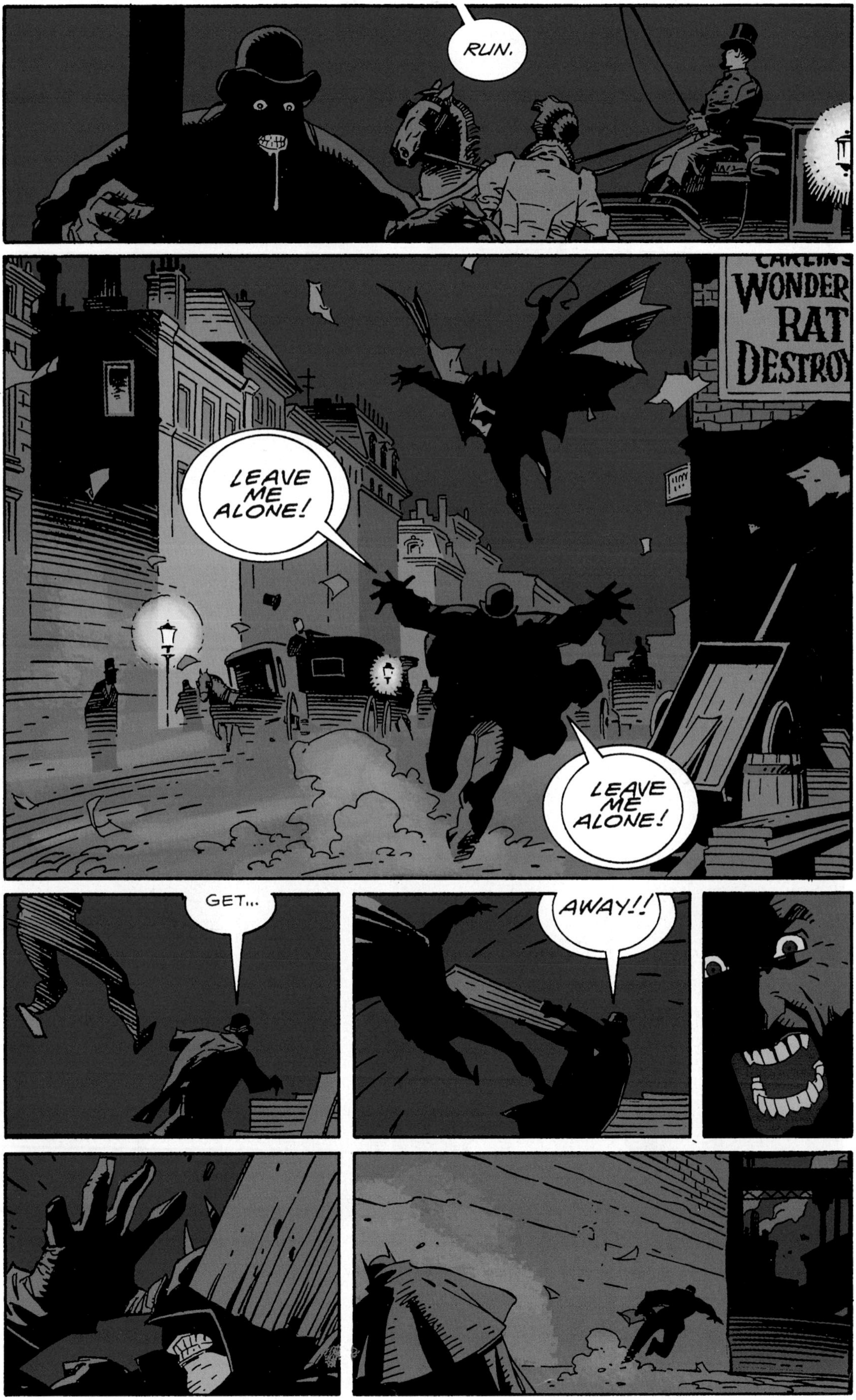
RUN.
WONDER
RAT
DESTROY
LEAVE ME ALONE!
LEAVE ME ALONE!
GET...
AWAY!!

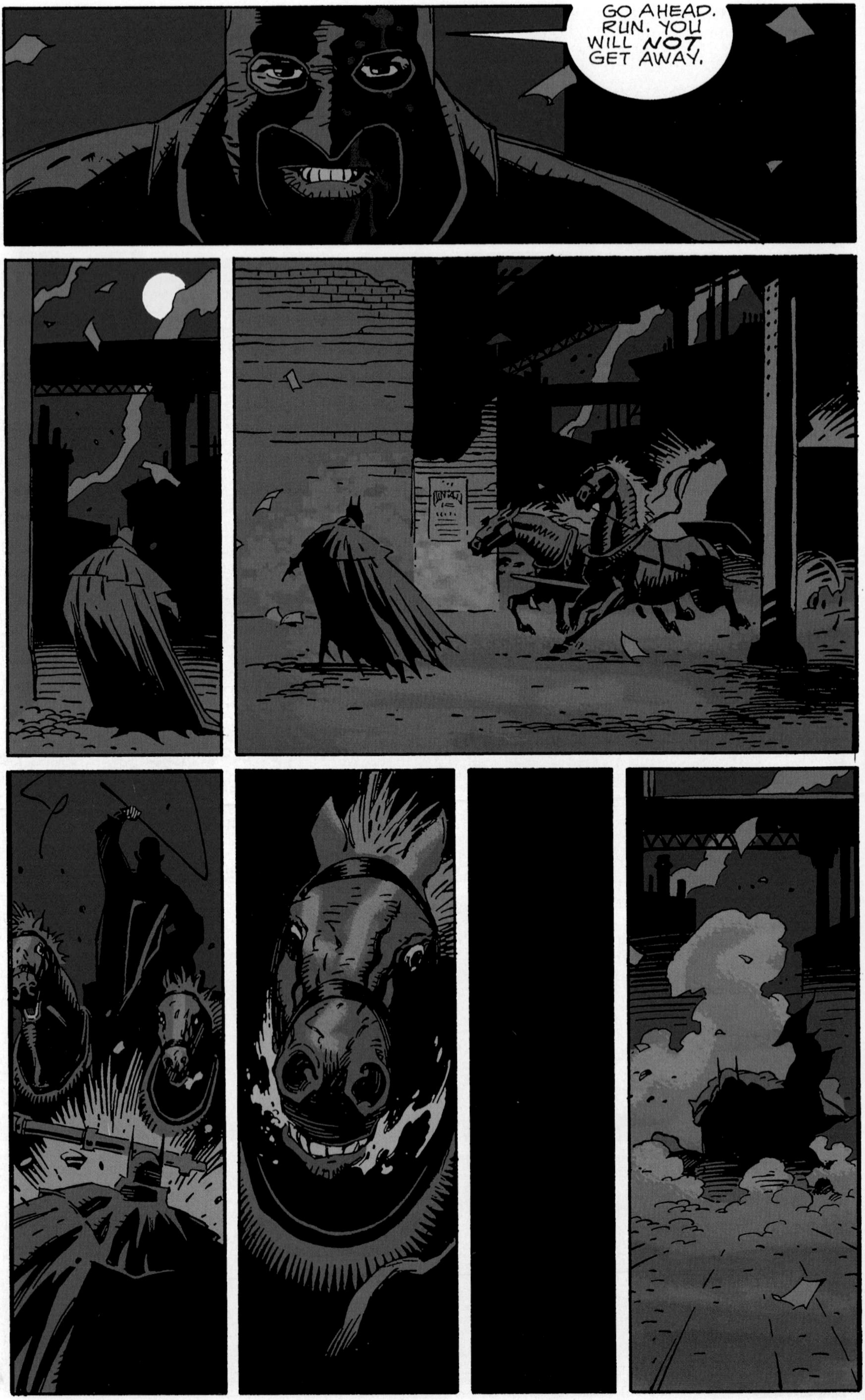
GO AHEAD. RUN. YOU WILL NOT GET AWAY.

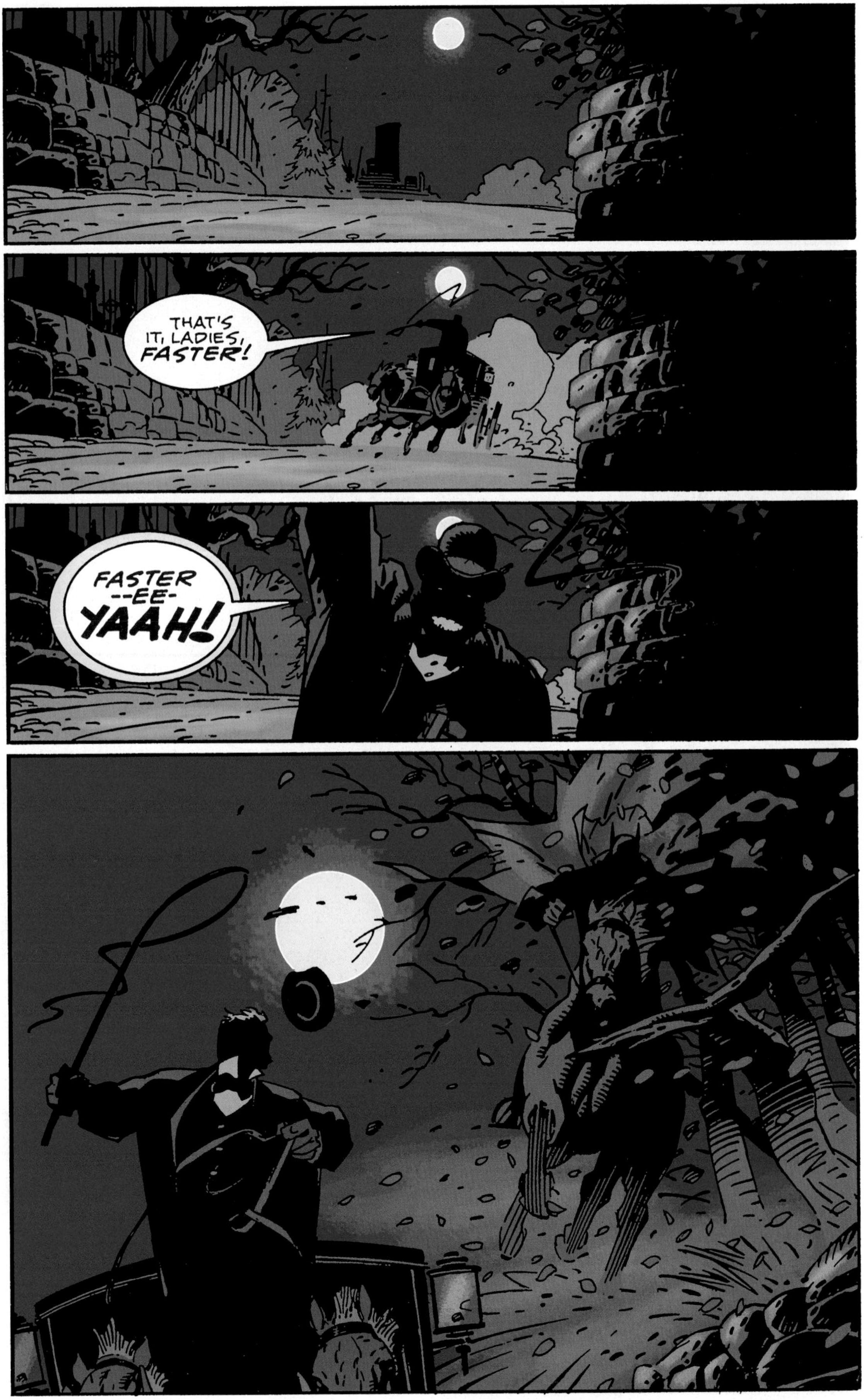
THAT'S IT, LADIES, FASTER!
FASTER --EE- YAAH!

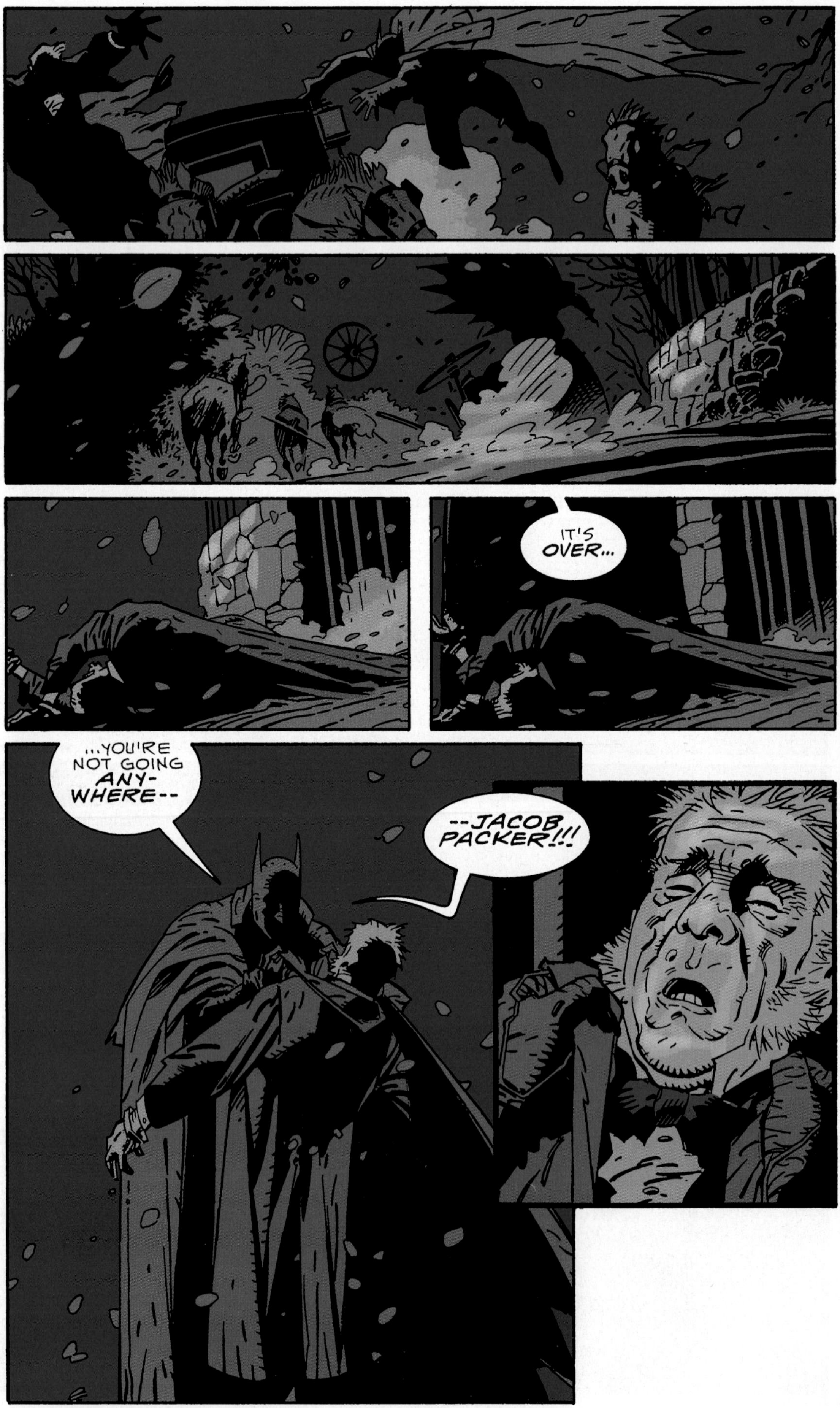
IT'S OVER...
...YOU'RE NOT GOING ANY-WHERE--
--JACOB PACKER!!!

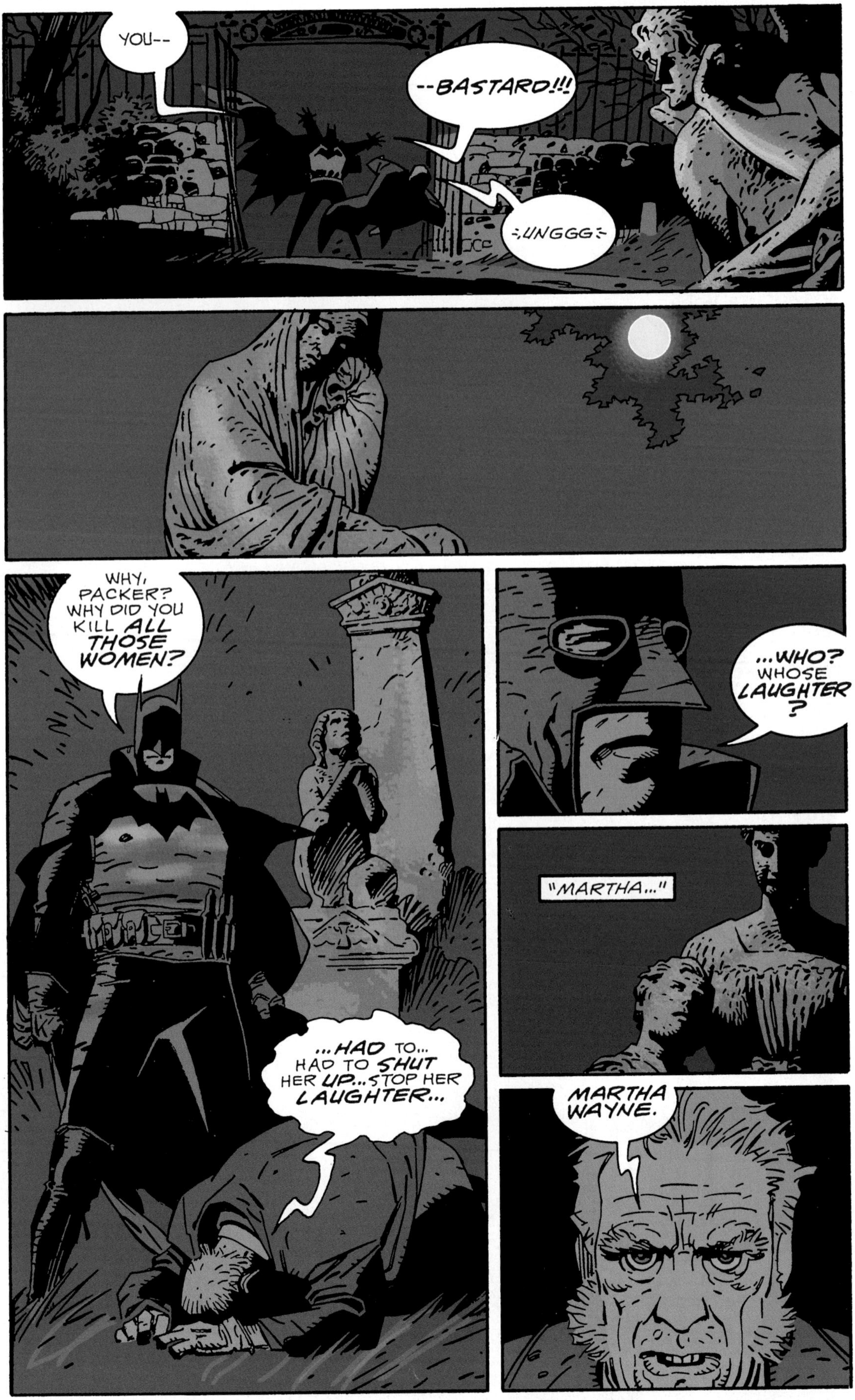
YOU--
--BASTARD!!!
UNGGG
WHY, PACKER? WHY DID YOU KILL ALL THOSE WOMEN?
...WHO? WHOSE LAUGHTER?
...HAD TO... HAD TO SHUT HER UP...STOP HER LAUGHTER...
"MARTHA..."
MARTHA WAYNE.

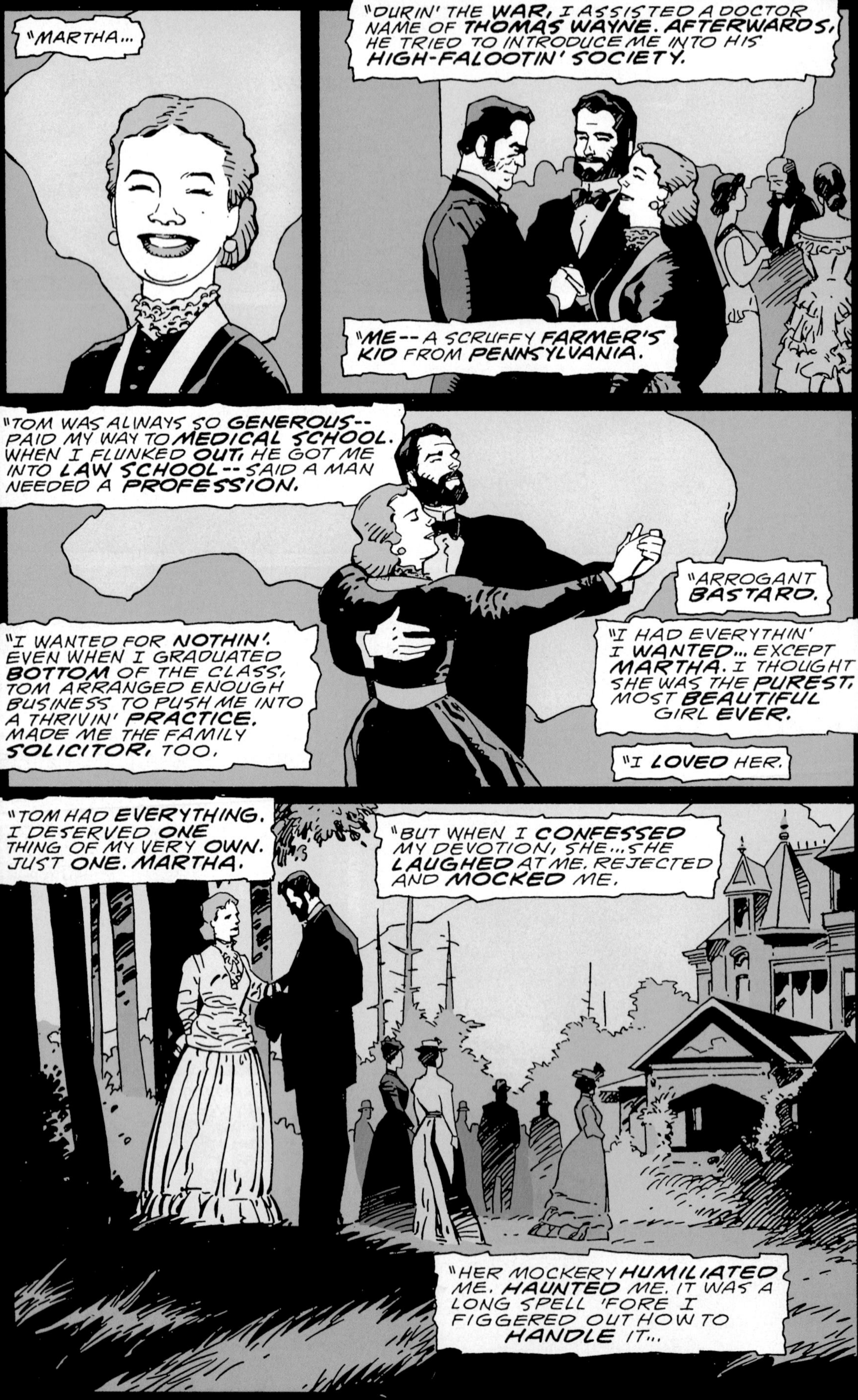
"MARTHA...
"DURIN' THE WAR, I ASSISTED A DOCTOR NAME OF THOMAS WAYNE. AFTERWARDS, HE TRIED TO INTRODUCE ME INTO HIS HIGH-FALOOTIN' SOCIETY.
"ME--A SCRUFFY FARMER'S KID FROM PENNSYLVANIA.
"TOM WAS ALWAYS SO GENEROUS--PAID MY WAY TO MEDICAL SCHOOL. WHEN I FLUNKED OUT, HE GOT ME INTO LAW SCHOOL--SAID A MAN NEEDED A PROFESSION.
"I WANTED FOR NOTHIN'. EVEN WHEN I GRADUATED BOTTOM OF THE CLASS, TOM ARRANGED ENOUGH BUSINESS TO PUSH ME INTO A THRIVIN' PRACTICE. MADE ME THE FAMILY SOLICITOR, TOO.
"ARROGANT BASTARD.
"I HAD EVERYTHIN' I WANTED... EXCEPT MARTHA. I THOUGHT SHE WAS THE PUREST, MOST BEAUTIFUL GIRL EVER.
"I LOVED HER.
"TOM HAD EVERYTHING. I DESERVED ONE THING OF MY VERY OWN. JUST ONE. MARTHA.
"BUT WHEN I CONFESSED MY DEVOTION, SHE...SHE LAUGHED AT ME. REJECTED AND MOCKED ME.
"HER MOCKERY HUMILIATED ME. HAUNTED ME. IT WAS A LONG SPELL 'FORE I FIGGERED OUT HOW TO HANDLE IT...

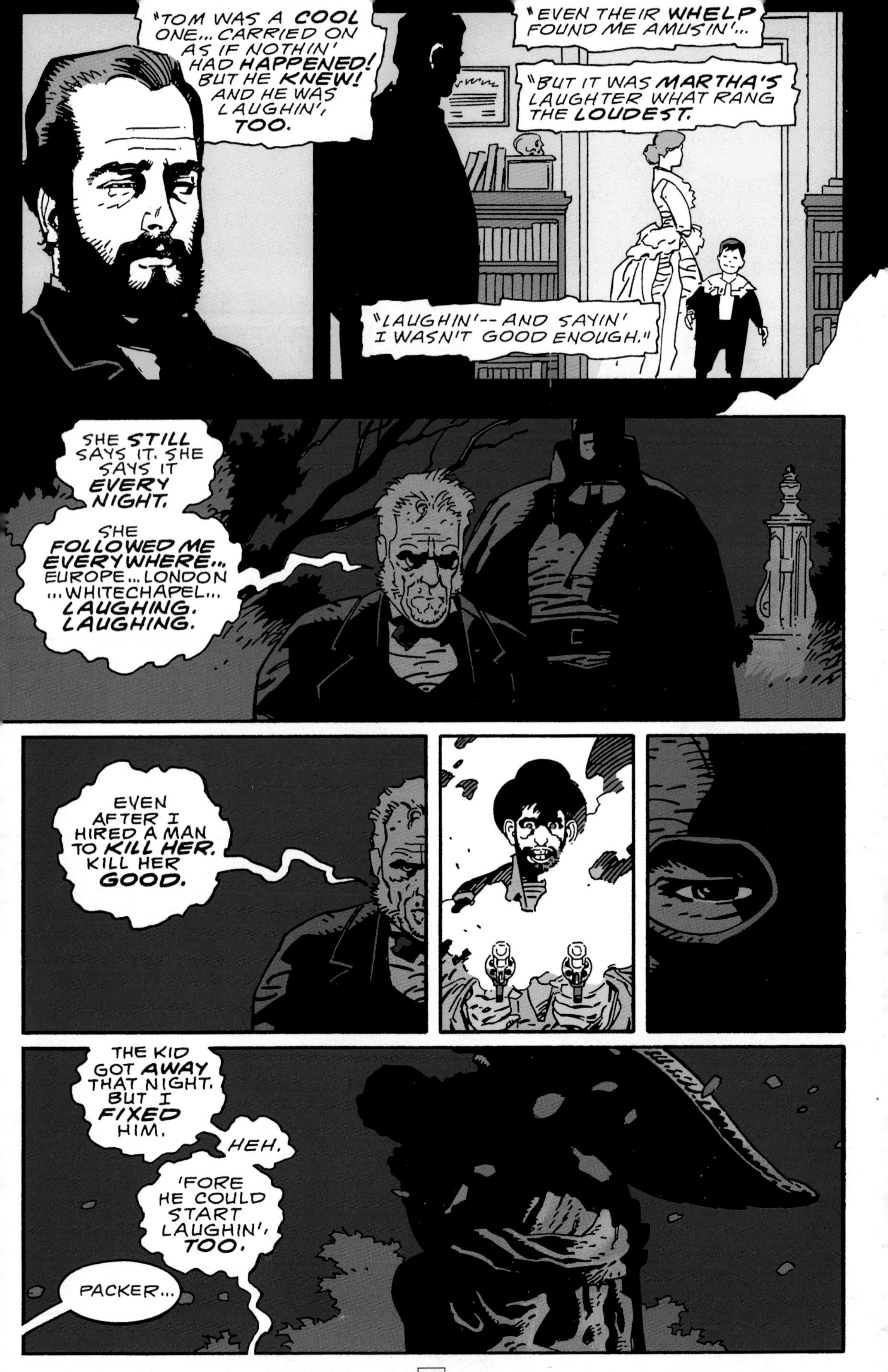

"TOM WAS A COOL ONE... CARRIED ON AS IF NOTHIN' HAD HAPPENED! BUT HE KNEW! AND HE WAS LAUGHIN', TOO.
"EVEN THEIR WHELP FOUND ME AMUSIN'...
"BUT IT WAS MARTHA'S LAUGHTER WHAT RANG THE LOUDEST.
"LAUGHIN'-- AND SAYIN' I WASN'T GOOD ENOUGH."
SHE STILL SAYS IT. SHE SAYS IT EVERY NIGHT.
SHE FOLLOWED ME EVERYWHERE... EUROPE... LONDON ...WHITECHAPEL... LAUGHING. LAUGHING.
EVEN AFTER I HIRED A MAN TO KILL HER. KILL HER GOOD.
THE KID GOT AWAY THAT NIGHT. BUT I FIXED HIM.
HEH.
'FORE HE COULD START LAUGHIN', TOO.
PACKER...

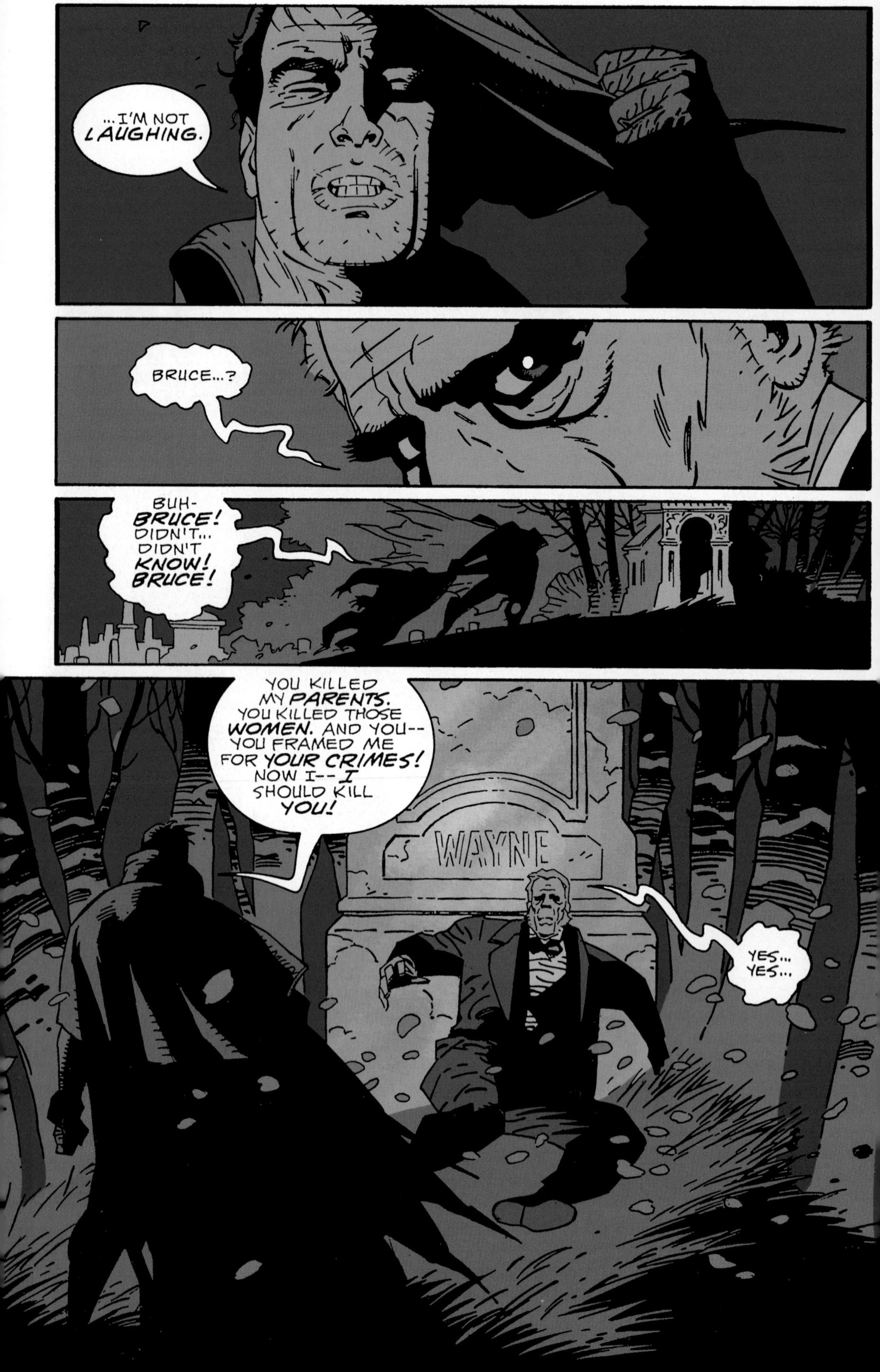
...I'M NOT LAUGHING.
BRUCE...?
BUH- BRUCE! DIDN'T... DIDN'T KNOW! BRUCE!
YOU KILLED MY PARENTS. YOU KILLED THOSE WOMEN. AND YOU-- YOU FRAMED ME FOR YOUR CRIMES! NOW I--I SHOULD KILL YOU!
WAYNE
YES... YES...

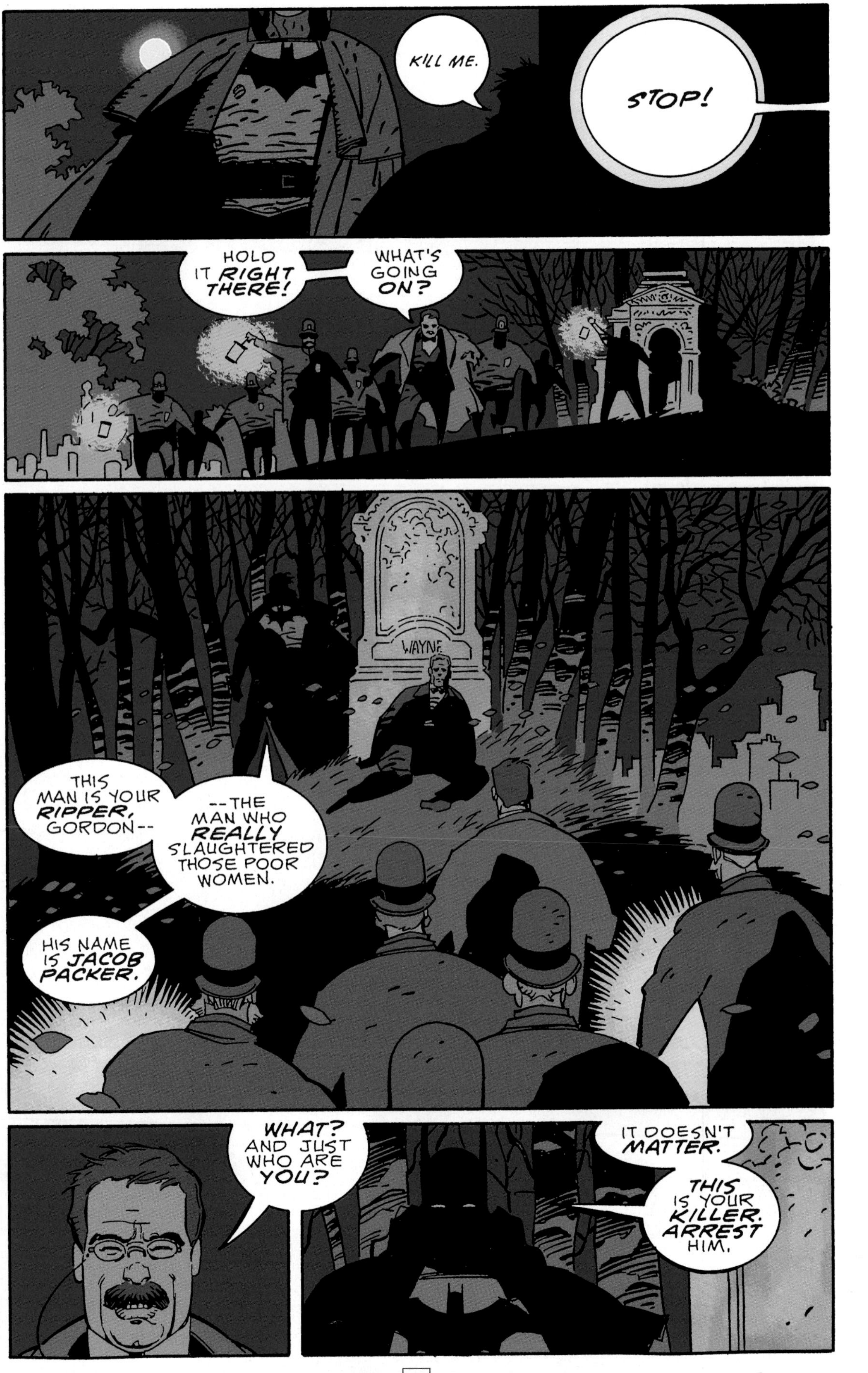
KILL ME.
STOP!
HOLD IT RIGHT THERE!
WHAT'S GOING ON?
WAYNE
THIS MAN IS YOUR RIPPER, GORDON--
--THE MAN WHO REALLY SLAUGHTERED THOSE POOR WOMEN.
HIS NAME IS JACOB PACKER.
WHAT? AND JUST WHO ARE YOU?
IT DOESN'T MATTER.
THIS IS YOUR KILLER. ARREST HIM.

'STRUE...
I'M YOUR MAN...
KILLED THE WOMEN
...HERE *ANO*
IN LONDON...

...EVEN
KILLED A
COUPLE O'
WHORES IN
PARIS WHAT
NO ONE EVER
CONNECTED...

...THEN
FRAMED
WAYNE.

...ALL THAT
BLOOD...
I'VE BEEN
VERY BAD.

I
SEE.

ALL
RIGHT.
BOTH OF
YOU ARE
COMING
WITH
US.

YES,
INDEEDIE...
VERY, *VERY*
BAD...

...HEH,
HEH...
YOURS
TRULY...

AAARRGHH!

JACK
THE
RIPPER!

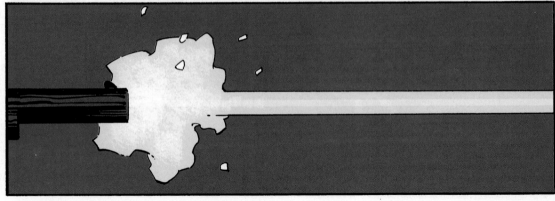

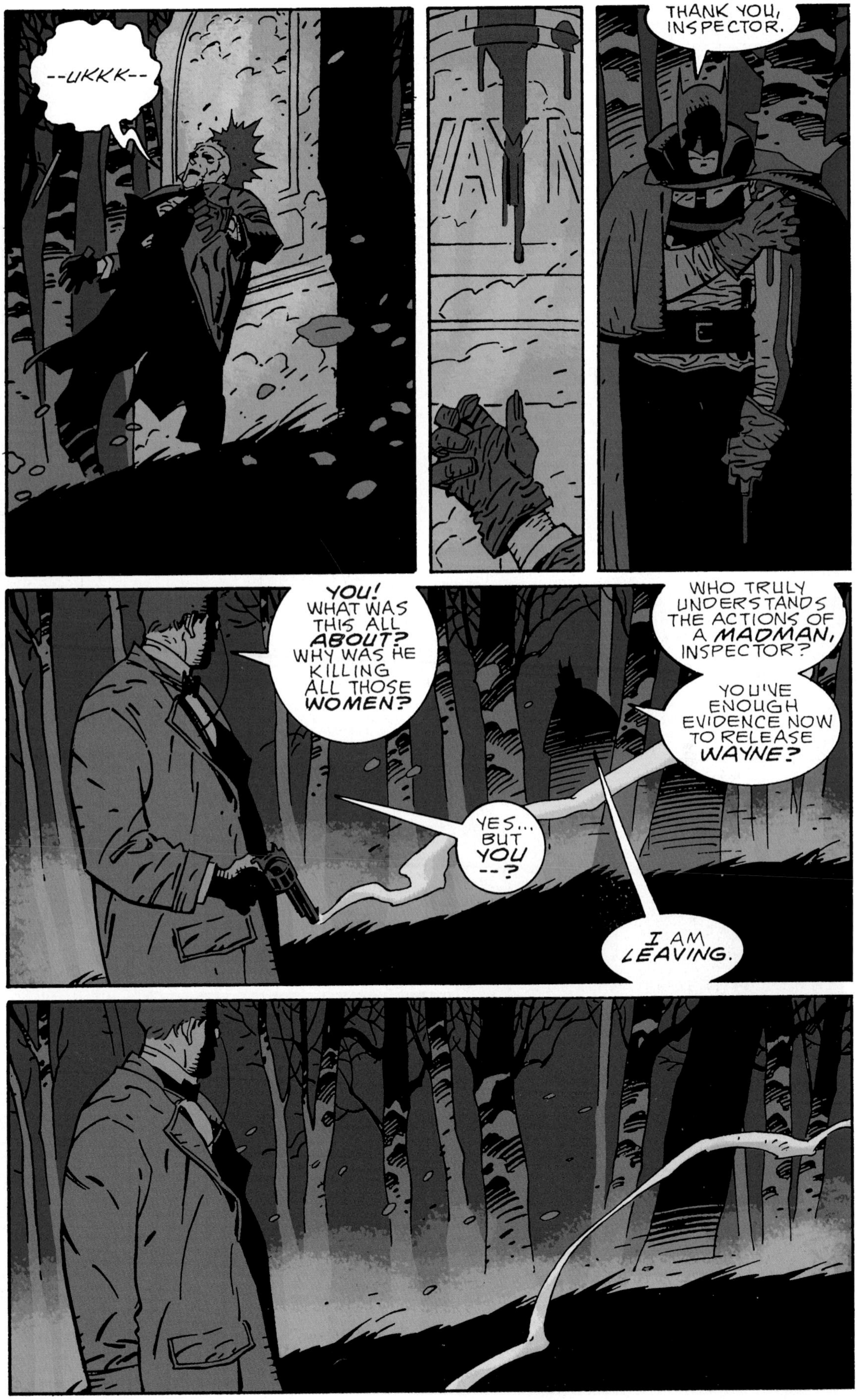
--UKKK--
THANK YOU, INSPECTOR.
YOU! WHAT WAS THIS ALL ABOUT? WHY WAS HE KILLING ALL THOSE WOMEN?
WHO TRULY UNDERSTANDS THE ACTIONS OF A MADMAN, INSPECTOR?
YOU'VE ENOUGH EVIDENCE NOW TO RELEASE WAYNE?
YES... BUT YOU --?
I AM LEAVING.

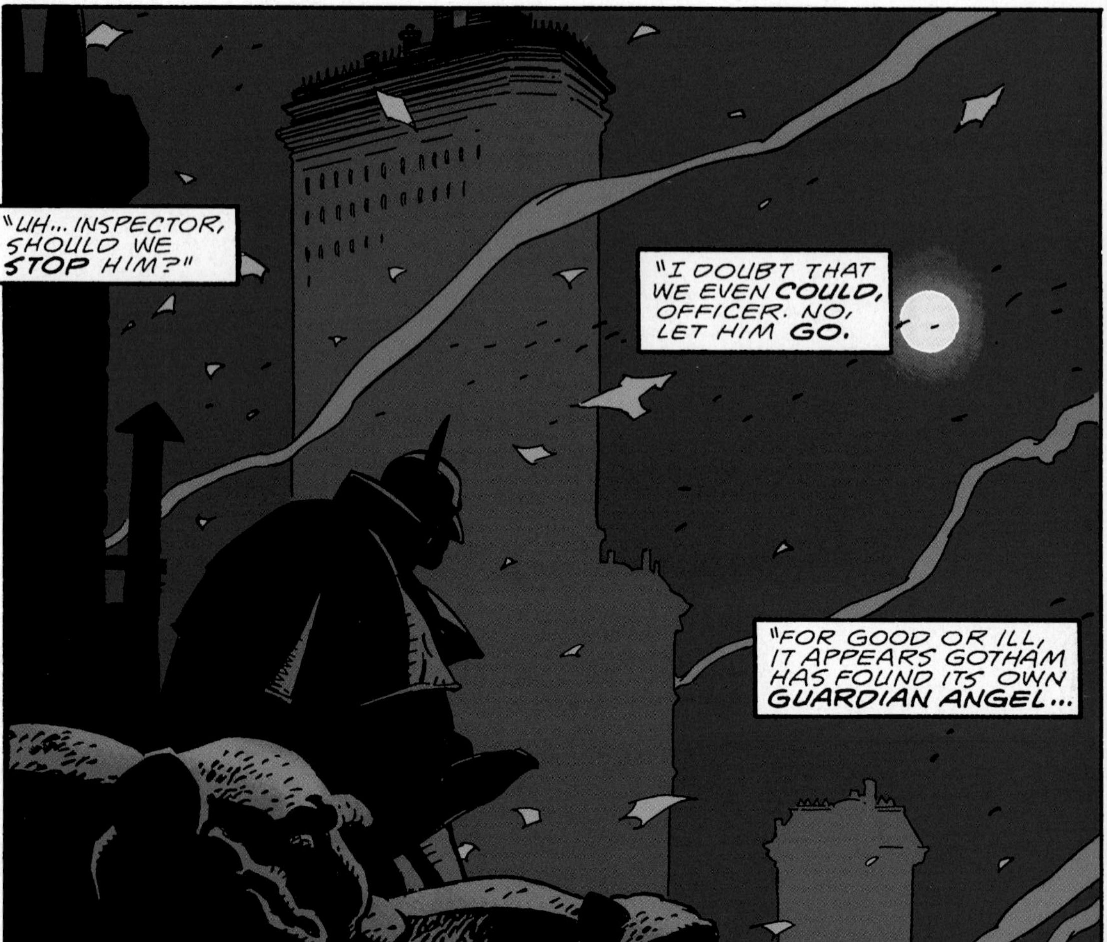
"UH... INSPECTOR, SHOULD WE STOP HIM?"
"I DOUBT THAT WE EVEN COULD, OFFICER. NO, LET HIM GO.
"FOR GOOD OR ILL, IT APPEARS GOTHAM HAS FOUND ITS OWN GUARDIAN ANGEL...
"...AND, GOD HELP US-- I SUSPECT WE'RE GOING TO NEED HIM."
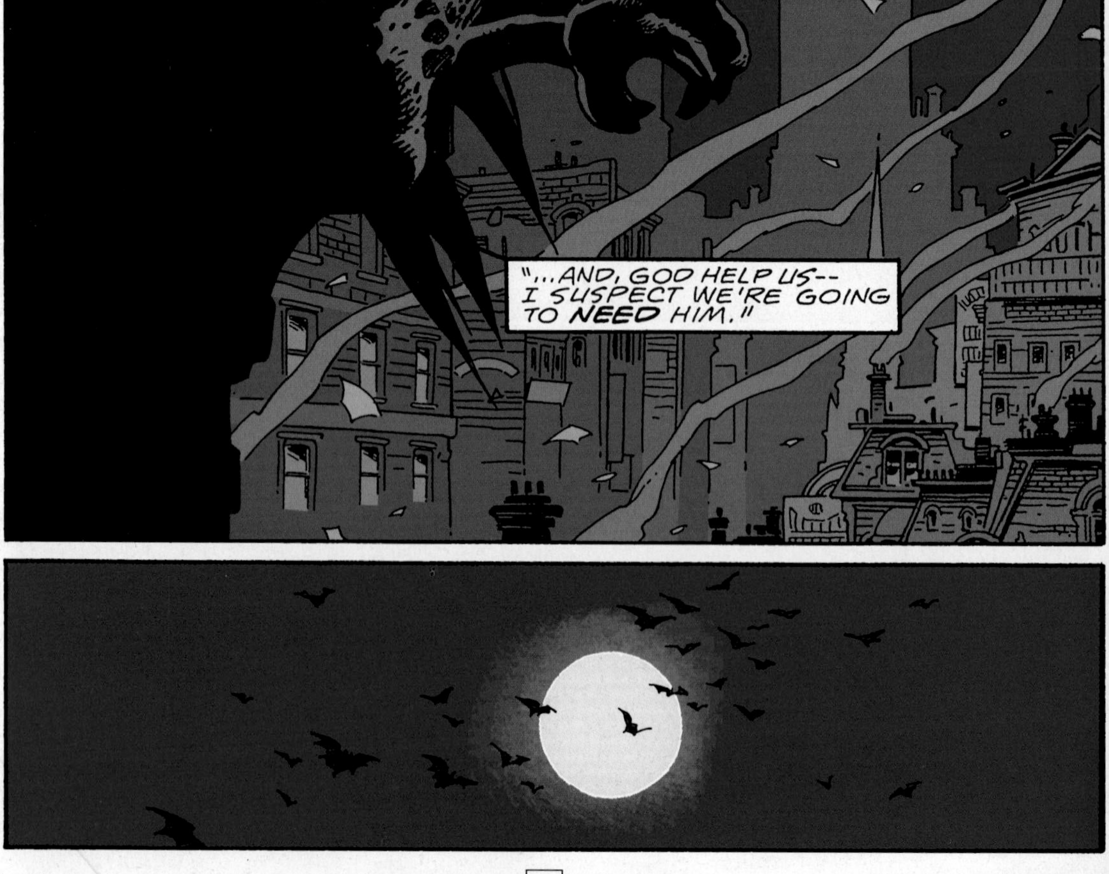

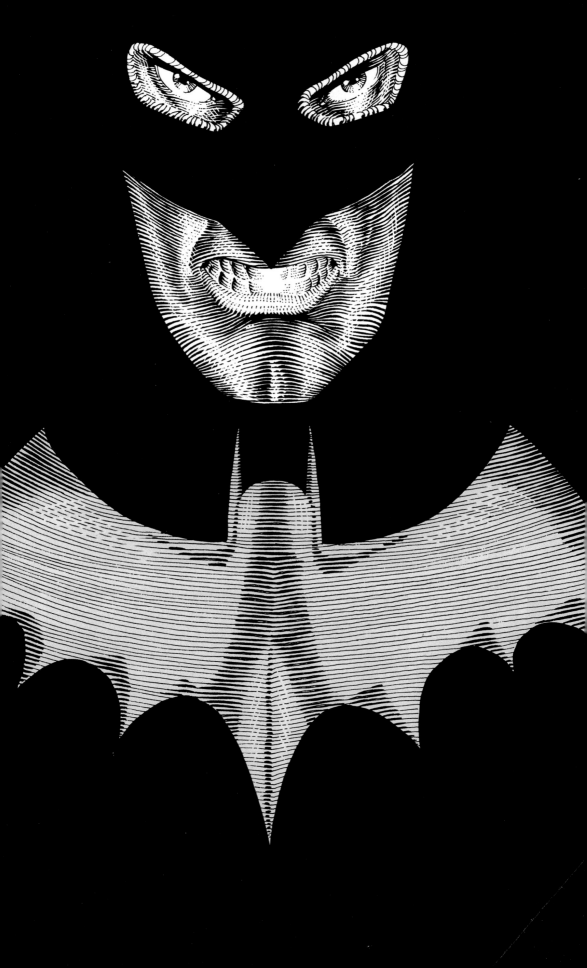

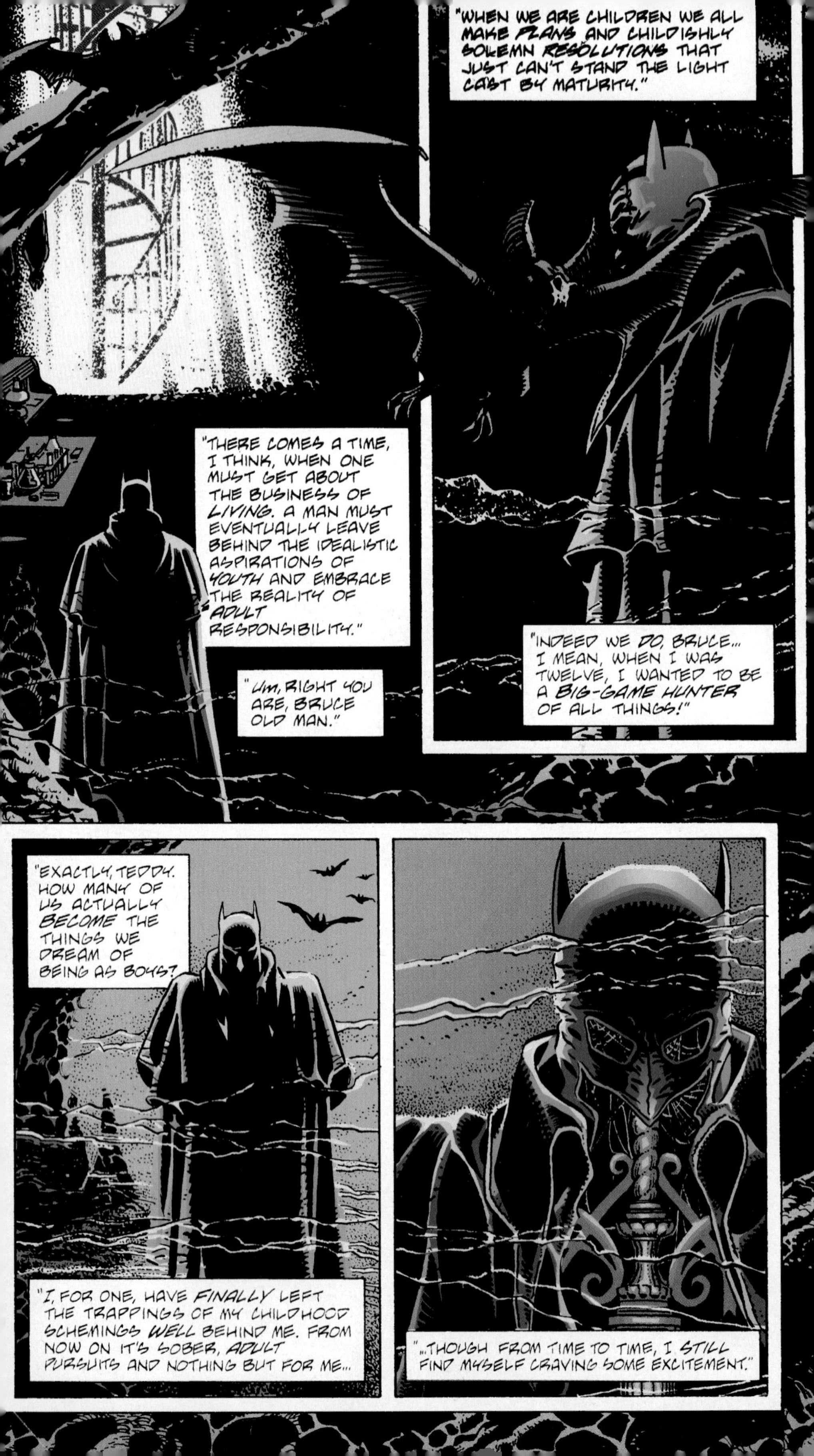
"WHEN WE ARE CHILDREN WE ALL MAKE PLANS AND CHILDISHLY SOLEMN RESOLUTIONS THAT JUST CAN'T STAND THE LIGHT CAST BY MATURITY."
"THERE COMES A TIME, I THINK, WHEN ONE MUST GET ABOUT THE BUSINESS OF LIVING. A MAN MUST EVENTUALLY LEAVE BEHIND THE IDEALISTIC ASPIRATIONS OF YOUTH AND EMBRACE THE REALITY OF ADULT RESPONSIBILITY."
"UM, RIGHT YOU ARE, BRUCE OLD MAN."
"INDEED WE DO, BRUCE... I MEAN, WHEN I WAS TWELVE, I WANTED TO BE A BIG-GAME HUNTER OF ALL THINGS!"
"EXACTLY, TEDDY. HOW MANY OF US ACTUALLY BECOME THE THINGS WE DREAM OF BEING AS BOYS?
"I, FOR ONE, HAVE FINALLY LEFT THE TRAPPINGS OF MY CHILDHOOD SCHEMINGS WELL BEHIND ME. FROM NOW ON IT'S SOBER, ADULT PURSUITS AND NOTHING BUT FOR ME...
"...THOUGH FROM TIME TO TIME, I STILL FIND MYSELF CRAVING SOME EXCITEMENT."

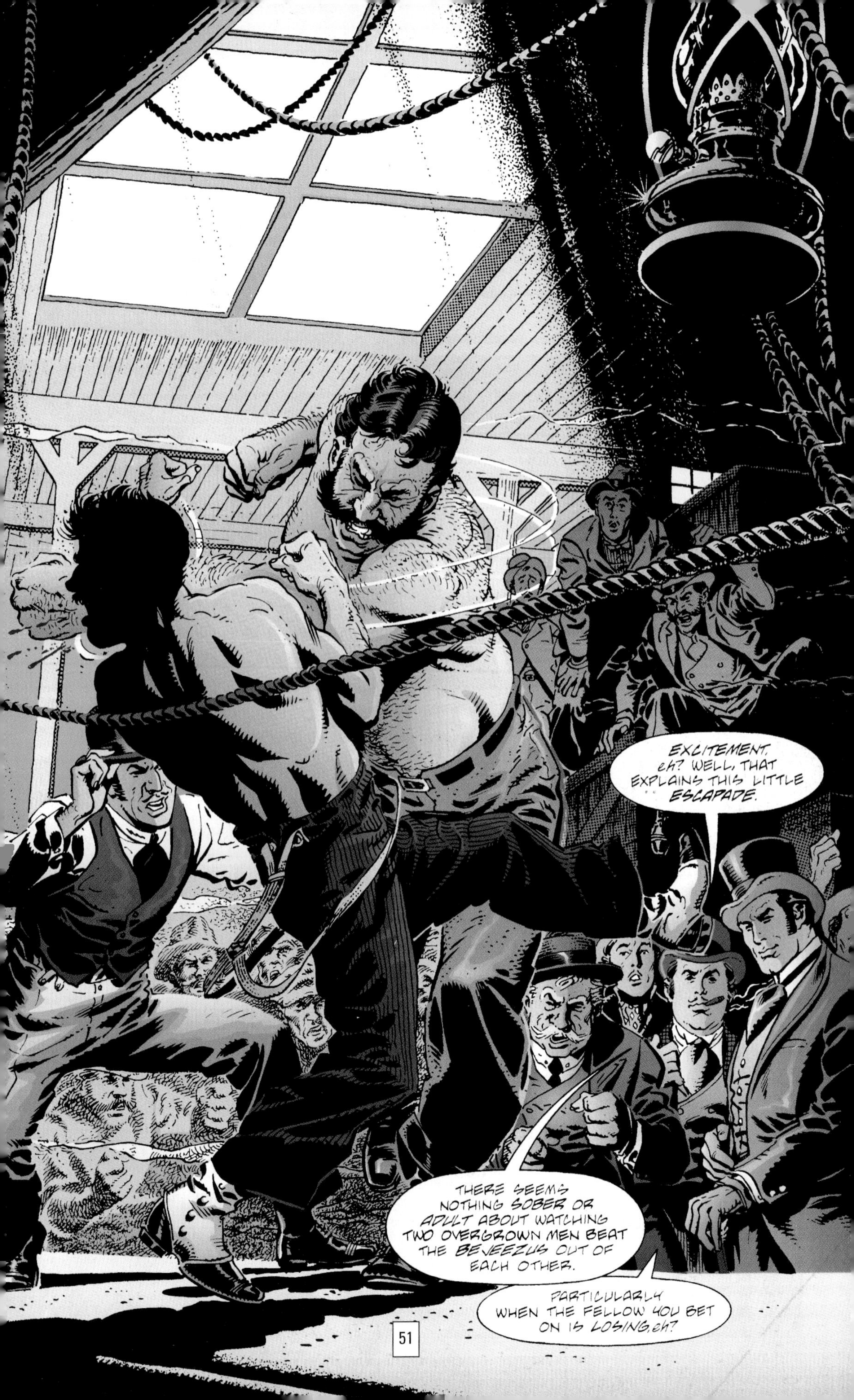
EXCITEMENT, eh? WELL, THAT EXPLAINS THIS LITTLE ESCAPADE.
THERE SEEMS NOTHING SOBER OR ADULT ABOUT WATCHING TWO OVERGROWN MEN BEAT THE BEJEEZUS OUT OF EACH OTHER.
PARTICULARLY WHEN THE FELLOW YOU BET ON IS LOSING, eh?

BESIDES, TEDDY, ISN'T *THIS* THE SORT OF THING WE RICH YOUNG *WASTRELS* ARE *EXPECTED* TO PURSUE WHEN WE BECOME ADULTS?!

I GUESS YOU'RE RI— *DAMNATION,* HE'S DOWN FOR *GOOD!!*

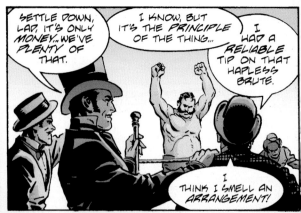

SETTLE DOWN, LAD, IT'S ONLY *MONEY...* WE'VE *PLENTY* OF THAT.

I *KNOW,* BUT IT'S THE *PRINCIPLE* OF THE THING...

I HAD A *RELIABLE* TIP ON THAT *HAPLESS* BRUTE.

I THINK I SMELL AN *ARRANGEMENT!*

THIS WAS NO *FAIR FIGHT,* YOU *HOOLIGANS!* THIS MATCH WAS *FIXED!*

TEDDY...

FIXED, eh? THEN AN *HONEST* LAD LIKE *YERSELF* SHOULD HAVE NO TROUBLE DEALING WITH DEXTER HERE... IN A *FAIR FIGHT!*

NOBODY CALLS ME A *CHEAT!*

WHAT *SAY,* MISTER *FAIR PLAY,* YOU *GAME?*

YES, YES... KILL THE LITTLE *SWELL!*

MY *MONEY'S* ON *DEXTER!*

KNOCK 'IM ON HIS *DUFF,* DEX!

BRING HIM *DOWN!*

MY FRIEND IS *UNINTERESTED* IN YOUR OFFER, I THINK... MAY I FIGHT IN HIS *PLACE?*

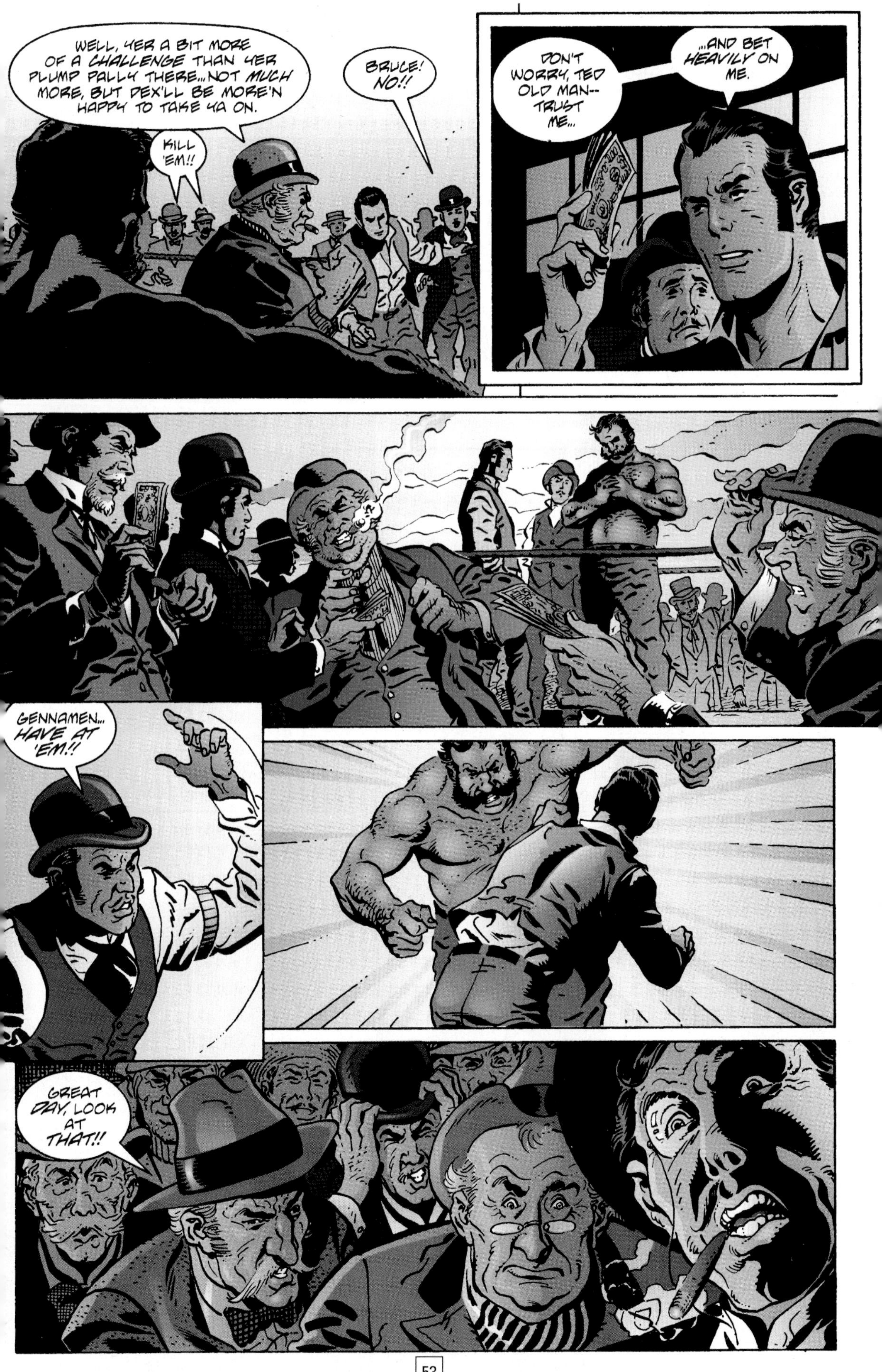
WELL, YER A BIT MORE OF A CHALLENGE THAN YER PLUMP PALLY THERE... NOT MUCH MORE, BUT DEX'LL BE MORE'N HAPPY TO TAKE YA ON.
KILL 'EM!!
BRUCE! NO!!
DON'T WORRY, TED OLD MAN-- TRUST ME...
...AND BET HEAVILY ON ME.
GENNAMEN... HAVE AT 'EM!!
GREAT DAY, LOOK AT THAT!!

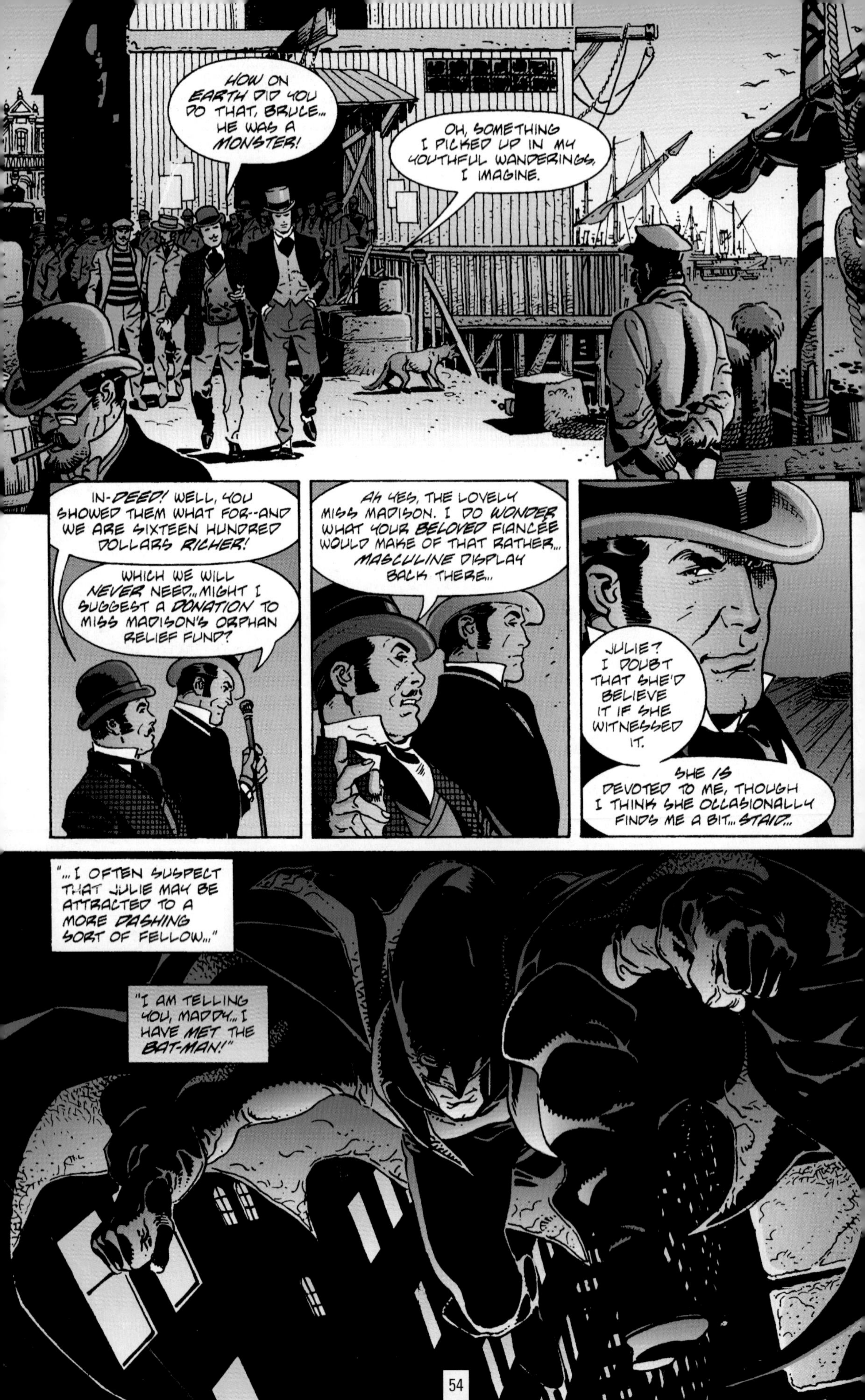
HOW ON EARTH DID YOU DO THAT, BRUCE... HE WAS A MONSTER!
OH, SOMETHING I PICKED UP IN MY YOUTHFUL WANDERINGS, I IMAGINE.
IN-DEED! WELL, YOU SHOWED THEM WHAT FOR--AND WE ARE SIXTEEN HUNDRED DOLLARS RICHER!
WHICH WE WILL NEVER NEED... MIGHT I SUGGEST A DONATION TO MISS MADISON'S ORPHAN RELIEF FUND?
AH YES, THE LOVELY MISS MADISON. I DO WONDER WHAT YOUR BELOVED FIANCÉE WOULD MAKE OF THAT RATHER... MASCULINE DISPLAY BACK THERE...
JULIE? I DOUBT THAT SHE'D BELIEVE IT IF SHE WITNESSED IT.
SHE IS DEVOTED TO ME, THOUGH I THINK SHE OCCASIONALLY FINDS ME A BIT... STAID...
"...I OFTEN SUSPECT THAT JULIE MAY BE ATTRACTED TO A MORE DASHING SORT OF FELLOW..."
"I AM TELLING YOU, MADDY... I HAVE MET THE BAT-MAN!"

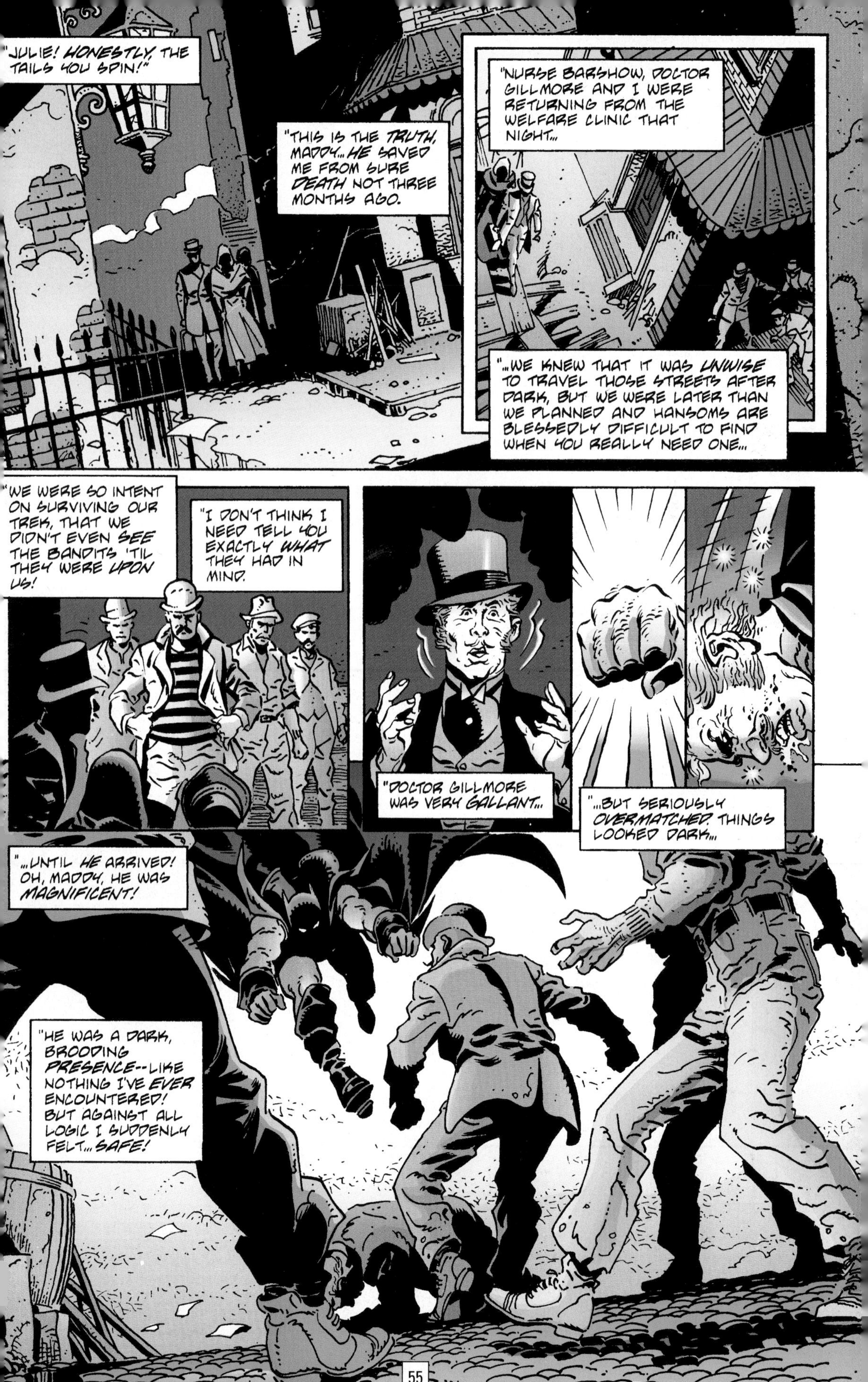
"JULIE! HONESTLY, THE TAILS YOU SPIN!"
"THIS IS THE TRUTH, MADDY... HE SAVED ME FROM SURE DEATH NOT THREE MONTHS AGO.
"NURSE BARSHOW, DOCTOR GILLMORE AND I WERE RETURNING FROM THE WELFARE CLINIC THAT NIGHT...
"...WE KNEW THAT IT WAS UNWISE TO TRAVEL THOSE STREETS AFTER DARK, BUT WE WERE LATER THAN WE PLANNED AND HANSOMS ARE BLESSEDLY DIFFICULT TO FIND WHEN YOU REALLY NEED ONE...
"WE WERE SO INTENT ON SURVIVING OUR TREK, THAT WE DIDN'T EVEN SEE THE BANDITS 'TIL THEY WERE UPON US!
"I DON'T THINK I NEED TELL YOU EXACTLY WHAT THEY HAD IN MIND.
"DOCTOR GILLMORE WAS VERY GALLANT...
"...BUT SERIOUSLY OVERMATCHED. THINGS LOOKED DARK...
"...UNTIL HE ARRIVED! OH, MADDY, HE WAS MAGNIFICENT!
"HE WAS A DARK, BROODING PRESENCE--LIKE NOTHING I'VE EVER ENCOUNTERED! BUT AGAINST ALL LOGIC I SUDDENLY FELT... SAFE!

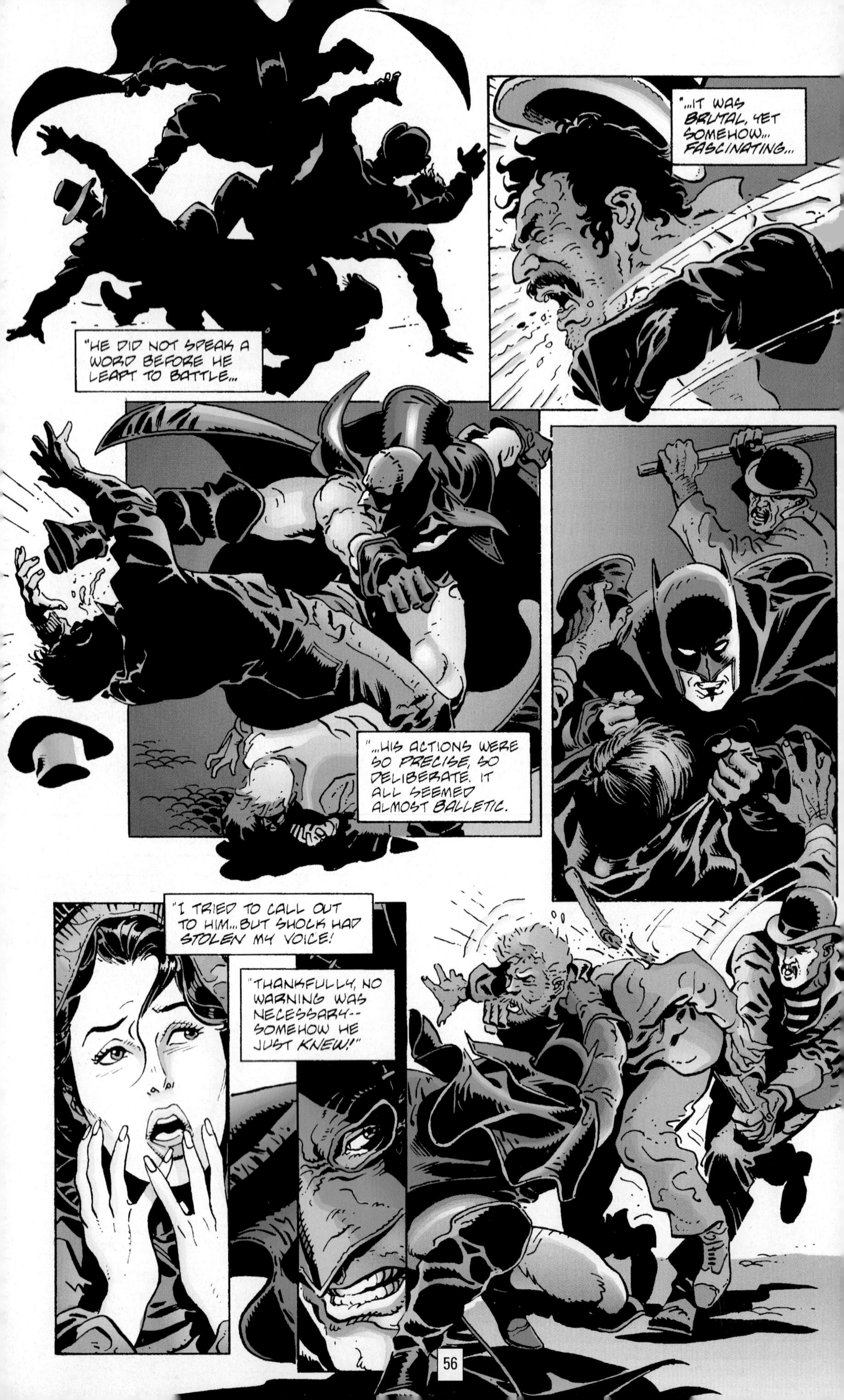
"HE DID NOT SPEAK A WORD BEFORE HE LEAPT TO BATTLE...
"...IT WAS BRUTAL, YET SOMEHOW... FASCINATING...
"...HIS ACTIONS WERE SO PRECISE, SO DELIBERATE. IT ALL SEEMED ALMOST BALLETIC.
"I TRIED TO CALL OUT TO HIM... BUT SHOCK HAD STOLEN MY VOICE!
"THANKFULLY, NO WARNING WAS NECESSARY-- SOMEHOW HE JUST KNEW!"

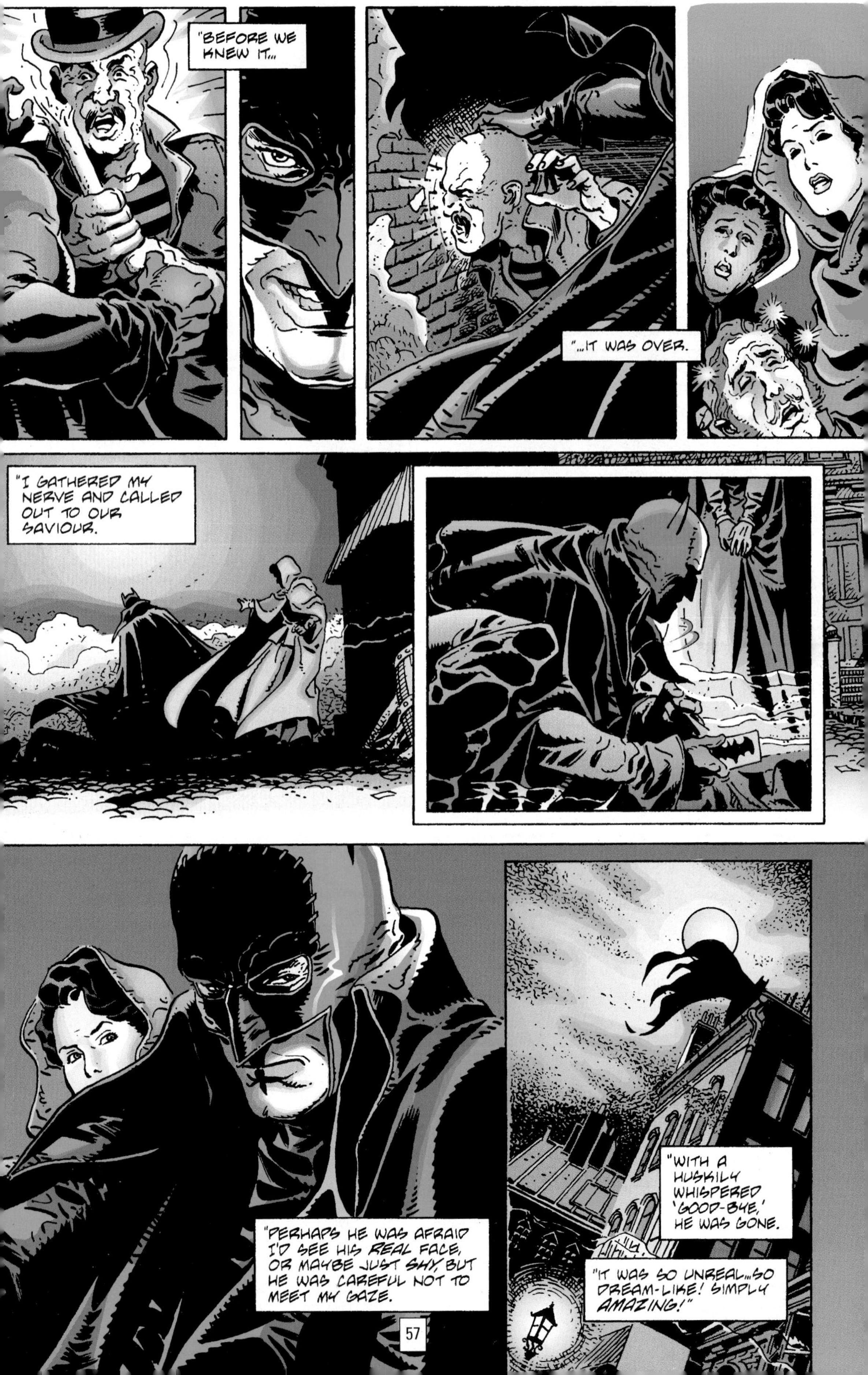
"BEFORE WE KNEW IT...
"...IT WAS OVER.
"I GATHERED MY NERVE AND CALLED OUT TO OUR SAVIOUR.
"PERHAPS HE WAS AFRAID I'D SEE HIS REAL FACE, OR MAYBE JUST SHY, BUT HE WAS CAREFUL NOT TO MEET MY GAZE.
"WITH A HUSKILY WHISPERED 'GOOD-BYE,' HE WAS GONE.
"IT WAS SO UNREAL...SO DREAM-LIKE! SIMPLY AMAZING!"

JULIE! THAT IS THE MOST *INCREDIBLE* THING I HAVE *EVER* HEARD...!

BUT ALL *TRUE*, MADDY, I SWEAR.

I SHOULD THINK YOU'D HAVE BEEN FRIGHTENED ABSOLUTELY *WITLESS*...

THEY SAY THAT THE *BAT* IS A *MONSTER*...A *VAMPIRE*...OR SOMETHING WORSE!

The **BAT-MAN MISSING?**

MAYOR PROMISES FAIR WILL GENERATE JOBS

THAT IS PATENTLY *RIDICULOUS.* I STOOD AS CLOSE TO HIM AS I AM TO YOU...

HE'S A *MAN,* NO QUESTION ABOUT THAT.

A VERY *SPECIAL* MAN, BUT A MAN TO BE SURE.

AND, I THINK, A MAN THIS CITY *NEEDS* VERY MUCH.

WE'RE MOVING INTO THE *FUTURE,* MADDY. THERE'S A NEW *CENTURY* JUST EIGHT YEARS AWAY...

THE WORLD IS MOVING FASTER. GETTING... *MEANER,* I THINK.

...WE NEED A... *GUARDIAN,* IF YOU WILL. SOMEONE TO KEEP US OFF THE *PRECIPICE*...AWAY FROM THE *ABYSS*...

...BUT NOW HE'S *VANISHED.*

"WHERE *IS* HE?"

DAMN IT, WHERE HAS HE GOTTEN TO?

HE SHOWS UP OUT OF NOWHERE TO SOLVE ONE OF THIS CITY'S *WORST* CRIMES...

--GETS ME NAMED COMMISSIONER-- AND TOLLIVER ELECTED MAYOR--BY *NOT* TAKING CREDIT FOR STOPPING THE *RIPPER*....

...SPENDS A *YEAR* SAVING THE CITY AGAIN AND AGAIN.

...AND THEN DISAPPEARS... *JUST* WHEN WE NEED HIM MOST.

SEE THE FUTURE!

THE AMERICAN DISCOVERY EXPOSITION

JOURNEY INTO THE TWENTIETH CENTURY AND BEYOND

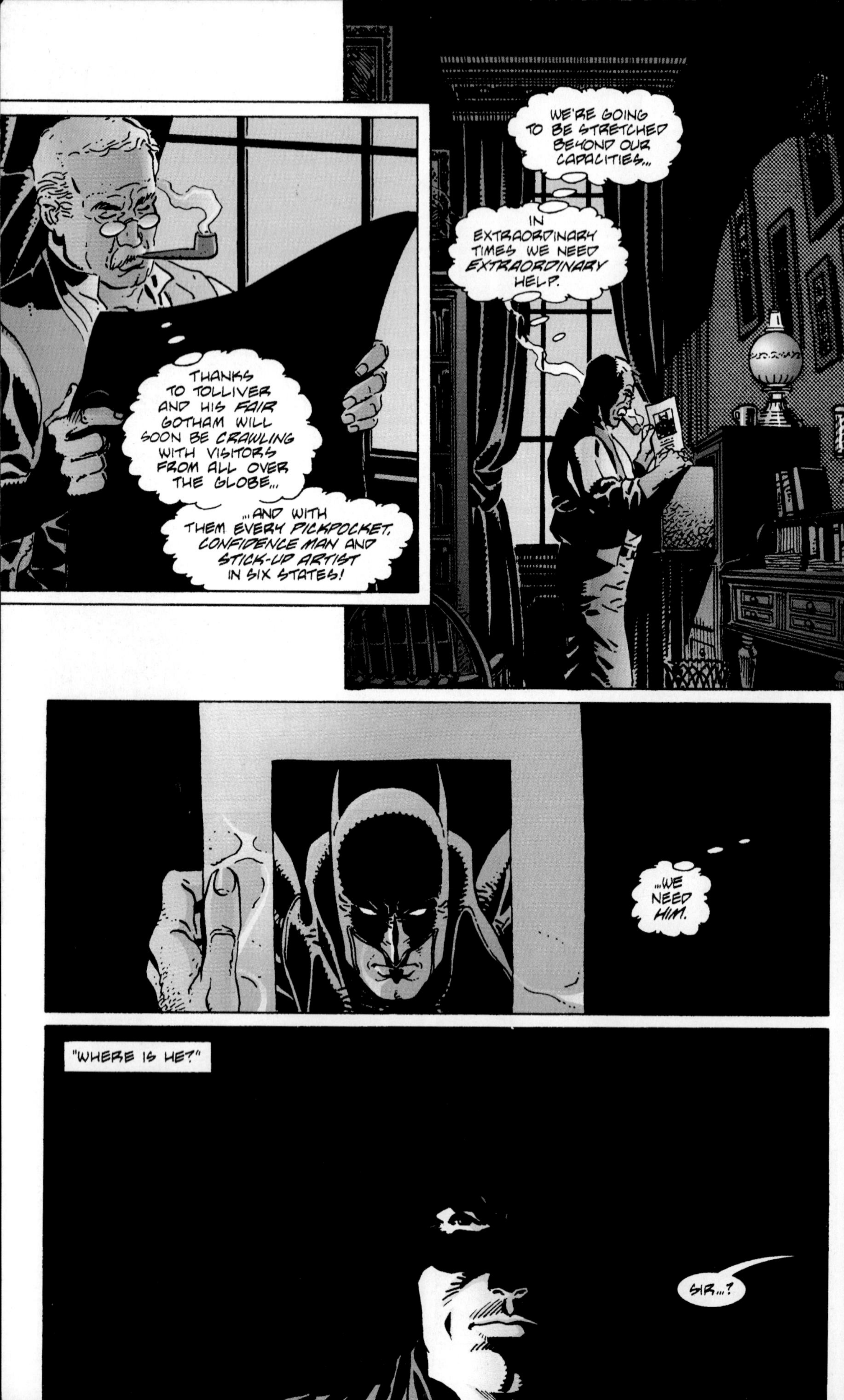
THANKS TO TOLLIVER AND HIS FAIR GOTHAM WILL SOON BE CRAWLING WITH VISITORS FROM ALL OVER THE GLOBE...
...AND WITH THEM EVERY PICKPOCKET, CONFIDENCE MAN AND STICK-UP ARTIST IN SIX STATES!
WE'RE GOING TO BE STRETCHED BEYOND OUR CAPACITIES...
IN EXTRAORDINARY TIMES WE NEED EXTRAORDINARY HELP.
...WE NEED HIM.
"WHERE IS HE?"
SIR...?

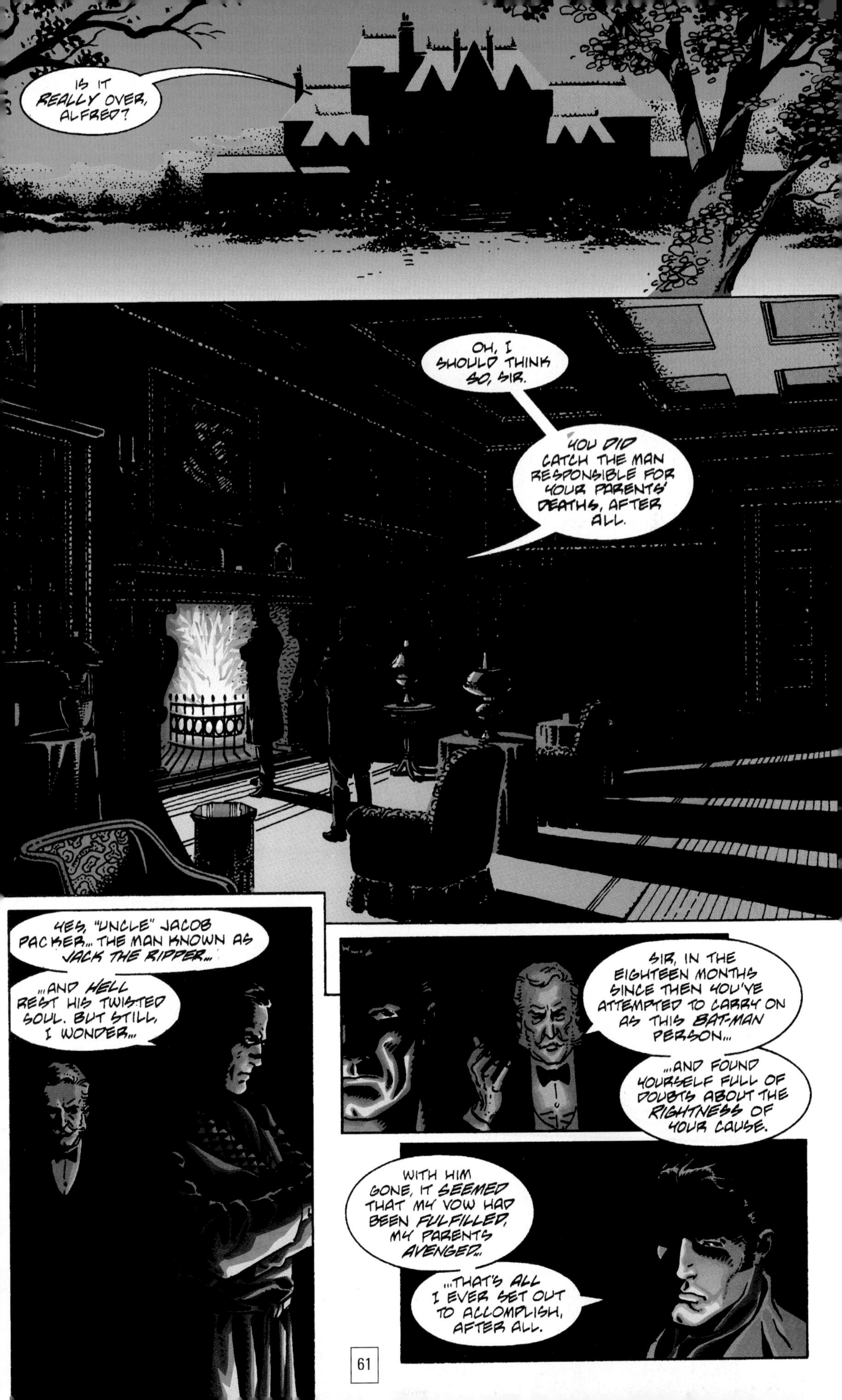
IS IT REALLY OVER, ALFRED?
OH, I SHOULD THINK SO, SIR.
YOU DID CATCH THE MAN RESPONSIBLE FOR YOUR PARENTS' DEATHS, AFTER ALL.
YES, "UNCLE" JACOB PACKER... THE MAN KNOWN AS JACK THE RIPPER...
...AND HELL REST HIS TWISTED SOUL. BUT STILL, I WONDER...
SIR, IN THE EIGHTEEN MONTHS SINCE THEN YOU'VE ATTEMPTED TO CARRY ON AS THIS BAT-MAN PERSON...
...AND FOUND YOURSELF FULL OF DOUBTS ABOUT THE RIGHTNESS OF YOUR CAUSE.
WITH HIM GONE, IT SEEMED THAT MY VOW HAD BEEN FULFILLED, MY PARENTS AVENGED...
...THAT'S ALL I EVER SET OUT TO ACCOMPLISH, AFTER ALL.

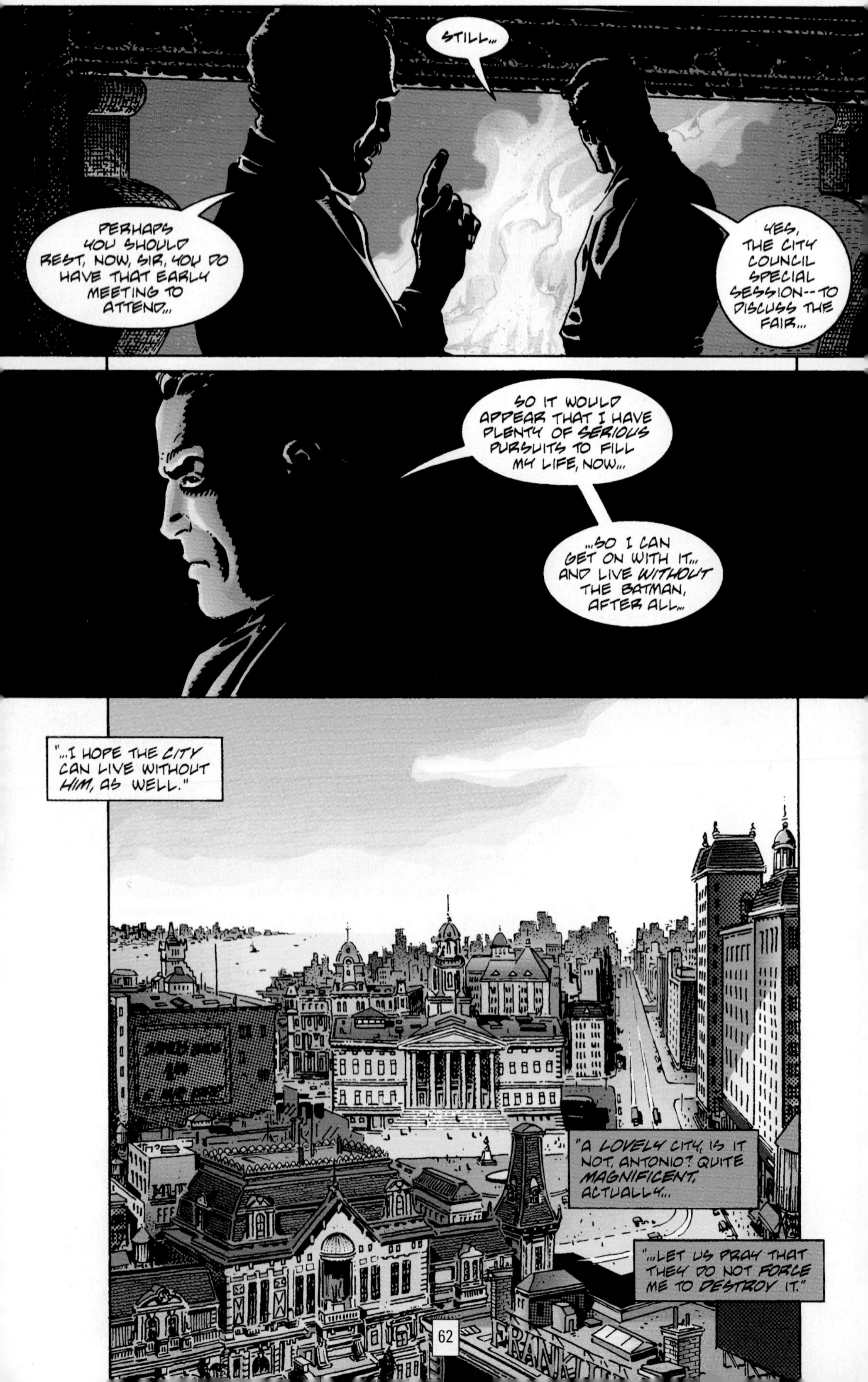
PERHAPS YOU SHOULD REST, NOW, SIR, YOU DO HAVE THAT EARLY MEETING TO ATTEND...
YES, THE CITY COUNCIL SPECIAL SESSION--TO DISCUSS THE FAIR...
STILL...
SO IT WOULD APPEAR THAT I HAVE PLENTY OF *SERIOUS* PURSUITS TO FILL MY LIFE, NOW...
...SO I CAN GET ON WITH IT... AND LIVE *WITHOUT* THE BATMAN, AFTER ALL...
"...I HOPE THE *CITY* CAN LIVE WITHOUT *HIM*, AS WELL."
"A *LOVELY* CITY, IS IT NOT, ANTONIO? QUITE *MAGNIFICENT*, ACTUALLY...
"...LET US PRAY THAT THEY DO NOT *FORCE* ME TO *DESTROY* IT."

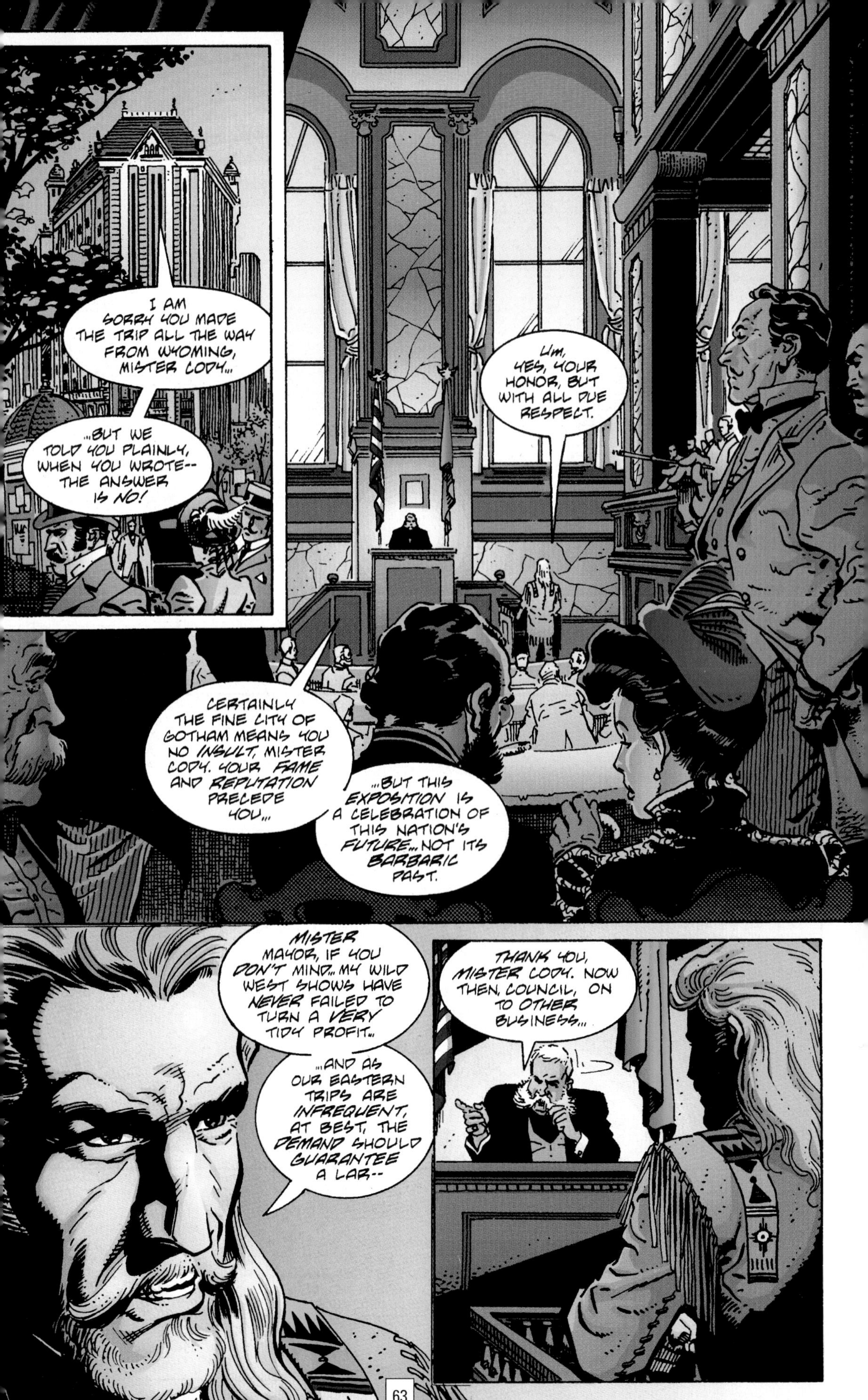
I AM SORRY YOU MADE THE TRIP ALL THE WAY FROM WYOMING, MISTER CODY...
...BUT WE TOLD YOU PLAINLY, WHEN YOU WROTE-- THE ANSWER IS NO!
UM, YES, YOUR HONOR, BUT WITH ALL DUE RESPECT.
CERTAINLY THE FINE CITY OF GOTHAM MEANS YOU NO INSULT, MISTER CODY. YOUR FAME AND REPUTATION PRECEDE YOU...
...BUT THIS EXPOSITION IS A CELEBRATION OF THIS NATION'S FUTURE... NOT ITS BARBARIC PAST.
MISTER MAYOR, IF YOU DON'T MIND... MY WILD WEST SHOWS HAVE NEVER FAILED TO TURN A VERY TIDY PROFIT...
...AND AS OUR EASTERN TRIPS ARE INFREQUENT, AT BEST, THE DEMAND SHOULD GUARANTEE A LAR--
THANK YOU, MISTER CODY. NOW THEN, COUNCIL, ON TO OTHER BUSINESS...

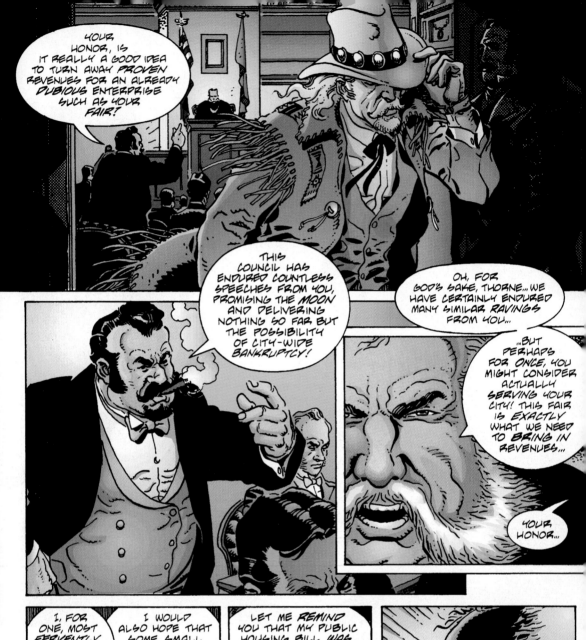

YOUR HONOR, IS IT REALLY A GOOD IDEA TO TURN AWAY *PROVEN* REVENUES FOR AN ALREADY *DUBIOUS* ENTERPRISE SUCH AS YOUR *FAIR?*

THIS COUNCIL HAS ENDURED COUNTLESS SPEECHES FROM YOU, PROMISING THE *MOON* AND DELIVERING NOTHING SO FAR BUT THE POSSIBILITY OF CITY-WIDE *BANKRUPTCY!*

OH, FOR GOD'S SAKE, THORNE... WE HAVE CERTAINLY ENDURED MANY SIMILAR *RAVINGS* FROM YOU...

...BUT PERHAPS FOR *ONCE,* YOU MIGHT CONSIDER ACTUALLY *SERVING* YOUR CITY! THIS FAIR IS *EXACTLY* WHAT WE NEED TO BRING IN REVENUES...

YOUR HONOR...

I, FOR ONE, MOST *FERVENTLY* HOPE YOU ARE RIGHT, MISTER MAYOR.

I WOULD ALSO HOPE THAT SOME SMALL PORTION OF THIS MUCH DEBATED REVENUE MIGHT FIND ITS WAY BACK INTO MY SLUM RENEWAL PROGRAM.

≥SIGH≤ YES, MR. CLAYPOOL

LET ME *REMIND* YOU THAT MY PUBLIC HOUSING BILL *WAS* TABLED TEMPORAR-ILY ONLY.

YES... YES... YES...

CAN'T *ANY* OF YOU LISTEN?!! THIS EXPOSITION *WILL* BRING IN THE MONEY... IT *WILL* PROVIDE HUNDREDS OF JOBS...

...BUT MORE *IMPORTANT,* IT WILL SHOW THE WORLD THAT GOTHAM HAS ITS EYES ON THE *FUTURE!*

FOOL!!

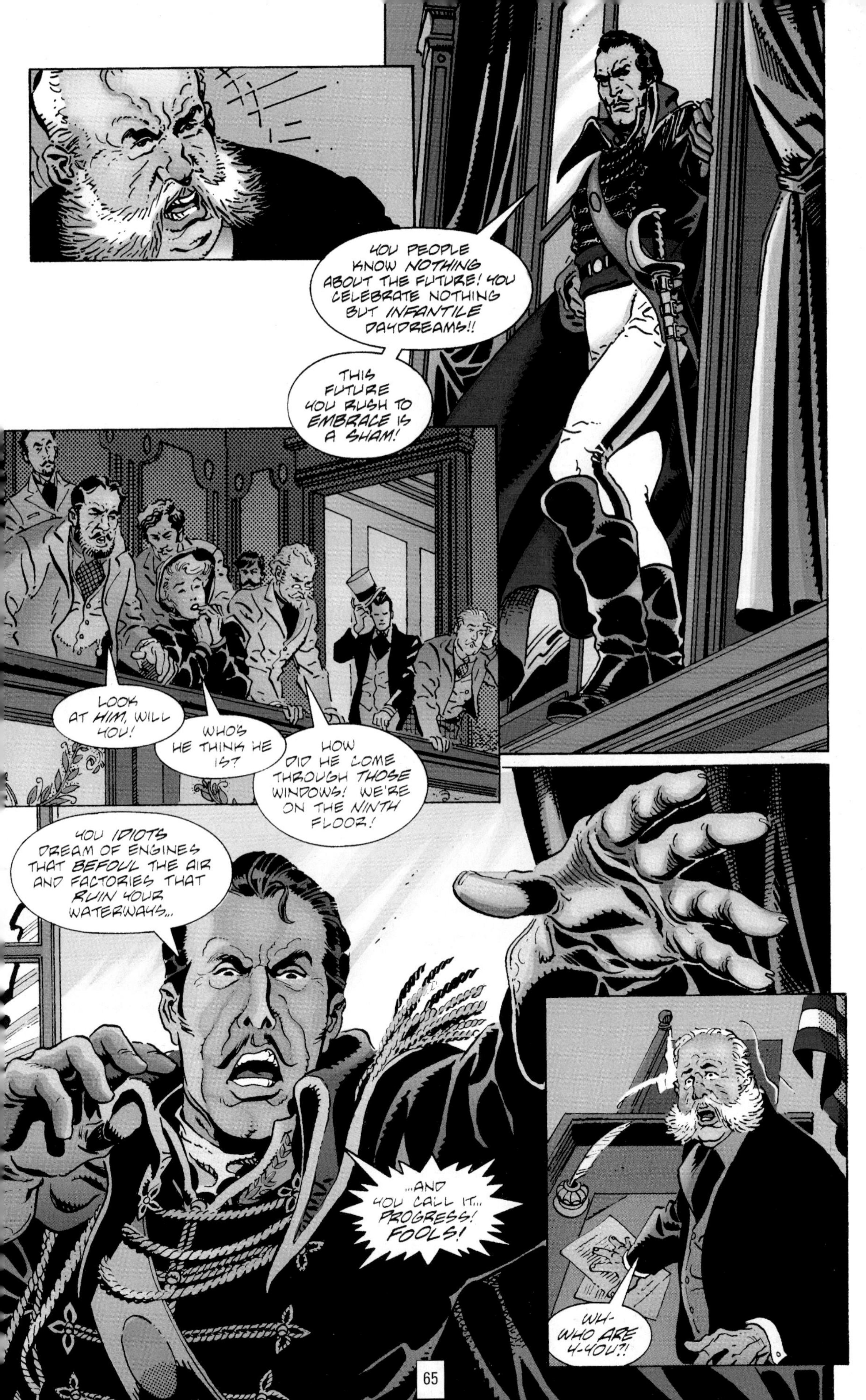
YOU PEOPLE KNOW NOTHING ABOUT THE FUTURE! YOU CELEBRATE NOTHING BUT INFANTILE DAYDREAMS!!
THIS FUTURE YOU RUSH TO EMBRACE IS A SHAM!
LOOK AT HIM, WILL YOU!
WHO'S HE THINK HE IS?
HOW DID HE COME THROUGH THOSE WINDOWS! WE'RE ON THE NINTH FLOOR!
YOU IDIOTS DREAM OF ENGINES THAT BEFOUL THE AIR AND FACTORIES THAT RUIN YOUR WATERWAYS...
...AND YOU CALL IT... PROGRESS! FOOLS!
WH-WHO ARE Y-YOU?!

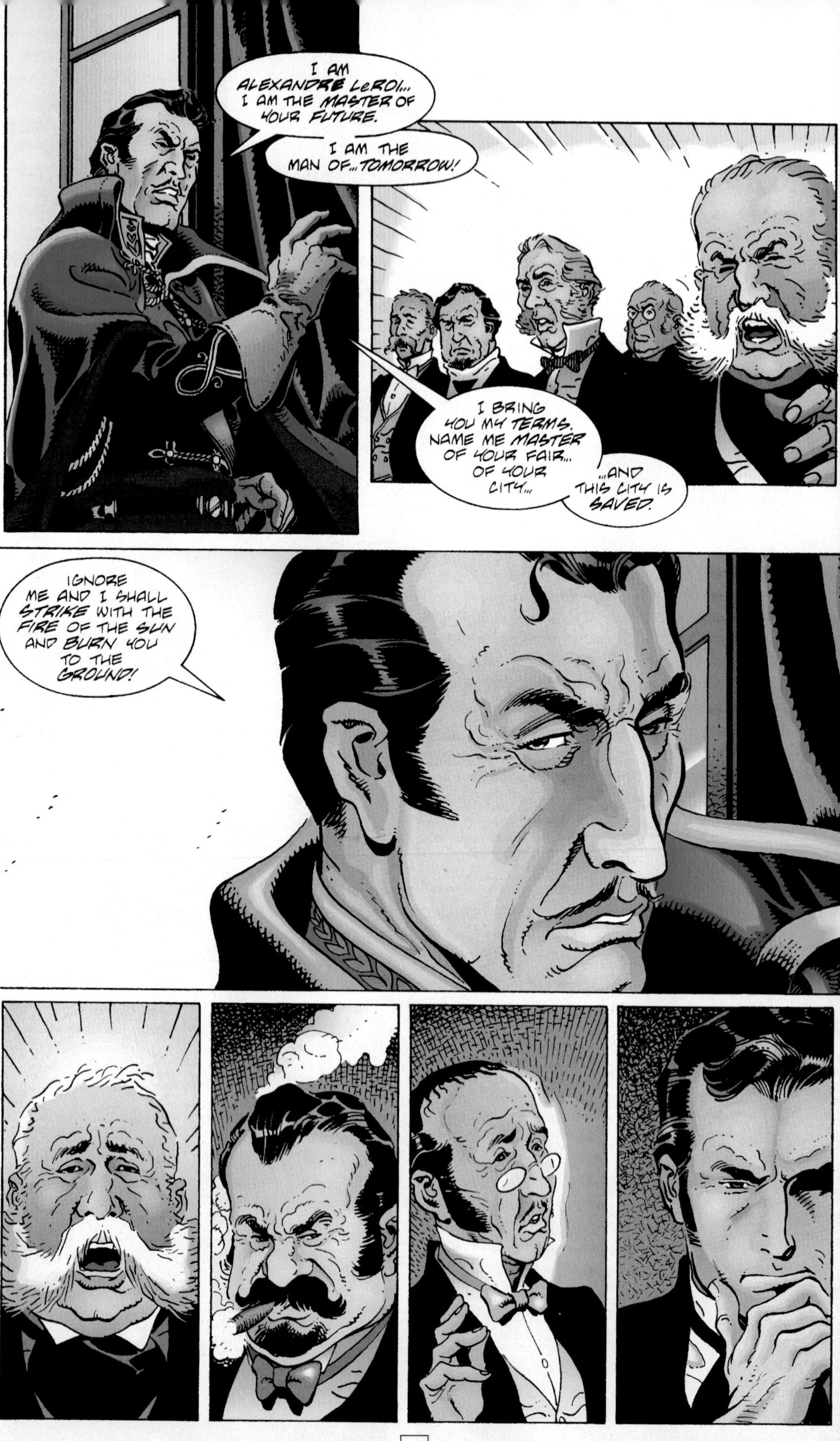
I AM ALEXANDRE LeROI... I AM THE MASTER OF YOUR FUTURE.
I AM THE MAN OF...TOMORROW!
I BRING YOU MY TERMS. NAME ME MASTER OF YOUR FAIR... OF YOUR CITY...
...AND THIS CITY IS SAVED.
IGNORE ME AND I SHALL STRIKE WITH THE FIRE OF THE SUN AND BURN YOU TO THE GROUND!

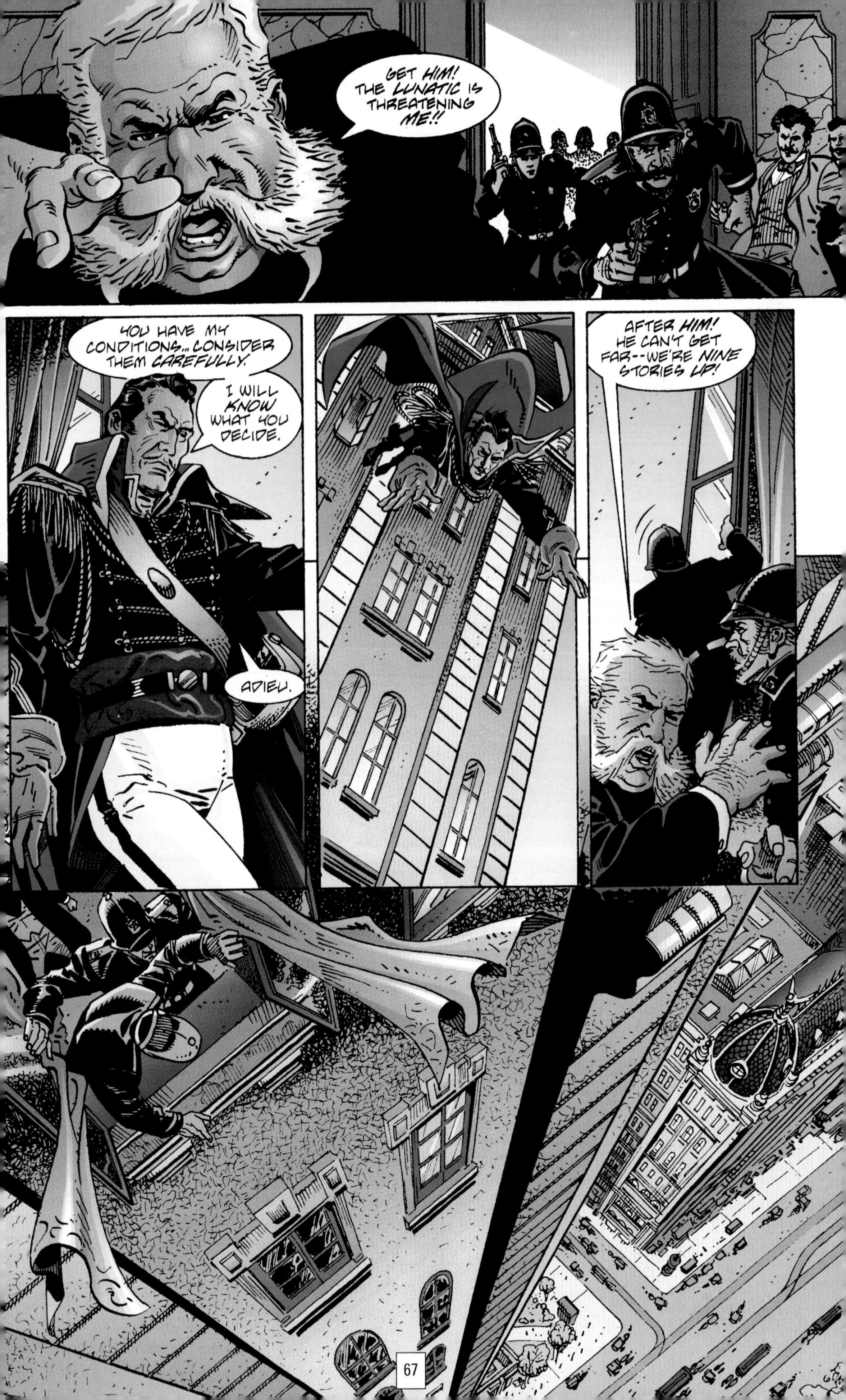
GET HIM! THE LUNATIC IS THREATENING ME!!
YOU HAVE MY CONDITIONS... CONSIDER THEM CAREFULLY.
I WILL KNOW WHAT YOU DECIDE.
ADIEU.
AFTER HIM! HE CAN'T GET FAR--WE'RE NINE STORIES UP!

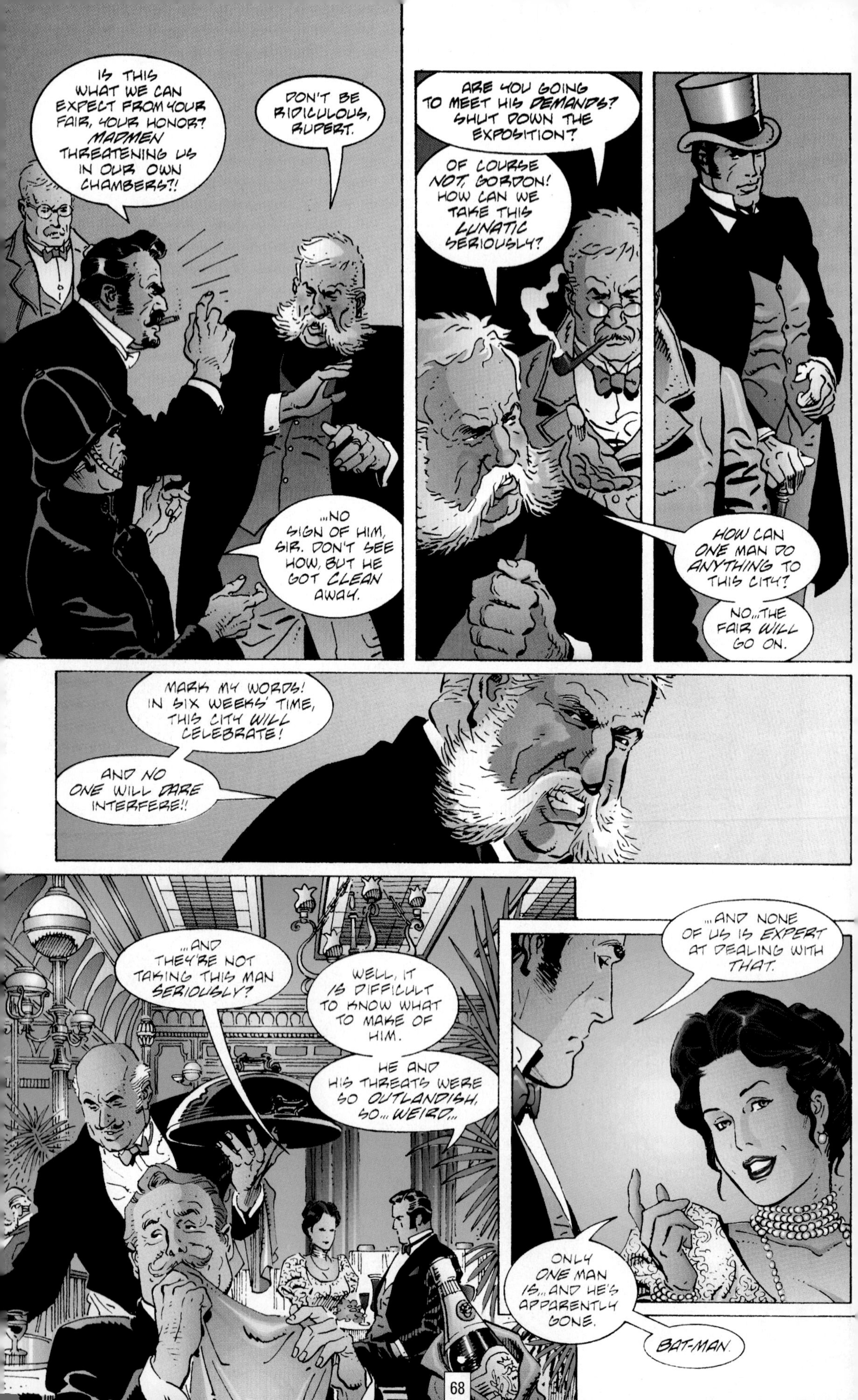
IS THIS WHAT WE CAN EXPECT FROM YOUR FAIR, YOUR HONOR? MADMEN THREATENING US IN OUR OWN CHAMBERS?!
DON'T BE RIDICULOUS, RUPERT.
...NO SIGN OF HIM, SIR. DON'T SEE HOW, BUT HE GOT CLEAN AWAY.
ARE YOU GOING TO MEET HIS DEMANDS? SHUT DOWN THE EXPOSITION?
OF COURSE NOT, GORDON! HOW CAN WE TAKE THIS LUNATIC SERIOUSLY?
HOW CAN ONE MAN DO ANYTHING TO THIS CITY?
NO...THE FAIR WILL GO ON.
MARK MY WORDS! IN SIX WEEKS' TIME, THIS CITY WILL CELEBRATE!
AND NO ONE WILL DARE INTERFERE!!
...AND THEY'RE NOT TAKING THIS MAN SERIOUSLY?
WELL, IT IS DIFFICULT TO KNOW WHAT TO MAKE OF HIM.
HE AND HIS THREATS WERE SO OUTLANDISH, SO... WEIRD...
...AND NONE OF US IS EXPERT AT DEALING WITH THAT.
ONLY ONE MAN IS...AND HE'S APPARENTLY GONE.
BAT-MAN.

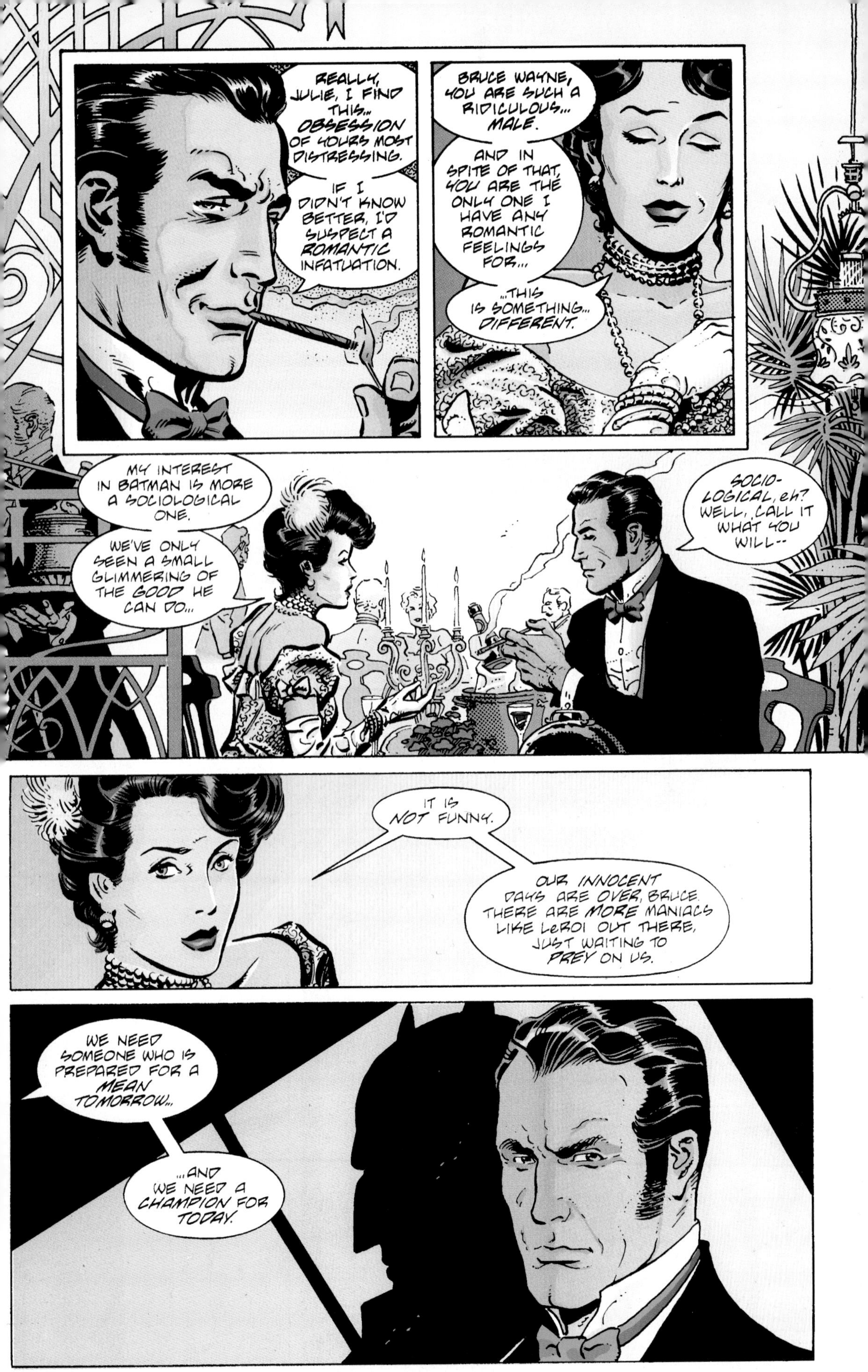
REALLY, JULIE, I FIND THIS... OBSESSION OF YOURS MOST DISTRESSING.
IF I DIDN'T KNOW BETTER, I'D SUSPECT A ROMANTIC INFATUATION.
BRUCE WAYNE, YOU ARE SUCH A RIDICULOUS... MALE.
AND IN SPITE OF THAT, YOU ARE THE ONLY ONE I HAVE ANY ROMANTIC FEELINGS FOR...
...THIS IS SOMETHING... DIFFERENT.
MY INTEREST IN BATMAN IS MORE A SOCIOLOGICAL ONE.
WE'VE ONLY SEEN A SMALL GLIMMERING OF THE GOOD HE CAN DO...
SOCIO-LOGICAL, eh? WELL, CALL IT WHAT YOU WILL--
IT IS NOT FUNNY.
OUR INNOCENT DAYS ARE OVER, BRUCE. THERE ARE MORE MANIACS LIKE LeROI OUT THERE, JUST WAITING TO PREY ON US.
WE NEED SOMEONE WHO IS PREPARED FOR A MEAN TOMORROW...
...AND WE NEED A CHAMPION FOR TODAY.

"WELL, ANTONIO, I AM OFF TO MEET OUR PARTNER, TO HEAR WHAT THE ANSWER WILL BE.

"...THOUGH PART OF ME *HOPES* THEY SAY NO.

"I DO LOVE TO SEE THINGS *BURN*."

AS I PREDICTED, THE FOOLS WILL NOT BOW.

A MATTER OF *LITTLE* IMPORT, MY FRIEND. I HAVE BEEN ANTICIPATING A TEST FOR MY NEW *SOLAR LENS*, ANYWAY.

YES, WELL, REMEMBER, WE HAVE A DEAL.

DO NOT FRET. LeROI ALWAYS KEEPS HIS WORD. OUR BARGAIN STANDS.

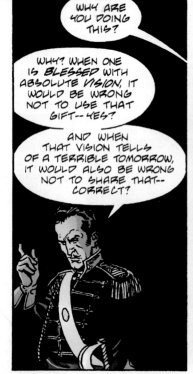

WHY ARE YOU DOING THIS?

WHY? WHEN ONE IS *BLESSED* WITH ABSOLUTE VISION, IT WOULD BE WRONG NOT TO USE THAT GIFT-- YES?

AND WHEN THAT VISION TELLS OF A TERRIBLE TOMORROW, IT WOULD ALSO BE WRONG NOT TO SHARE THAT-- CORRECT?

THIS INSIGHT I POSSESS GIVES ME A *CLEAR* PICTURE OF THE *DARK ROAD* WE NOW TRAVEL...

I ALONE CAN GUIDE MANKIND OFF THIS RECKLESS PATH.

MAN IS SO ENAMORED OF THE FUTURE THAT HE WILL SACRIFICE ALL HIS RESOURCES--

--SACRIFICE EVERYTHING HE NEEDS-- TO MACHINES OF CONVENIENCE TO GET THERE.

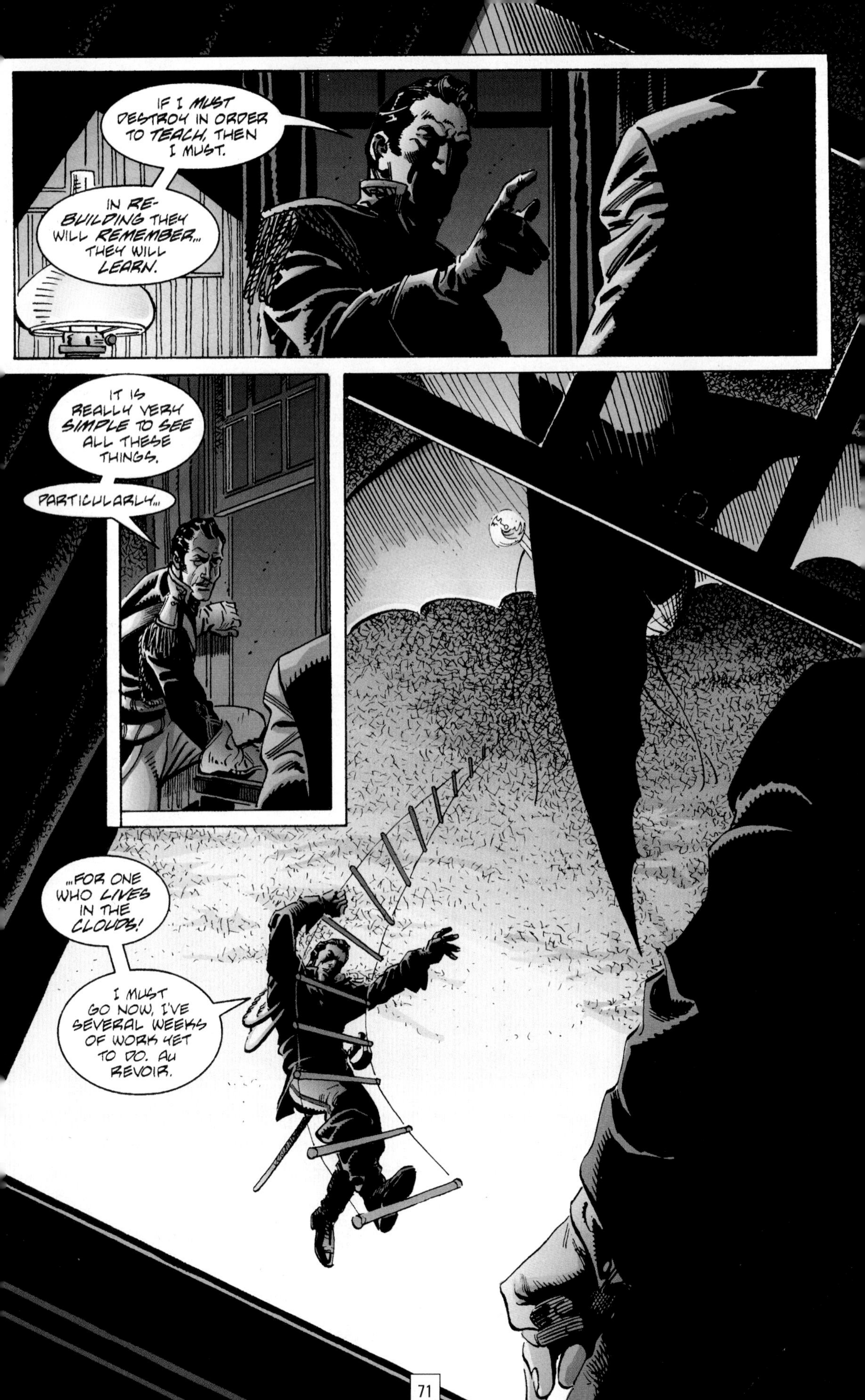
IF I MUST DESTROY IN ORDER TO TEACH, THEN I MUST.
IN RE-BUILDING THEY WILL REMEMBER... THEY WILL LEARN.
IT IS REALLY VERY SIMPLE TO SEE ALL THESE THINGS.
PARTICULARLY...
...FOR ONE WHO LIVES IN THE CLOUDS!
I MUST GO NOW, I'VE SEVERAL WEEKS OF WORK YET TO DO. AU REVOIR.

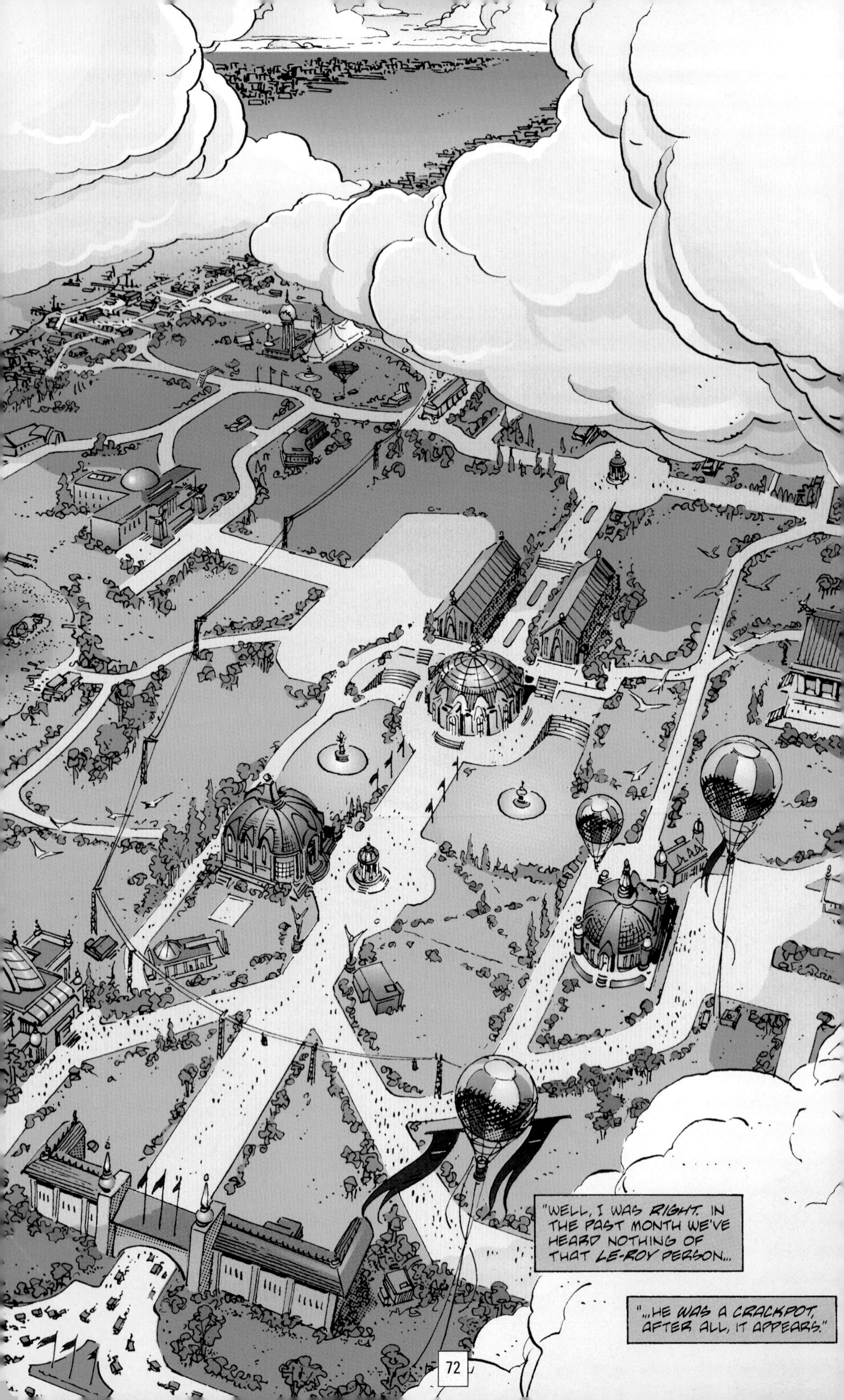
"WELL, I WAS RIGHT. IN THE PAST MONTH WE'VE HEARD NOTHING OF THAT LE-ROY PERSON...
"...HE WAS A CRACKPOT, AFTER ALL, IT APPEARS."

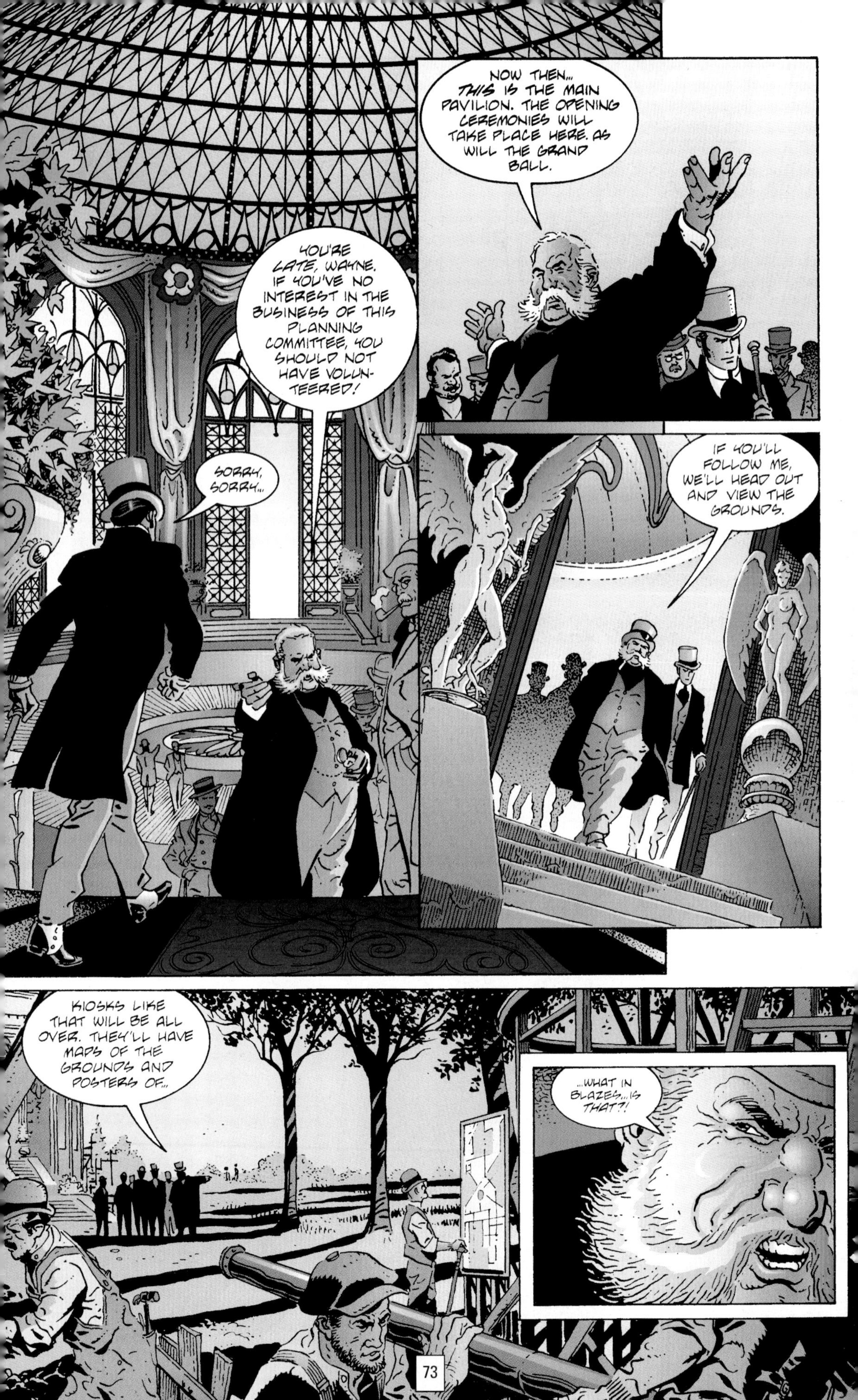

YOU'RE LATE, WAYNE. IF YOU'VE NO INTEREST IN THE BUSINESS OF THIS PLANNING COMMITTEE, YOU SHOULD NOT HAVE VOLUNTEERED!
SORRY, SORRY...
NOW THEN... THIS IS THE MAIN PAVILION. THE OPENING CEREMONIES WILL TAKE PLACE HERE. AS WILL THE GRAND BALL.
IF YOU'LL FOLLOW ME, WE'LL HEAD OUT AND VIEW THE GROUNDS.
KIOSKS LIKE THAT WILL BE ALL OVER. THEY'LL HAVE MAPS OF THE GROUNDS AND POSTERS OF...
...WHAT IN BLAZES... IS THAT?!

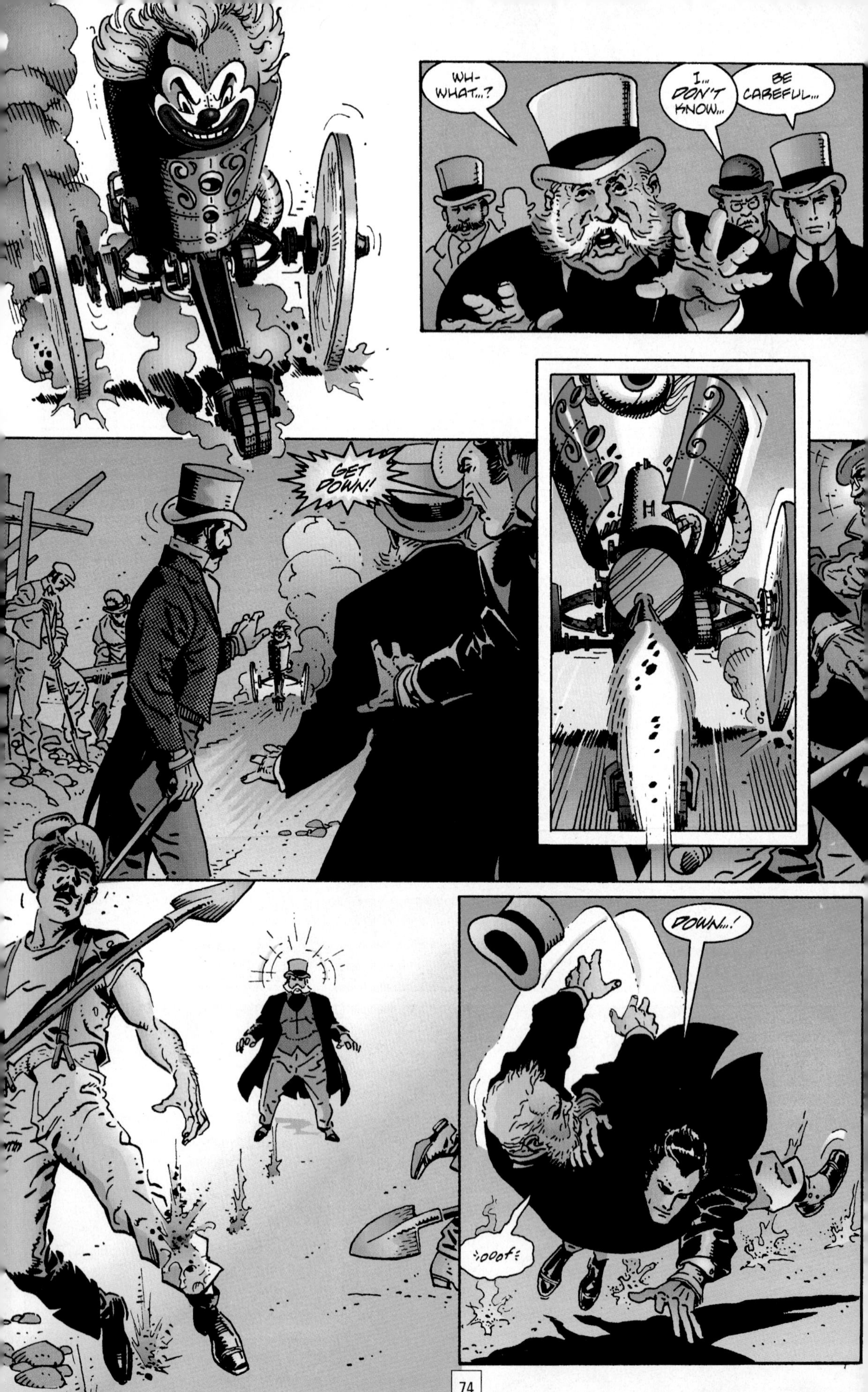
WH-WHAT...?
I... DON'T KNOW...
BE CAREFUL...
GET DOWN!
DOWN...!
OOOF

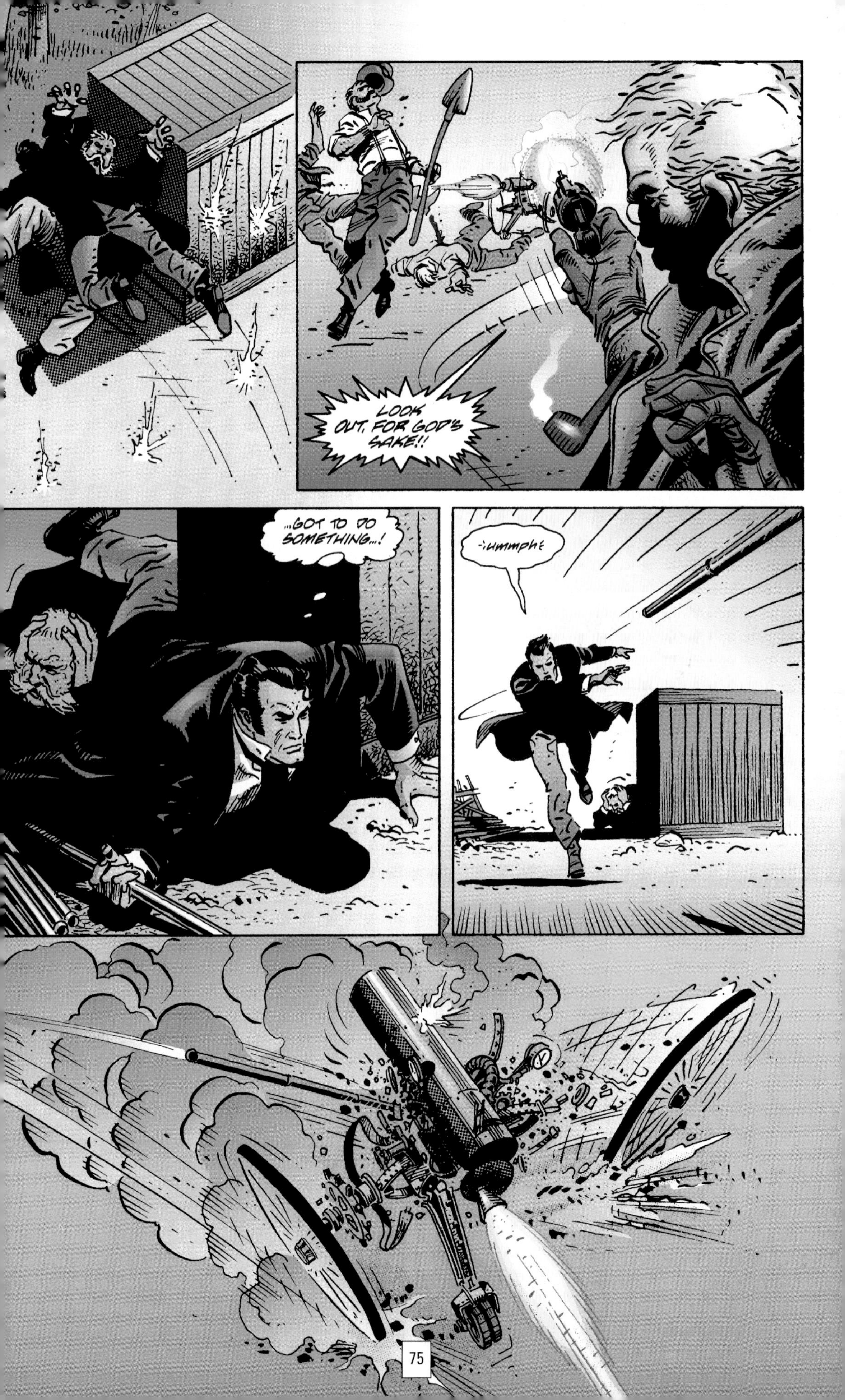
LOOK OUT, FOR GOD'S SAKE!!
...GOT TO DO SOMETHING...!
ummph

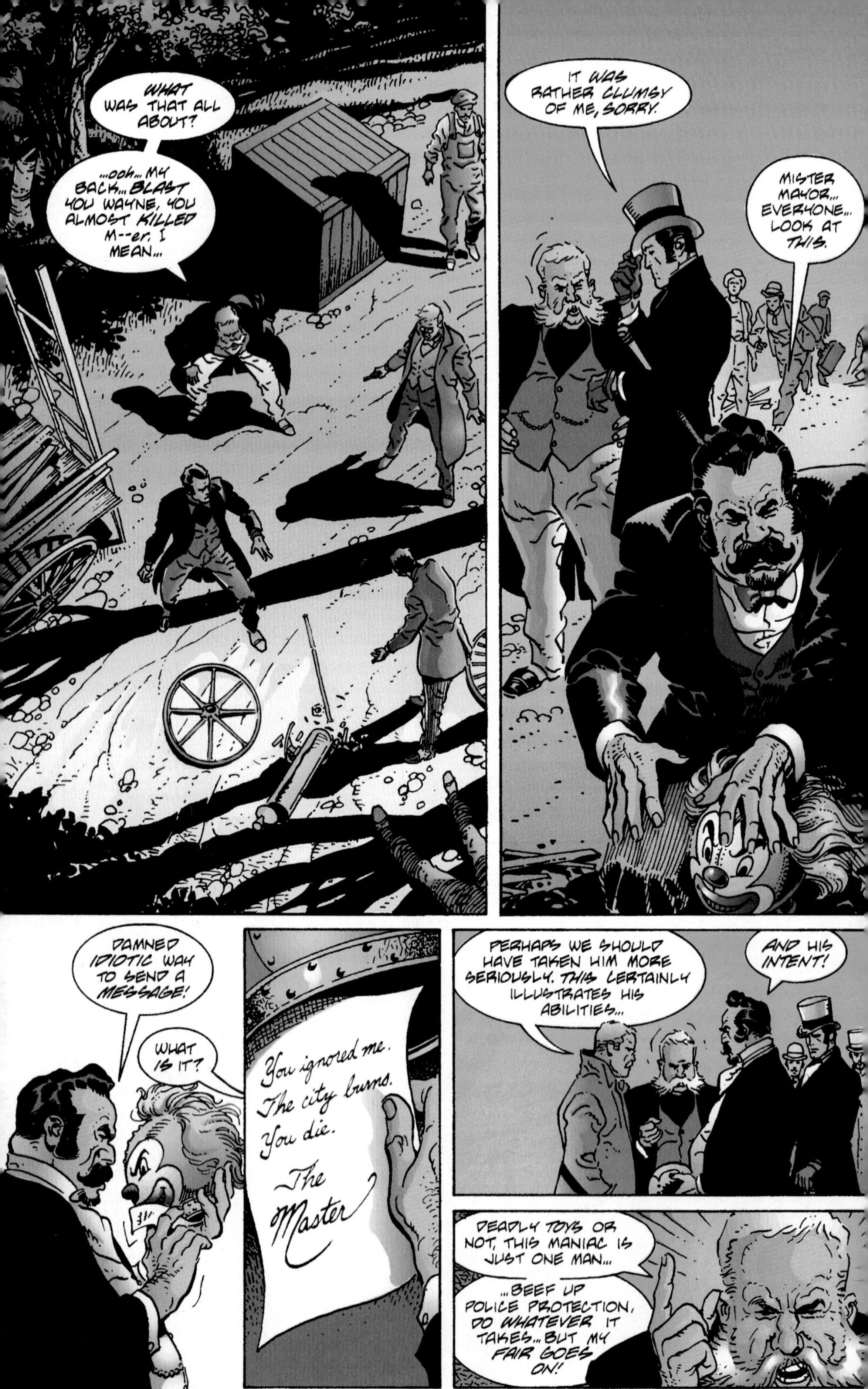
WHAT WAS THAT ALL ABOUT?
...ooh... MY BACK... BLAST YOU WAYNE, YOU ALMOST KILLED M--er, I MEAN...
IT WAS RATHER CLUMSY OF ME, SORRY.
MISTER MAYOR... EVERYONE... LOOK AT THIS.
DAMNED IDIOTIC WAY TO SEND A MESSAGE!
WHAT IS IT?
You ignored me. The city burns. You die. The Master
PERHAPS WE SHOULD HAVE TAKEN HIM MORE SERIOUSLY. THIS CERTAINLY ILLUSTRATES HIS ABILITIES...
AND HIS INTENT!
DEADLY TOYS OR NOT, THIS MANIAC IS JUST ONE MAN...
...BEEF UP POLICE PROTECTION, DO WHATEVER IT TAKES... BUT MY FAIR GOES ON!

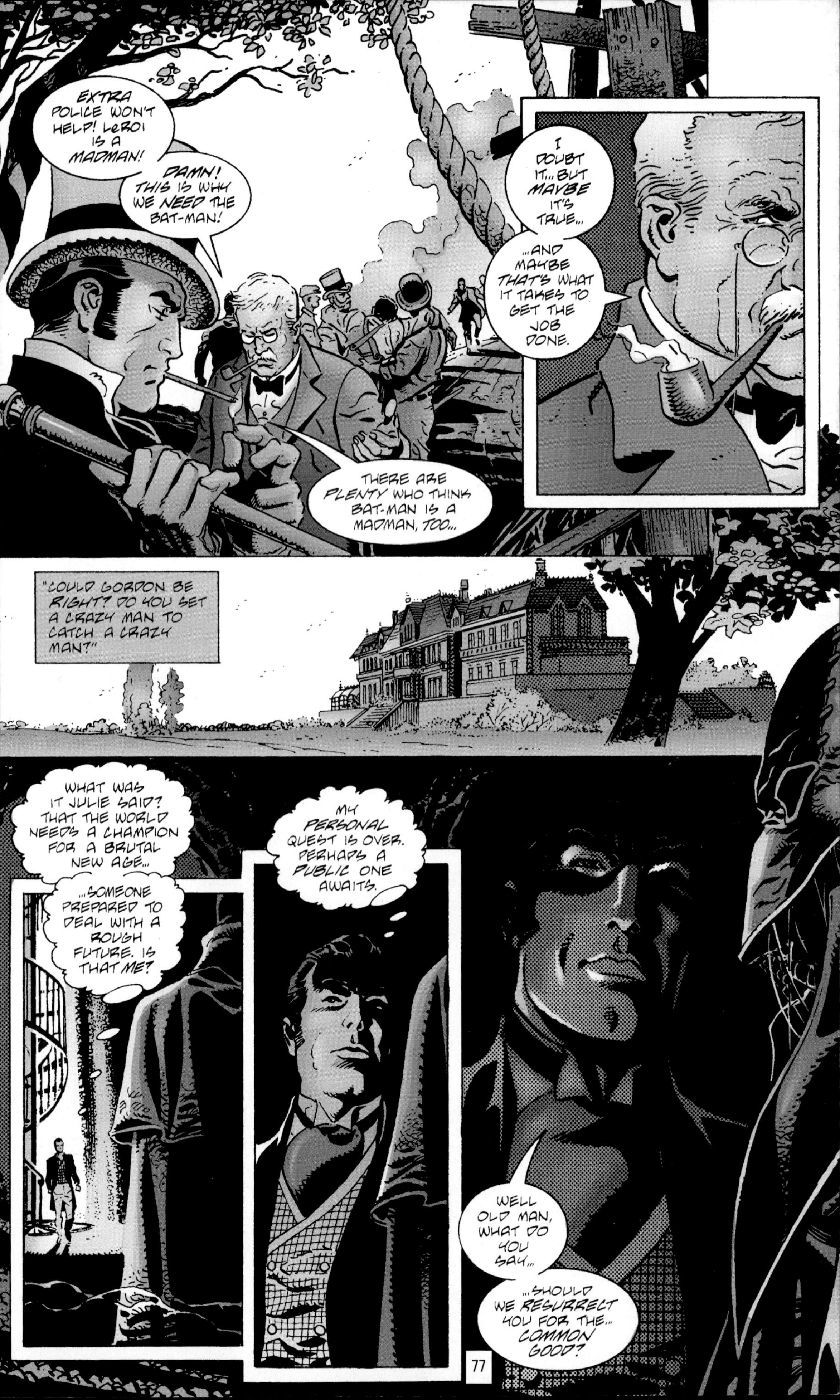

EXTRA POLICE WON'T HELP! LeROI IS A MADMAN!
DAMN! THIS IS WHY WE NEED THE BAT-MAN!
THERE ARE PLENTY WHO THINK BAT-MAN IS A MADMAN, TOO...
I DOUBT IT... BUT MAYBE IT'S TRUE...
...AND MAYBE THAT'S WHAT IT TAKES TO GET THE JOB DONE.
"COULD GORDON BE RIGHT? DO YOU GET A CRAZY MAN TO CATCH A CRAZY MAN?"
WHAT WAS IT JULIE SAID? THAT THE WORLD NEEDS A CHAMPION FOR A BRUTAL NEW AGE...
...SOMEONE PREPARED TO DEAL WITH A ROUGH FUTURE. IS THAT ME?
MY PERSONAL QUEST IS OVER. PERHAPS A PUBLIC ONE AWAITS.
WELL OLD MAN, WHAT DO YOU SAY...
...SHOULD WE RESURRECT YOU FOR THE... COMMON GOOD?

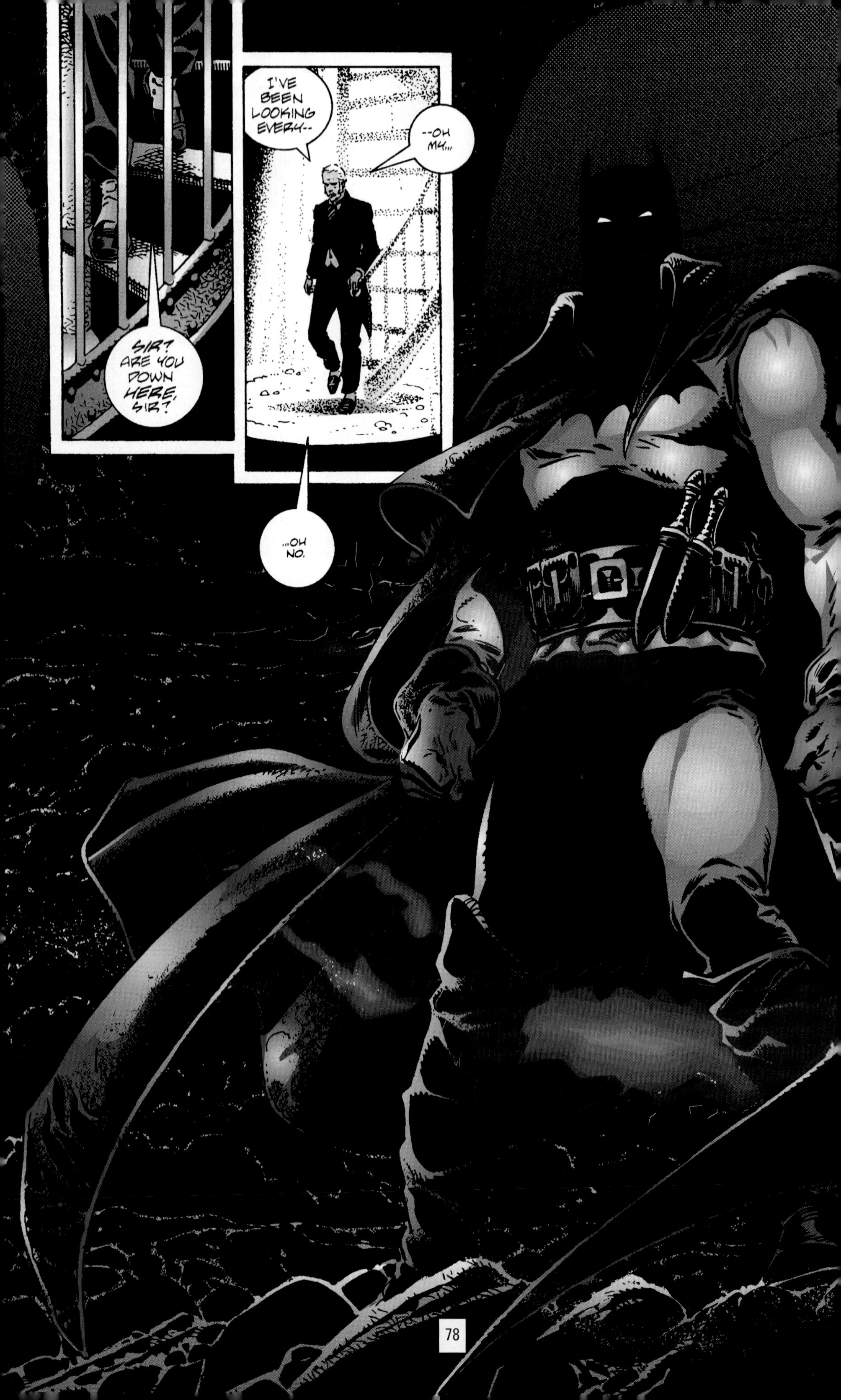
SIR? ARE YOU DOWN HERE, SIR?
I'VE BEEN LOOKING EVERY--
--OH MY...
...OH NO.

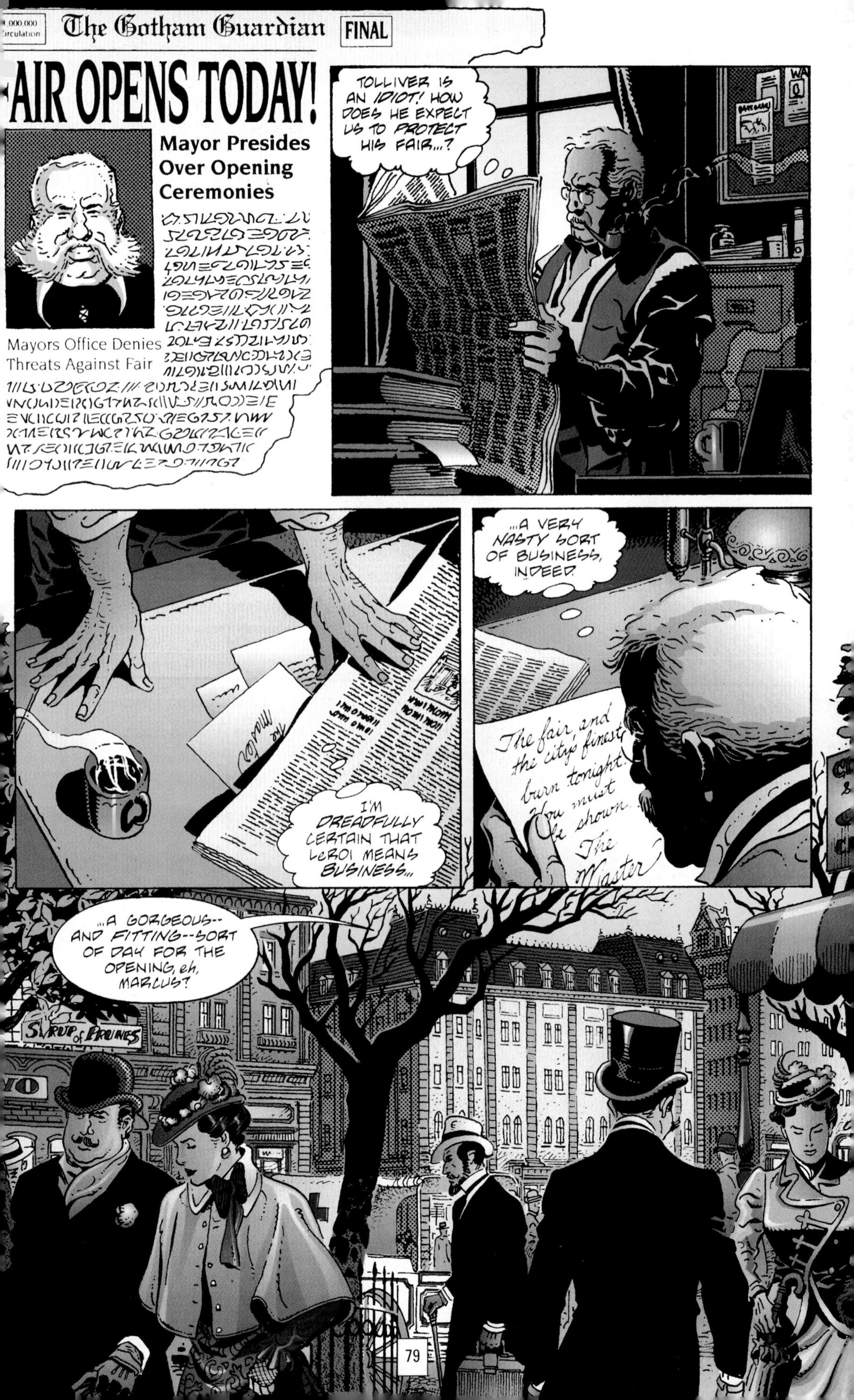

The Gotham Guardian
FINAL
Circulation
AIR OPENS TODAY!
Mayor Presides Over Opening Ceremonies
Mayors Office Denies Threats Against Fair
TOLLIVER IS AN IDIOT! HOW DOES HE EXPECT US TO PROTECT HIS FAIR...?
I'M DREADFULLY CERTAIN THAT LeROI MEANS BUSINESS...
...A VERY NASTY SORT OF BUSINESS, INDEED.
The fair, and the city's finest burn tonight. You must shown. The Master
...A GORGEOUS--AND FITTING--SORT OF DAY FOR THE OPENING, eh, MARCUS?
SYRUP of PRUNES

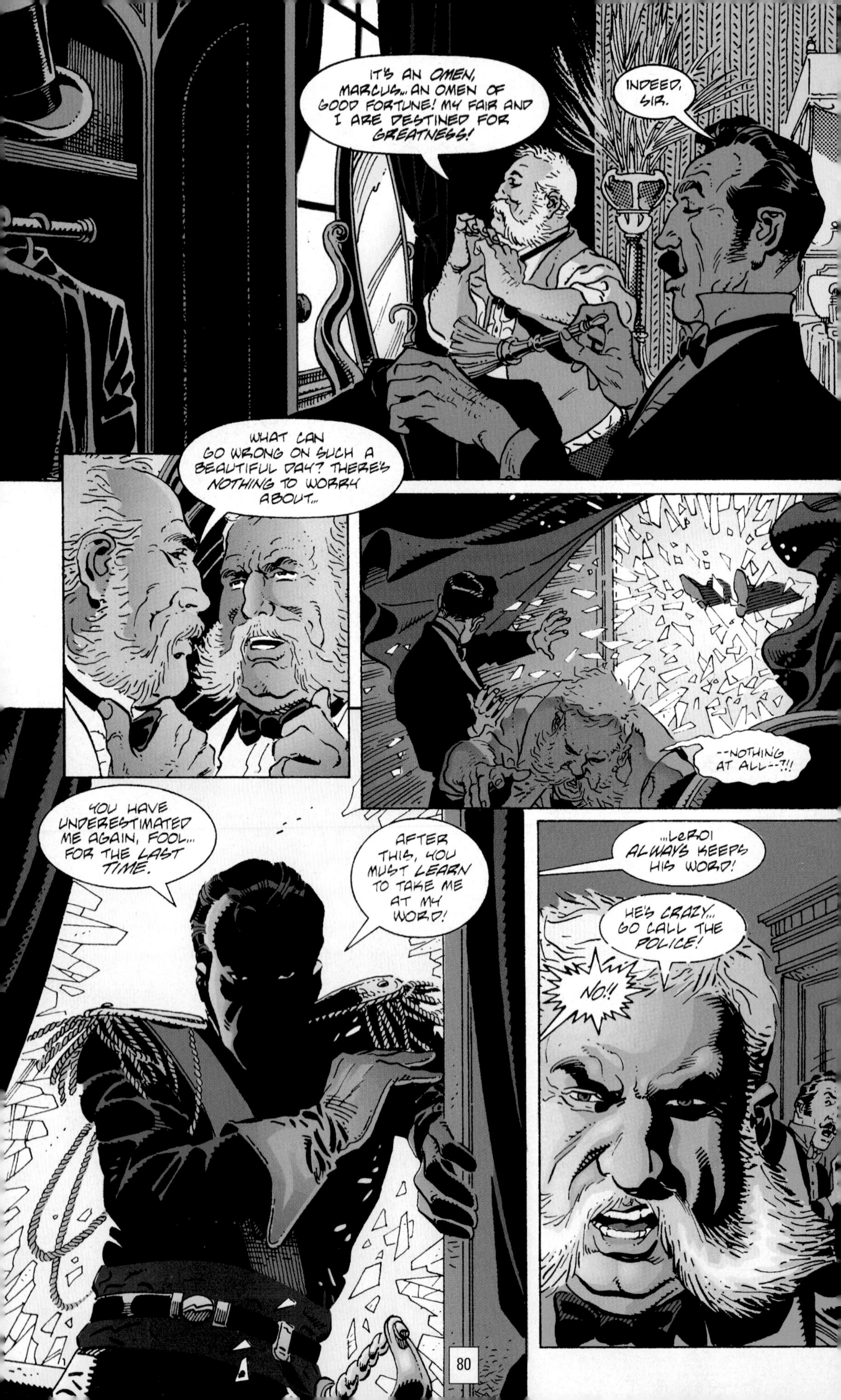

IT'S AN OMEN, MARCUS... AN OMEN OF GOOD FORTUNE! MY FAIR AND I ARE DESTINED FOR GREATNESS!
INDEED, SIR.
WHAT CAN GO WRONG ON SUCH A BEAUTIFUL DAY? THERE'S NOTHING TO WORRY ABOUT...
--NOTHING AT ALL--?!!
YOU HAVE UNDERESTIMATED ME AGAIN, FOOL... FOR THE LAST TIME.
AFTER THIS, YOU MUST LEARN TO TAKE ME AT MY WORD!
...LeROI ALWAYS KEEPS HIS WORD!
HE'S CRAZY... GO CALL THE POLICE!
NO!!

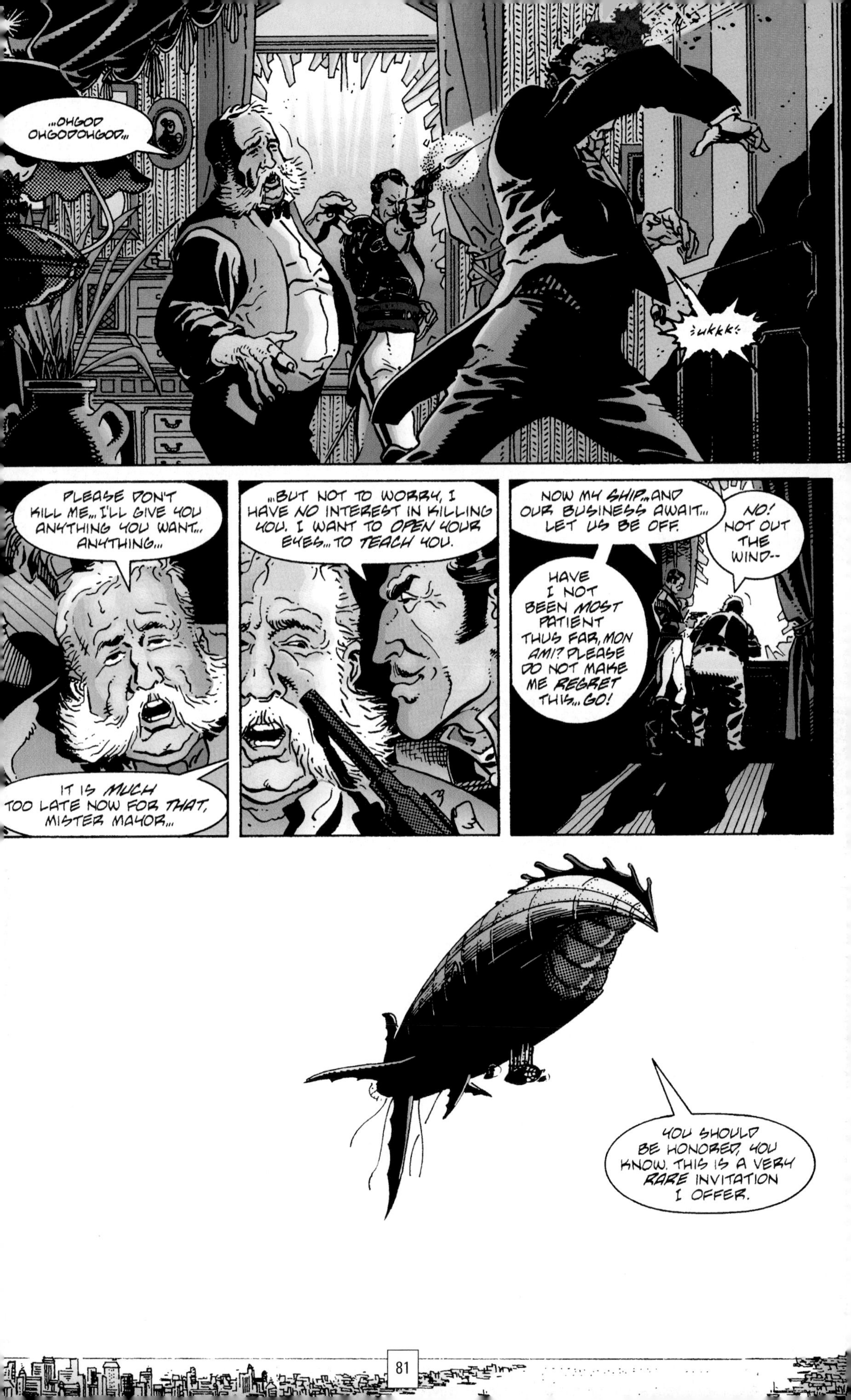
...OHGOD OHGODOHGOD...
:ukkk:
PLEASE DON'T KILL ME... I'LL GIVE YOU ANYTHING YOU WANT... ANYTHING...
IT IS MUCH TOO LATE NOW FOR THAT, MISTER MAYOR...
...BUT NOT TO WORRY, I HAVE NO INTEREST IN KILLING YOU. I WANT TO OPEN YOUR EYES... TO TEACH YOU.
NOW MY SHIP... AND OUR BUSINESS AWAIT... LET US BE OFF.
NO! NOT OUT THE WIND--
HAVE I NOT BEEN MOST PATIENT THUS FAR, MON AMI? PLEASE DO NOT MAKE ME REGRET THIS... GO!
YOU SHOULD BE HONORED, YOU KNOW. THIS IS A VERY RARE INVITATION I OFFER.

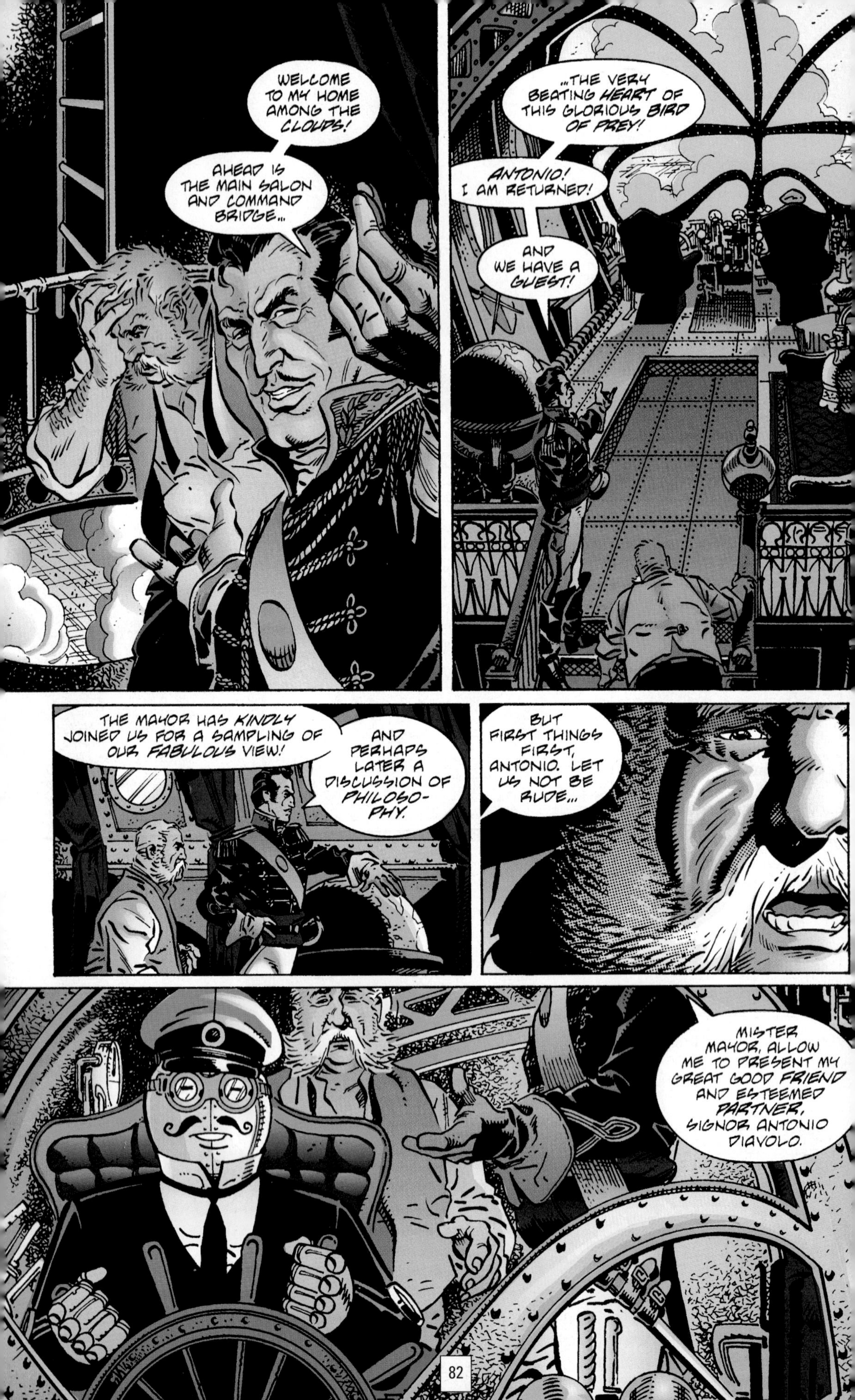
WELCOME TO MY HOME AMONG THE CLOUDS!
AHEAD IS THE MAIN SALON AND COMMAND BRIDGE...
...THE VERY BEATING HEART OF THIS GLORIOUS BIRD OF PREY!
ANTONIO! I AM RETURNED!
AND WE HAVE A GUEST!
THE MAYOR HAS KINDLY JOINED US FOR A SAMPLING OF OUR FABULOUS VIEW!
AND PERHAPS LATER A DISCUSSION OF PHILOSO-PHY.
BUT FIRST THINGS FIRST, ANTONIO. LET US NOT BE RUDE...
MISTER MAYOR, ALLOW ME TO PRESENT MY GREAT GOOD FRIEND AND ESTEEMED PARTNER, SIGNOR ANTONIO DIAVOLO.

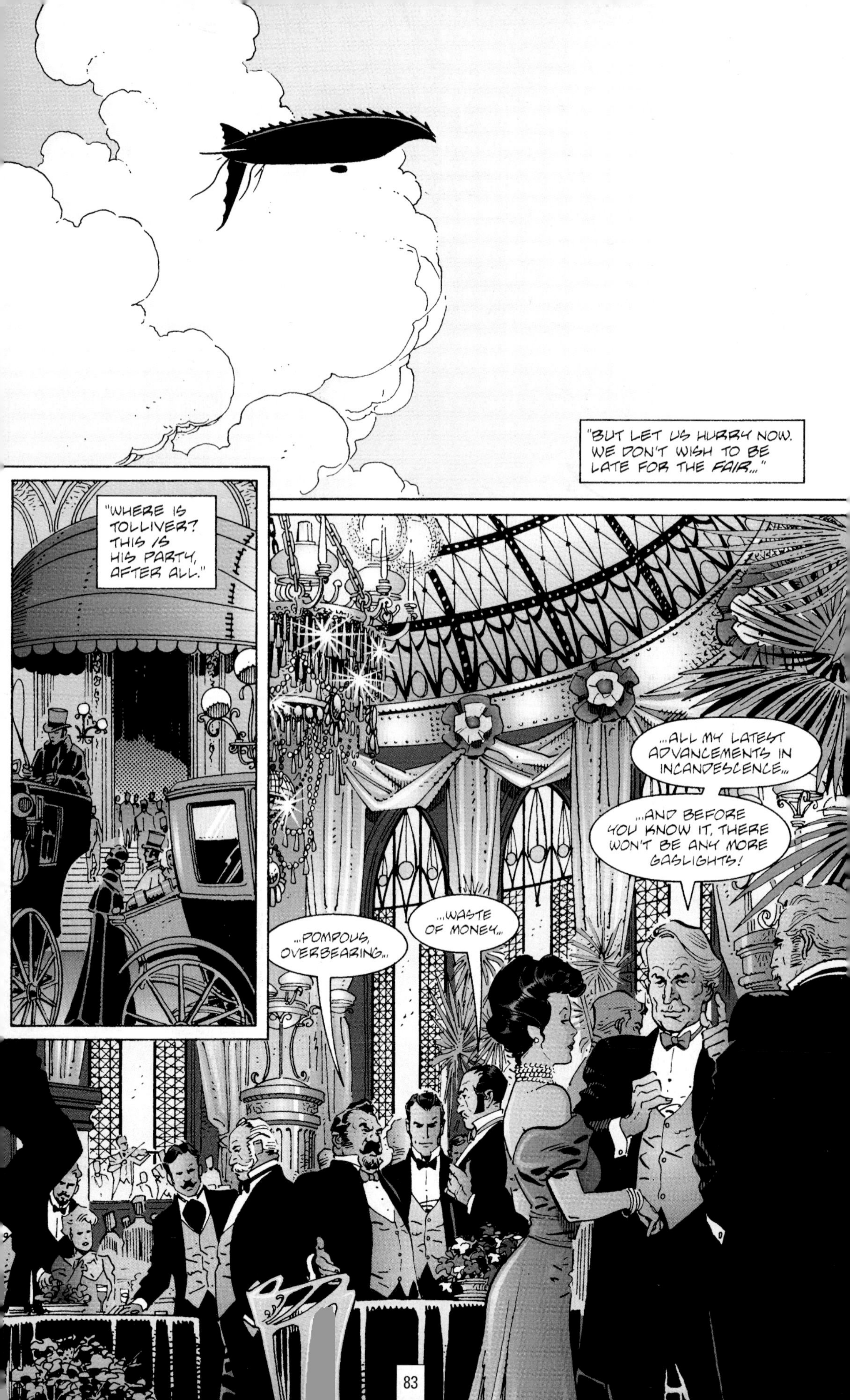
"BUT LET US HURRY NOW. WE DON'T WISH TO BE LATE FOR THE FAIR..."
"WHERE IS TOLLIVER? THIS IS HIS PARTY, AFTER ALL."
...ALL MY LATEST ADVANCEMENTS IN INCANDESCENCE...
...AND BEFORE YOU KNOW IT, THERE WON'T BE ANY MORE GASLIGHTS!
...POMPOUS, OVERBEARING...
...WASTE OF MONEY...

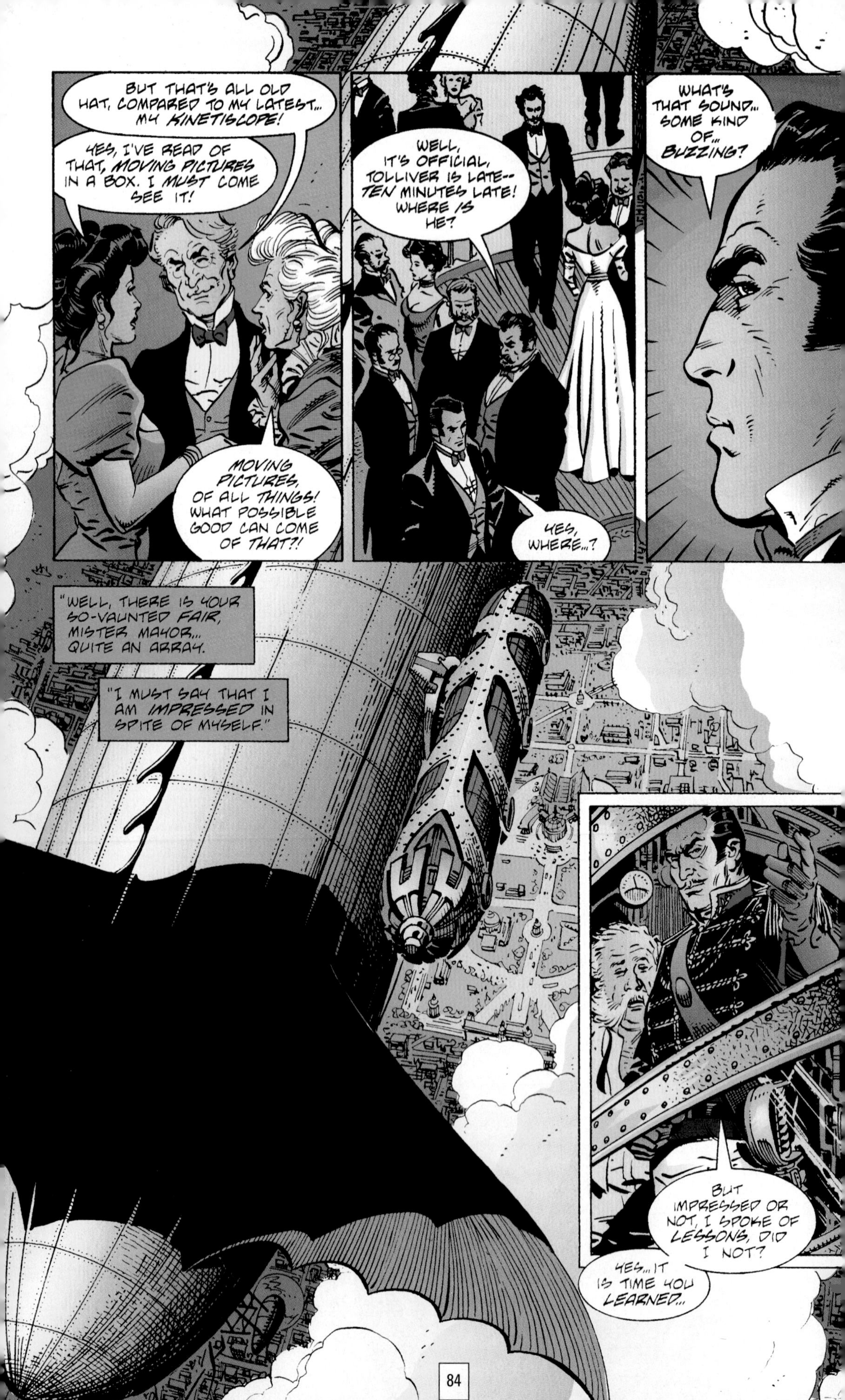

BUT THAT'S ALL OLD HAT, COMPARED TO MY LATEST... MY KINETISCOPE!
YES, I'VE READ OF THAT, MOVING PICTURES IN A BOX. I MUST COME SEE IT!
MOVING PICTURES, OF ALL THINGS! WHAT POSSIBLE GOOD CAN COME OF THAT?!
WELL, IT'S OFFICIAL, TOLLIVER IS LATE-- TEN MINUTES LATE! WHERE IS HE?
YES, WHERE...?
WHAT'S THAT SOUND... SOME KIND OF... BUZZING?
"WELL, THERE IS YOUR SO-VAUNTED FAIR, MISTER MAYOR... QUITE AN ARRAY.
"I MUST SAY THAT I AM IMPRESSED IN SPITE OF MYSELF."
BUT IMPRESSED OR NOT, I SPOKE OF LESSONS, DID I NOT?
YES... IT IS TIME YOU LEARNED...

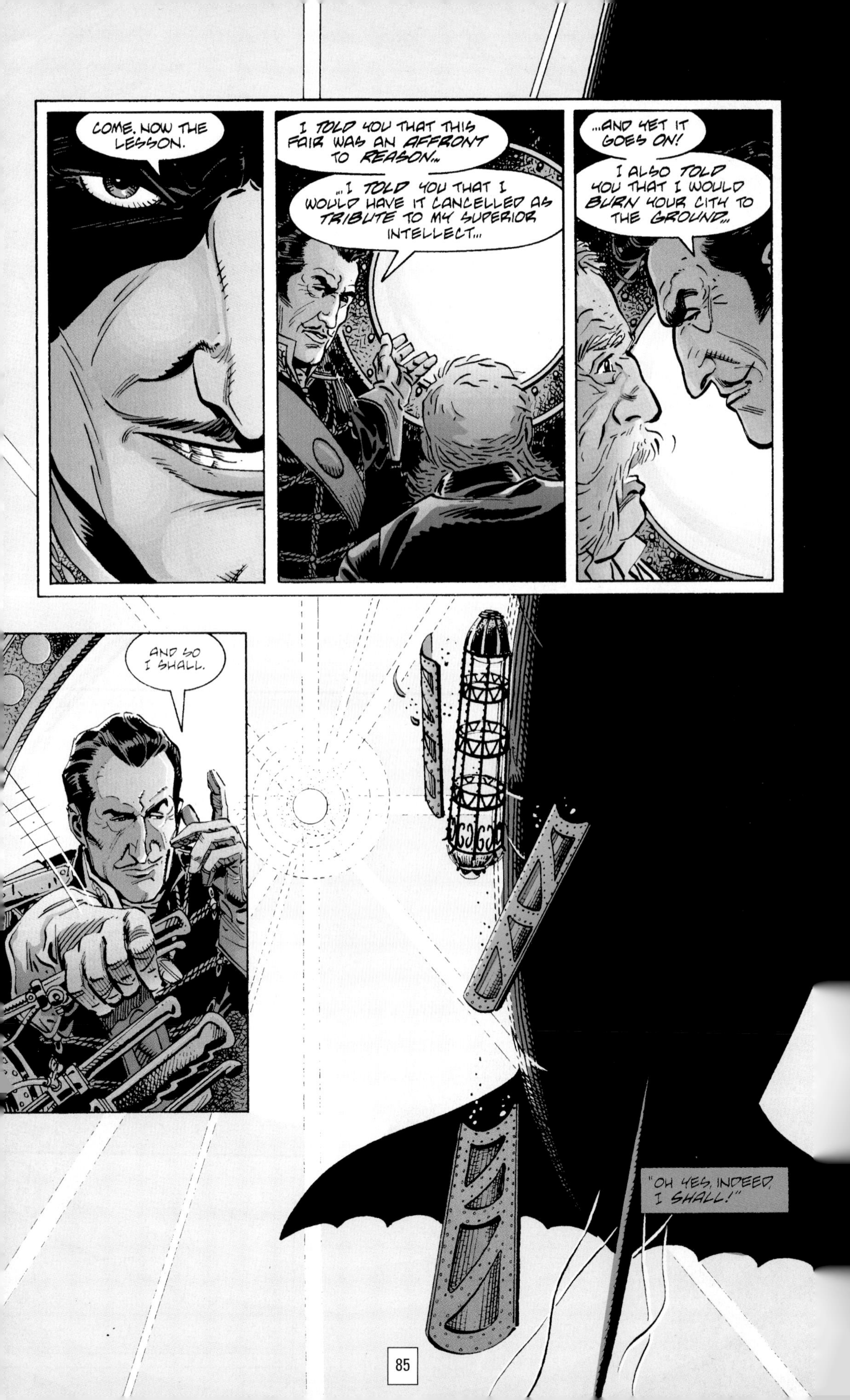
COME. NOW THE LESSON.
I TOLD YOU THAT THIS FAIR WAS AN AFFRONT TO REASON...
...I TOLD YOU THAT I WOULD HAVE IT CANCELLED AS TRIBUTE TO MY SUPERIOR INTELLECT...
...AND YET IT GOES ON!
I ALSO TOLD YOU THAT I WOULD BURN YOUR CITY TO THE GROUND...
AND SO I SHALL.
"OH YES, INDEED, I SHALL!"

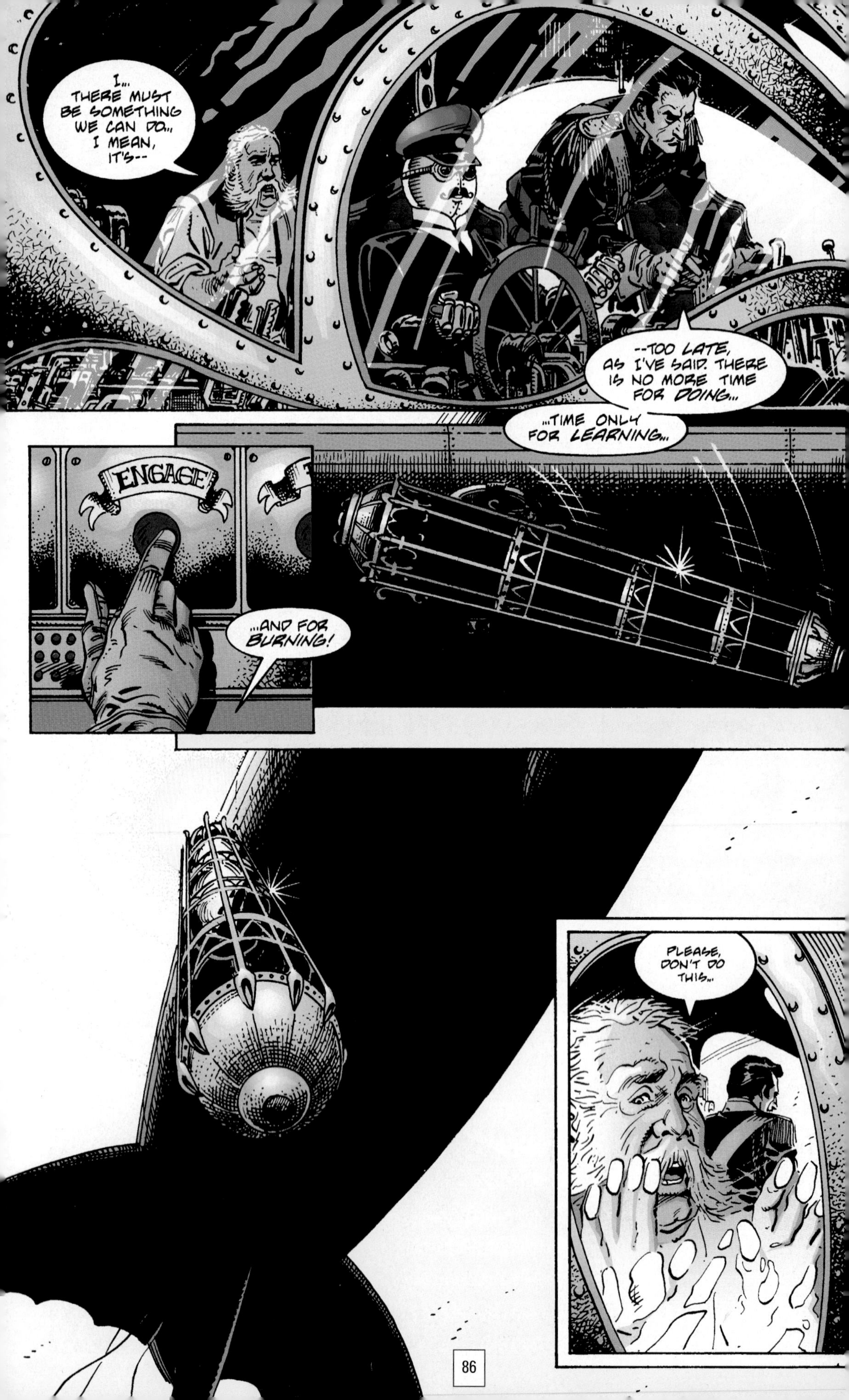
I... THERE MUST BE SOMETHING WE CAN DO... I MEAN, IT'S--
--TOO LATE, AS I'VE SAID. THERE IS NO MORE TIME FOR DOING...
...TIME ONLY FOR LEARNING...
ENGAGE
...AND FOR BURNING!
PLEASE, DON'T DO THIS...

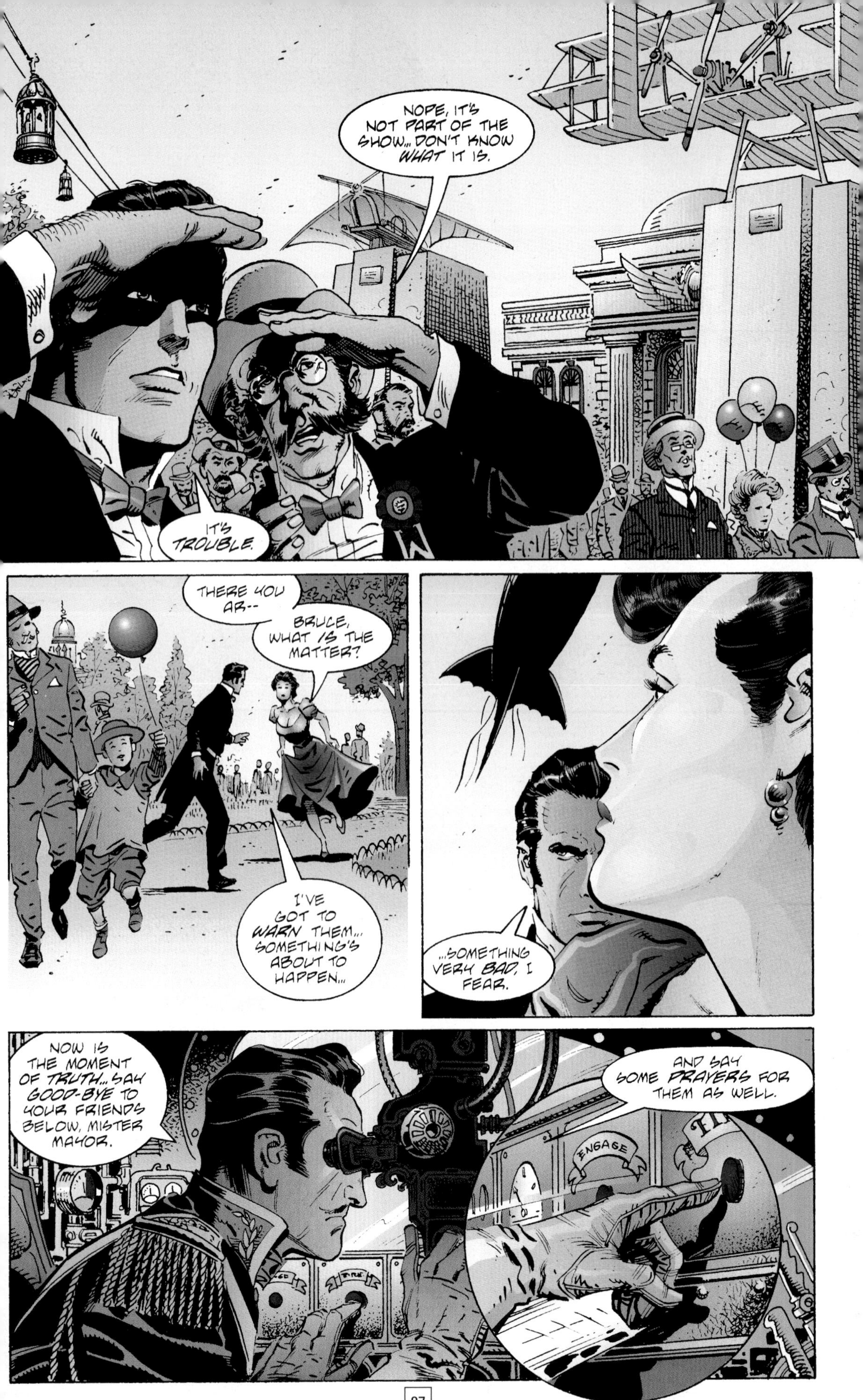
NOPE, IT'S NOT PART OF THE SHOW... DON'T KNOW WHAT IT IS.
IT'S TROUBLE.
THERE YOU AR--
BRUCE, WHAT IS THE MATTER?
I'VE GOT TO WARN THEM... SOMETHING'S ABOUT TO HAPPEN...
...SOMETHING VERY BAD, I FEAR.
NOW IS THE MOMENT OF TRUTH... SAY GOOD-BYE TO YOUR FRIENDS BELOW, MISTER MAYOR.
AND SAY SOME PRAYERS FOR THEM AS WELL.
ENGAGE

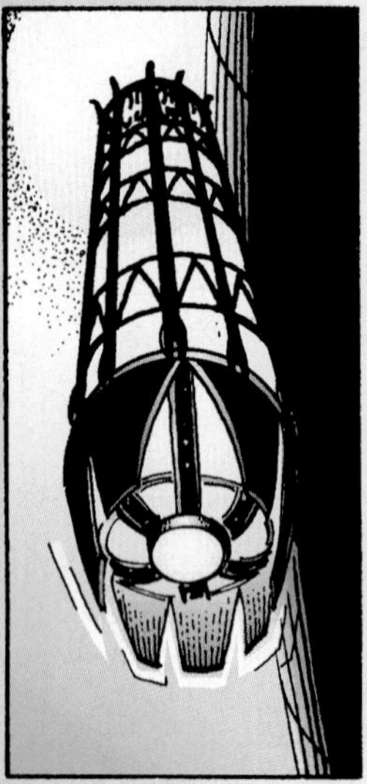

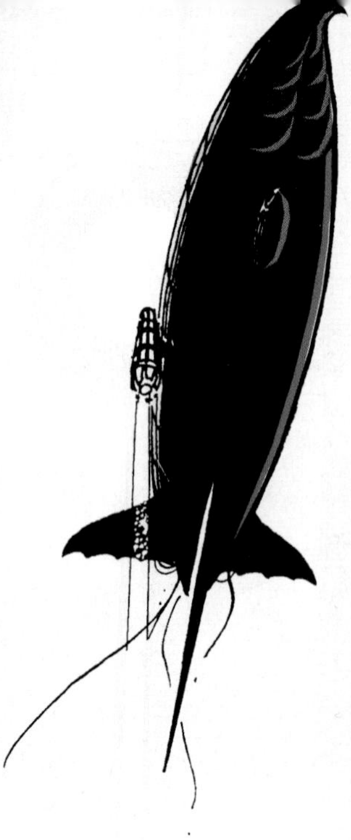

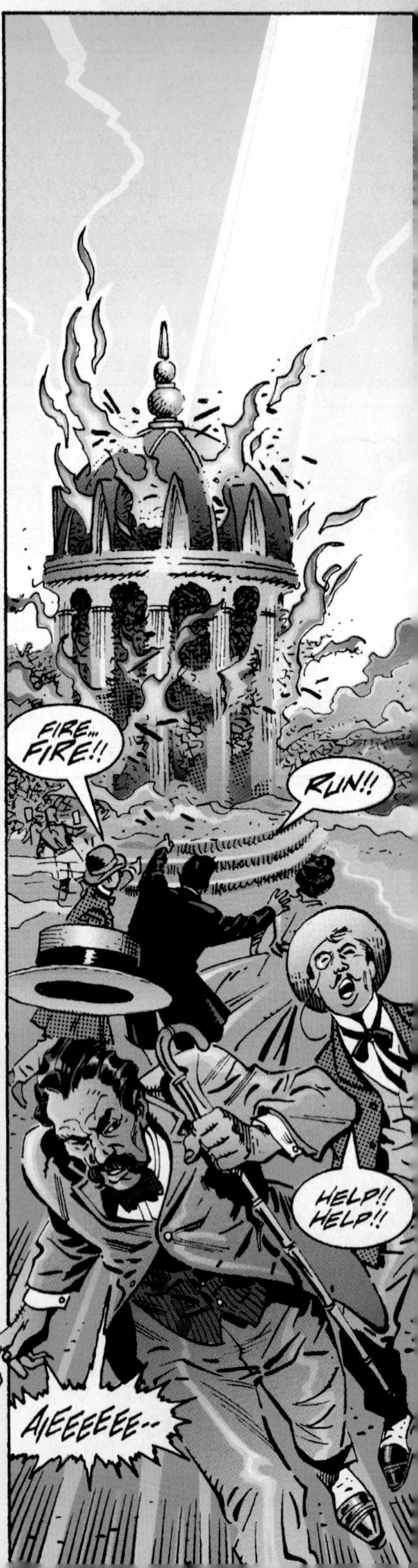
FIRE... FIRE!!
RUN!!
HELP!! HELP!!
AIEEEEEE--

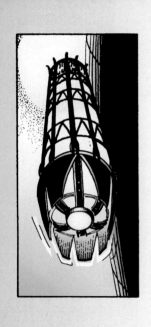

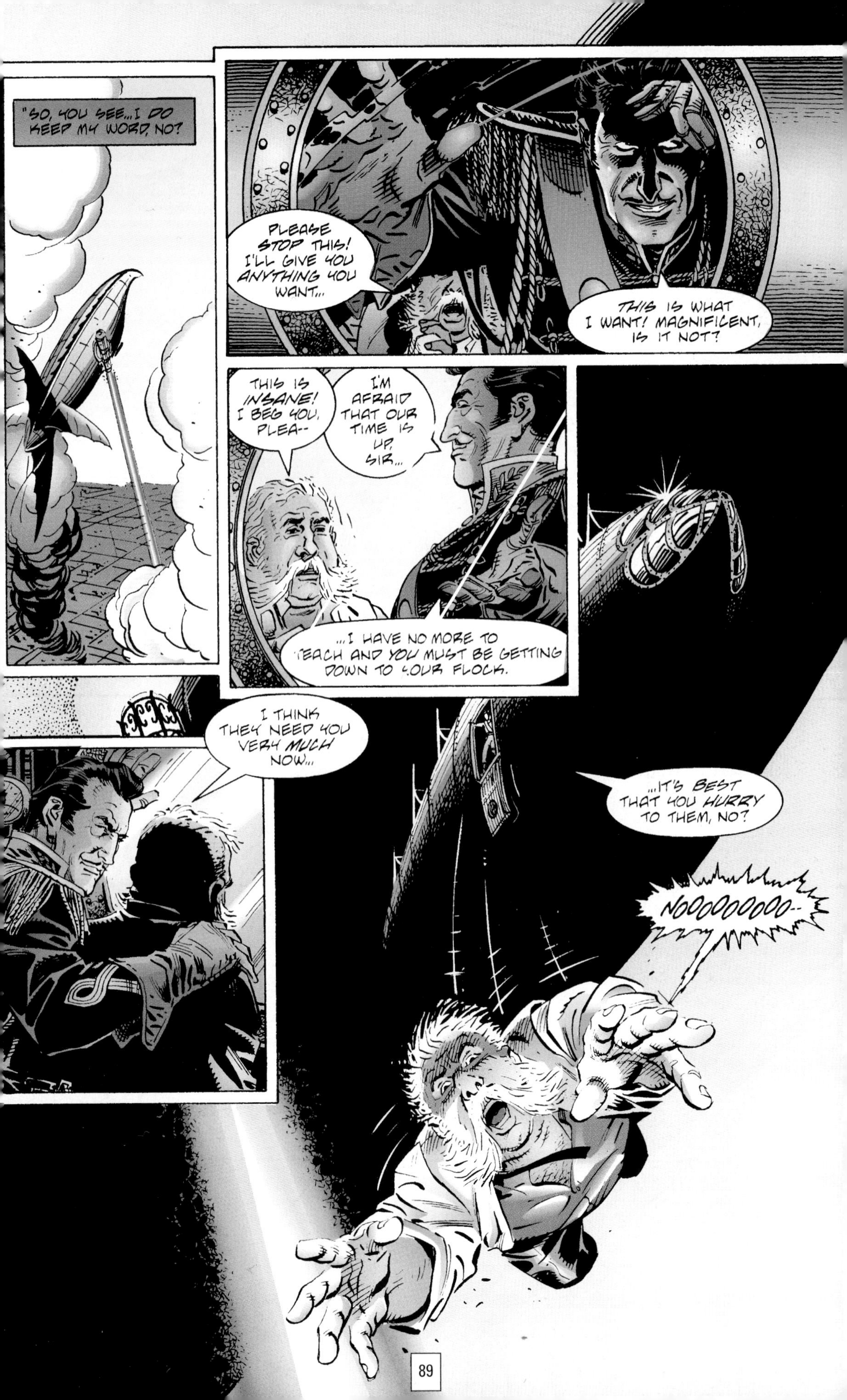
"SO, YOU SEE...I DO KEEP MY WORD, NO?
PLEASE STOP THIS! I'LL GIVE YOU ANYTHING YOU WANT...
THIS IS WHAT I WANT! MAGNIFICENT, IS IT NOT?
THIS IS INSANE! I BEG YOU, PLEA--
I'M AFRAID THAT OUR TIME IS UP, SIR...
...I HAVE NO MORE TO TEACH AND YOU MUST BE GETTING DOWN TO YOUR FLOCK.
I THINK THEY NEED YOU VERY MUCH NOW...
...IT'S BEST THAT YOU HURRY TO THEM, NO?
NOOOOOOOOO--

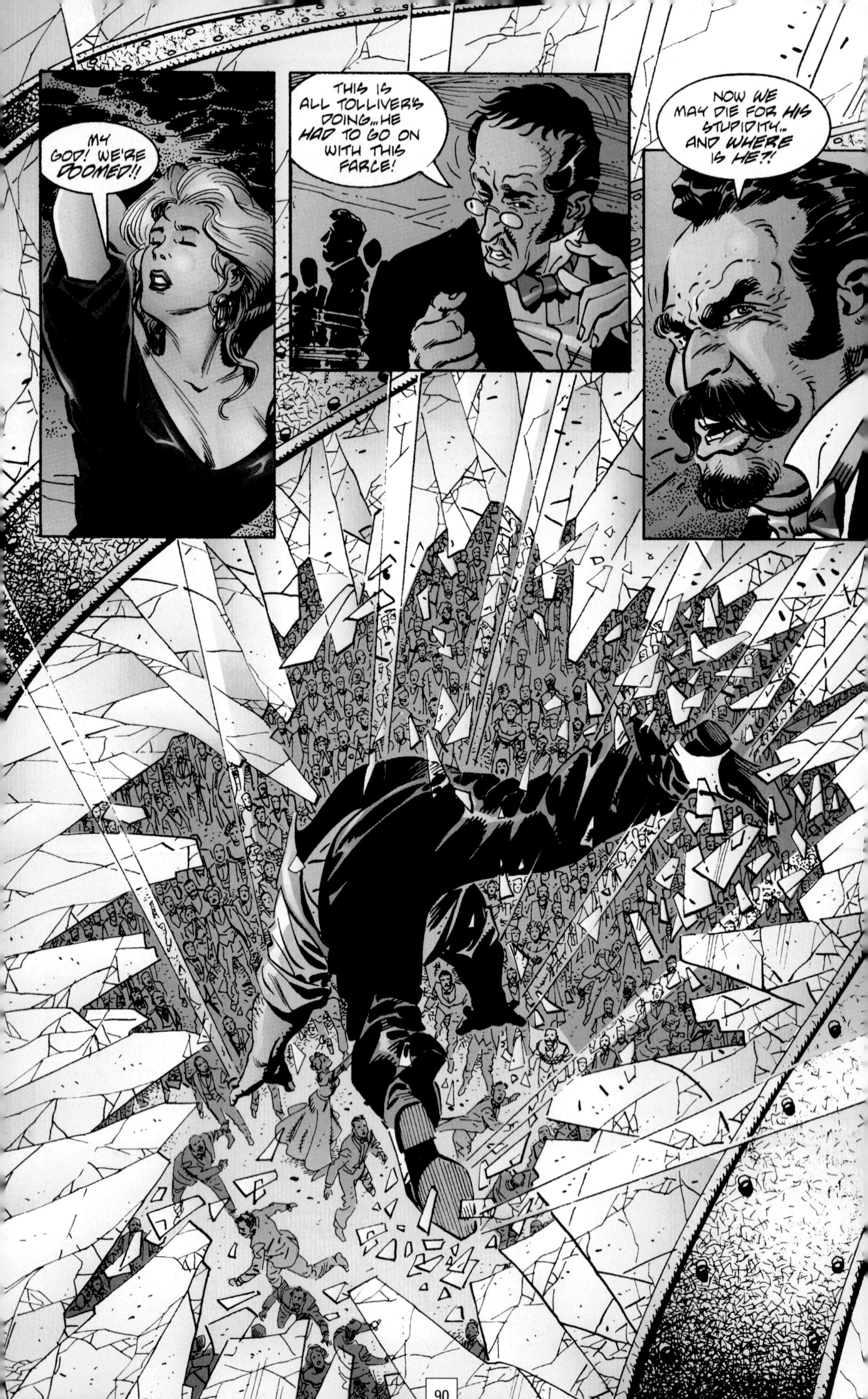
MY GOD! WE'RE DOOMED!!
THIS IS ALL TOLLIVER'S DOING... HE HAD TO GO ON WITH THIS FARCE!
NOW WE MAY DIE FOR HIS STUPIDITY... AND WHERE IS HE?!

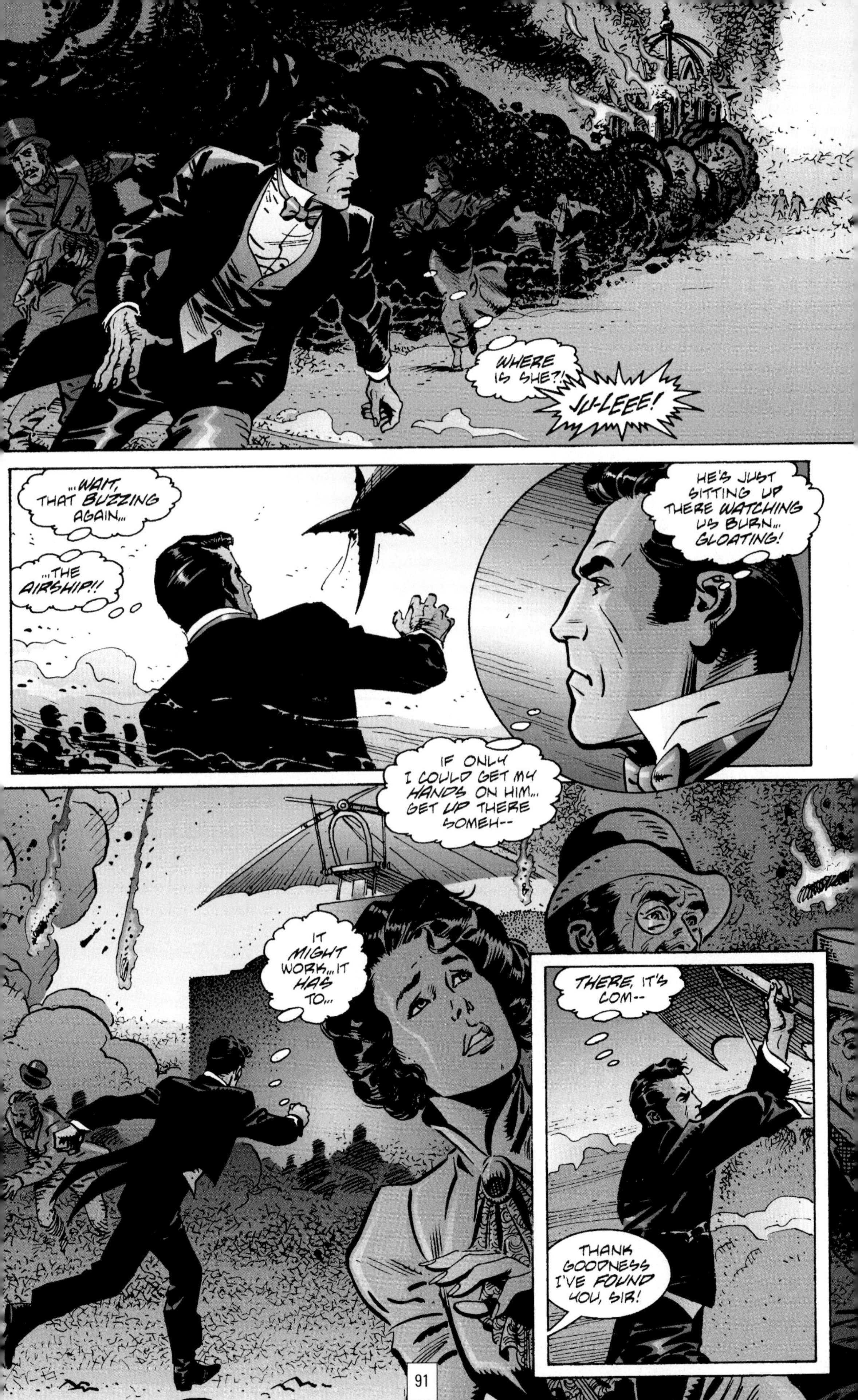
WHERE IS SHE?!
JU-LEEE!
...WAIT, THAT BUZZING AGAIN...
...THE AIRSHIP!!
HE'S JUST SITTING UP THERE WATCHING US BURN... GLOATING!
IF ONLY I COULD GET MY HANDS ON HIM... GET UP THERE SOMEH--
IT MIGHT WORK... IT HAS TO...
THERE, IT'S COM--
THANK GOODNESS I'VE FOUND YOU, SIR!

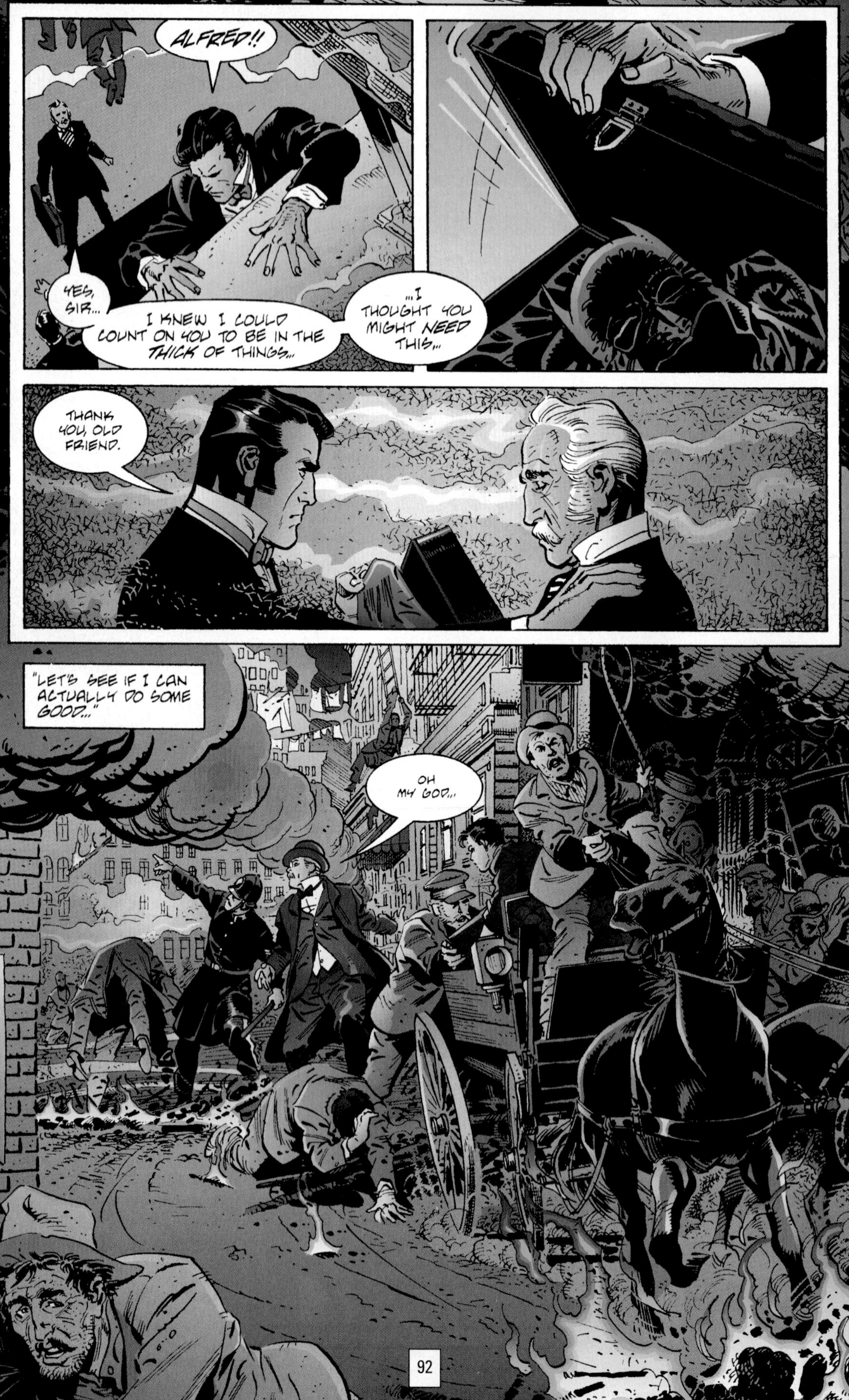
ALFRED!!
YES, SIR...
I KNEW I COULD COUNT ON YOU TO BE IN THE THICK OF THINGS...
...I THOUGHT YOU MIGHT NEED THIS...
THANK YOU, OLD FRIEND.
"LET'S SEE IF I CAN ACTUALLY DO SOME GOOD..."
OH MY GOD...

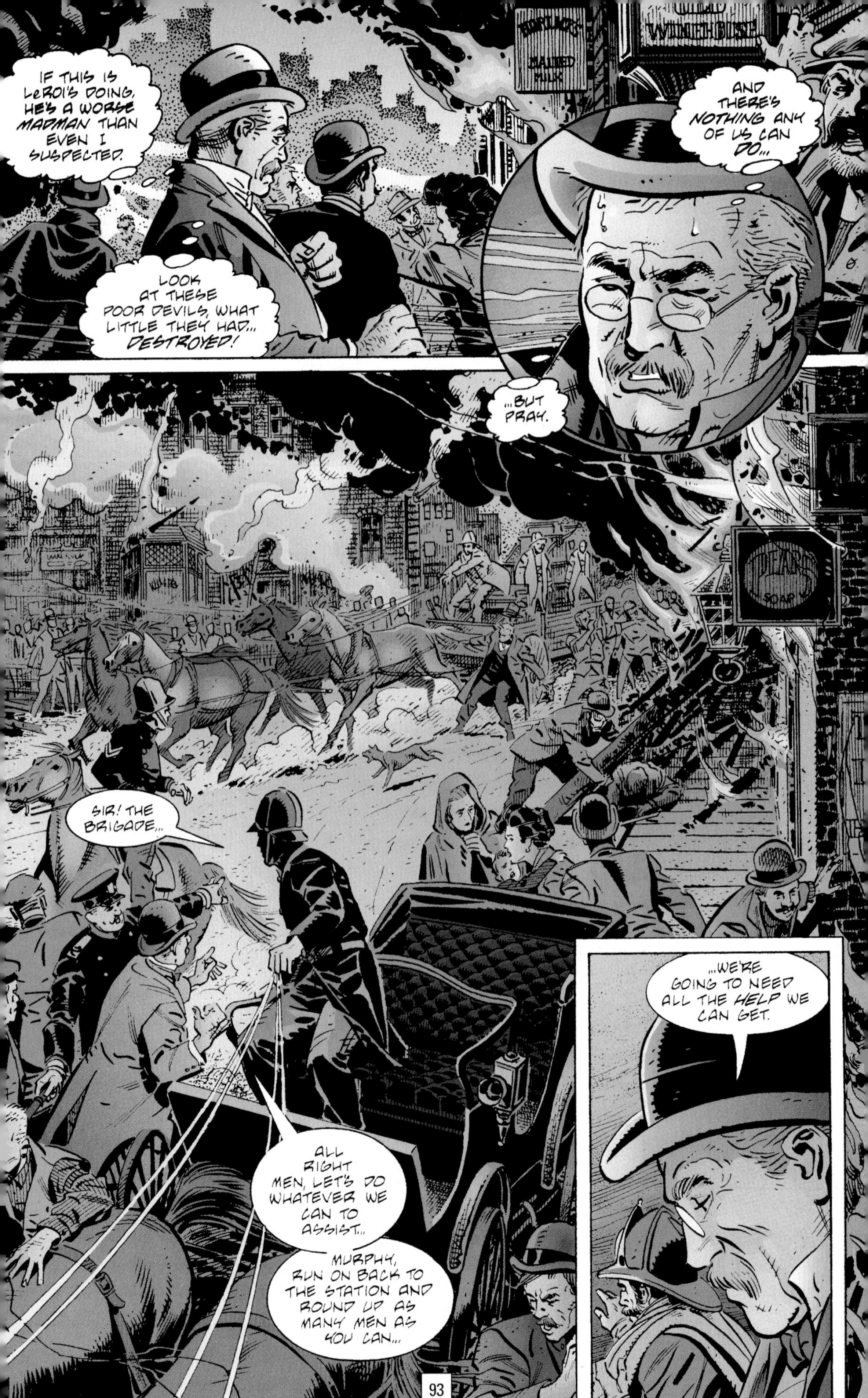
IF THIS IS LeROI'S DOING, HE'S A WORSE MADMAN THAN EVEN I SUSPECTED.
LOOK AT THESE POOR DEVILS, WHAT LITTLE THEY HAD... DESTROYED!
AND THERE'S NOTHING ANY OF US CAN DO...
...BUT PRAY.
SIR! THE BRIGADE...
ALL RIGHT MEN, LET'S DO WHATEVER WE CAN TO ASSIST...
MURPHY, RUN ON BACK TO THE STATION AND ROUND UP AS MANY MEN AS YOU CAN...
...WE'RE GOING TO NEED ALL THE HELP WE CAN GET.

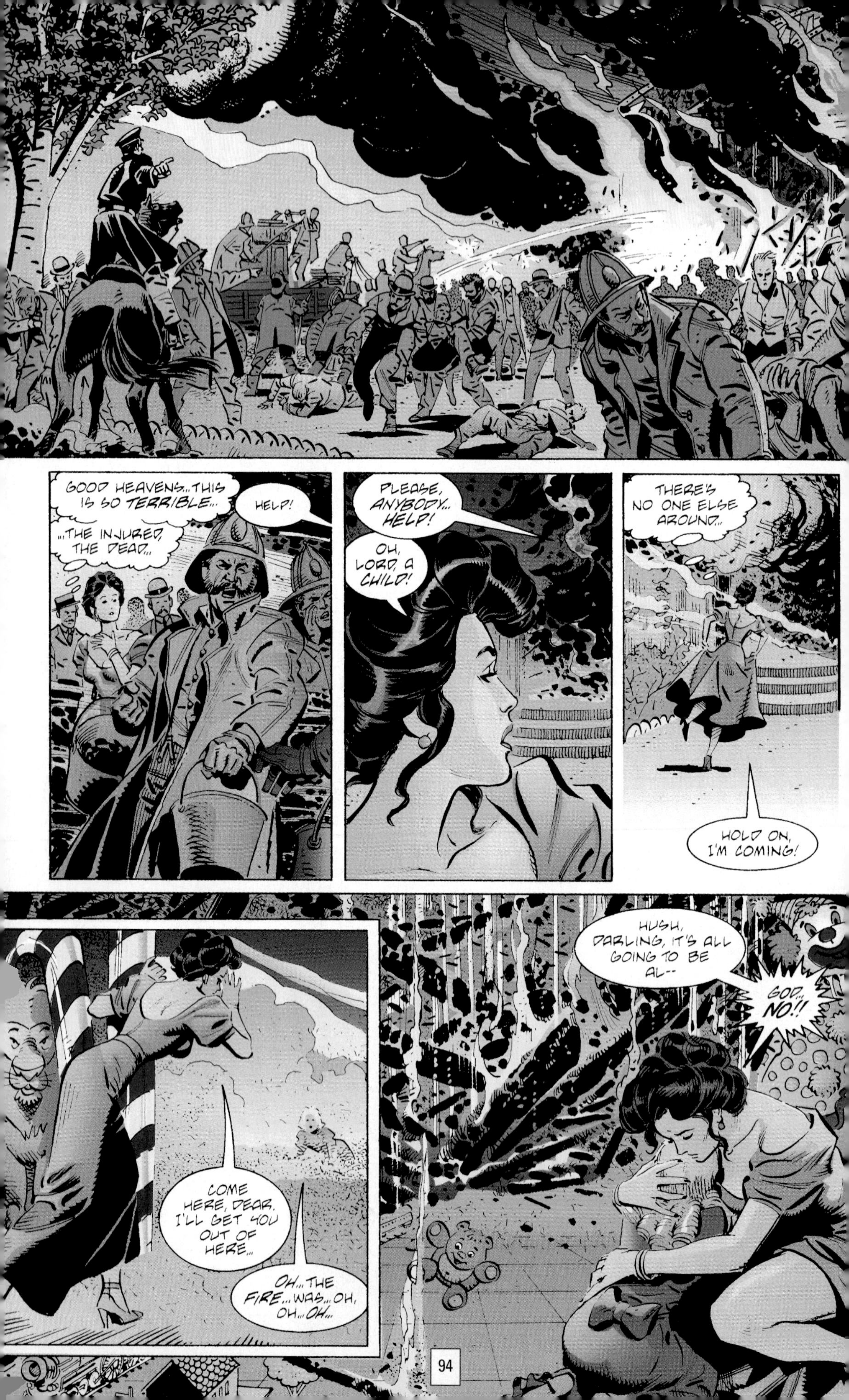
GOOD HEAVENS... THIS IS SO TERRIBLE...
...THE INJURED, THE DEAD...
HELP!
PLEASE, ANYBODY... HELP!
OH, LORD, A CHILD!
THERE'S NO ONE ELSE AROUND...
HOLD ON, I'M COMING!
COME HERE, DEAR. I'LL GET YOU OUT OF HERE...
OH... THE FIRE... WAS... OH, OH... OH...
HUSH, DARLING, IT'S ALL GOING TO BE AL--
GOD... NO!!

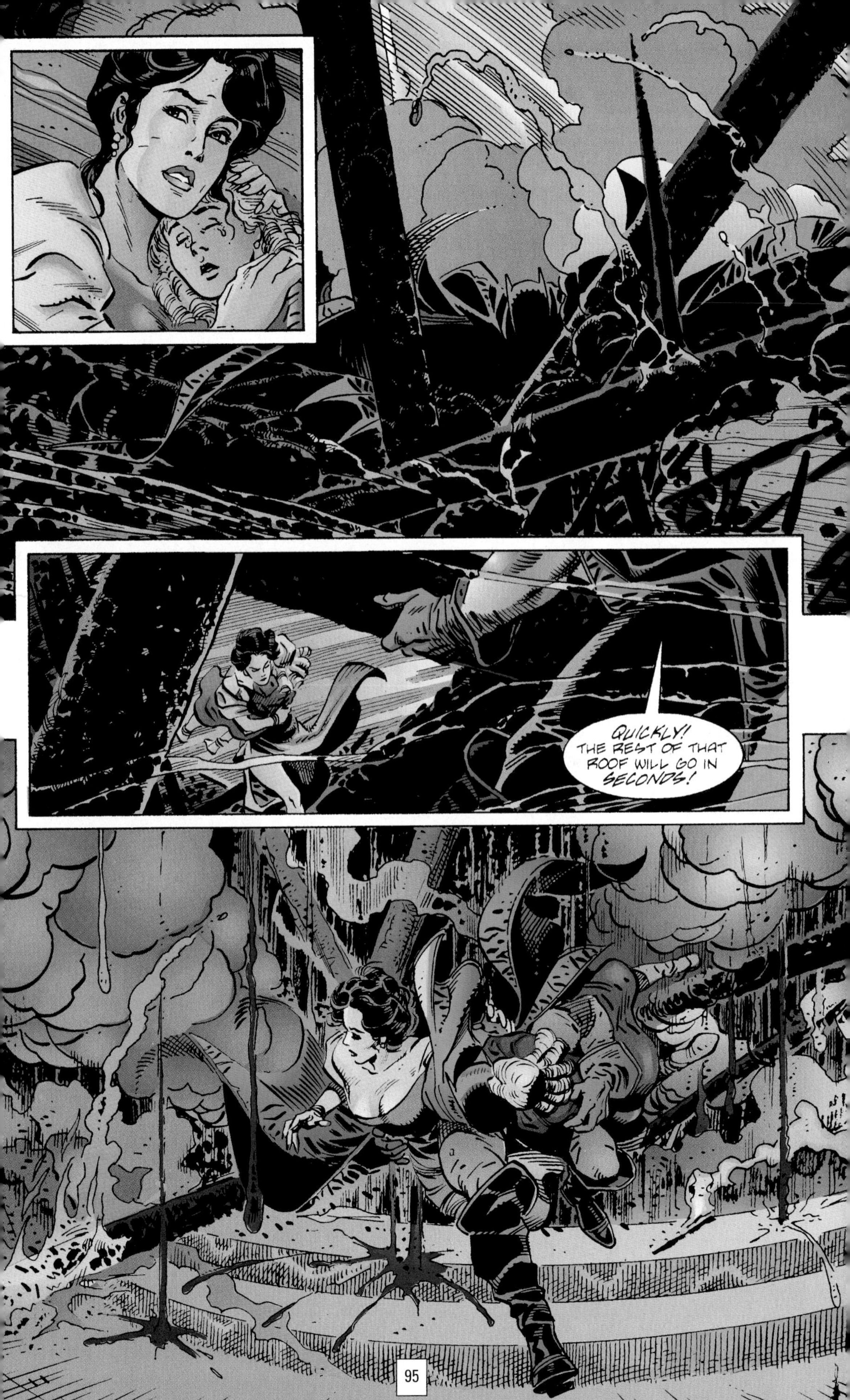
QUICKLY! THE REST OF THAT ROOF WILL GO IN SECONDS!

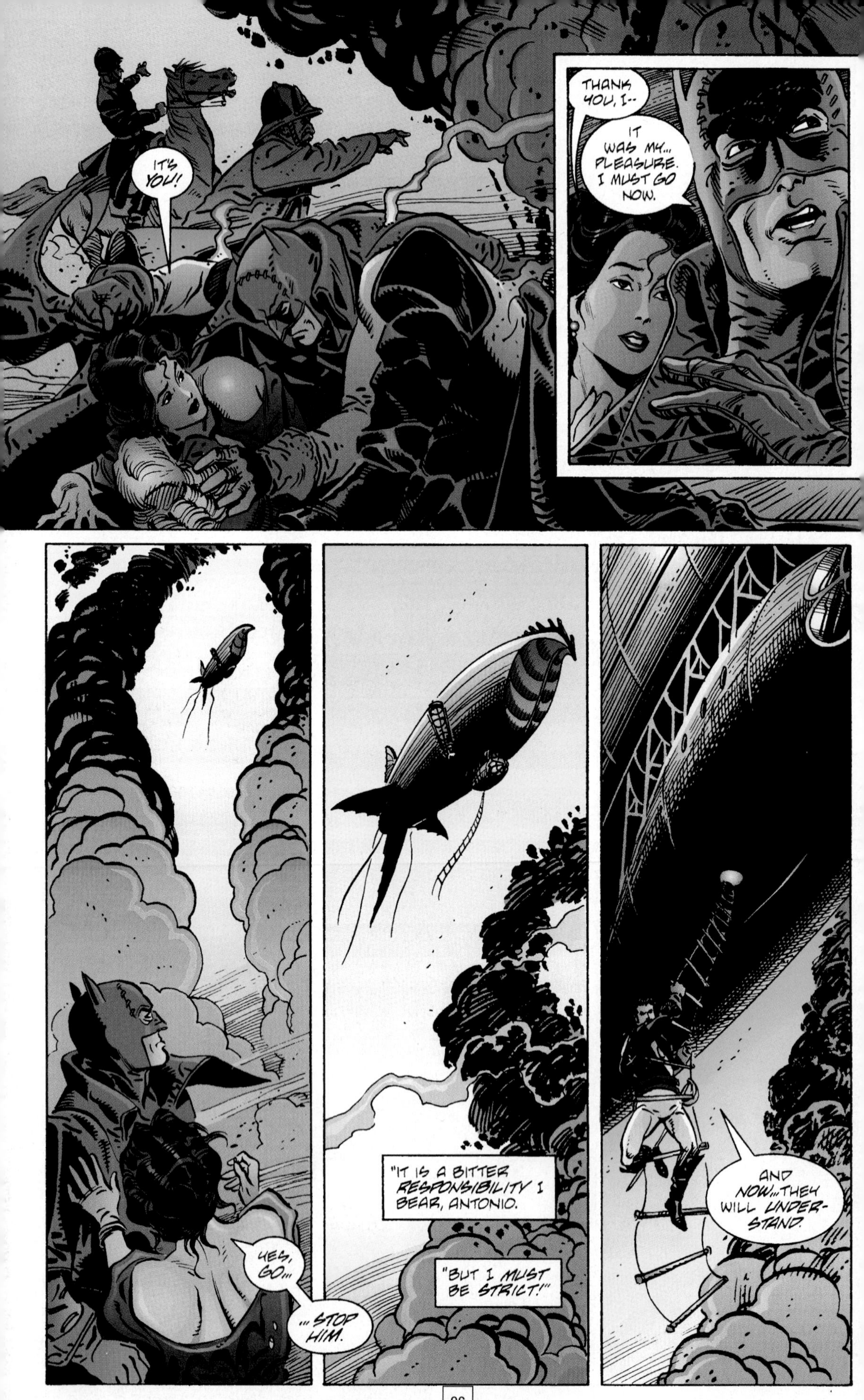
IT'S YOU!
THANK YOU, I--
IT WAS MY... PLEASURE. I MUST GO NOW.
YES, GO...
...STOP HIM.
"IT IS A BITTER RESPONSIBILITY I BEAR, ANTONIO.
"BUT I MUST BE STRICT!"
AND NOW...THEY WILL UNDERSTAND.

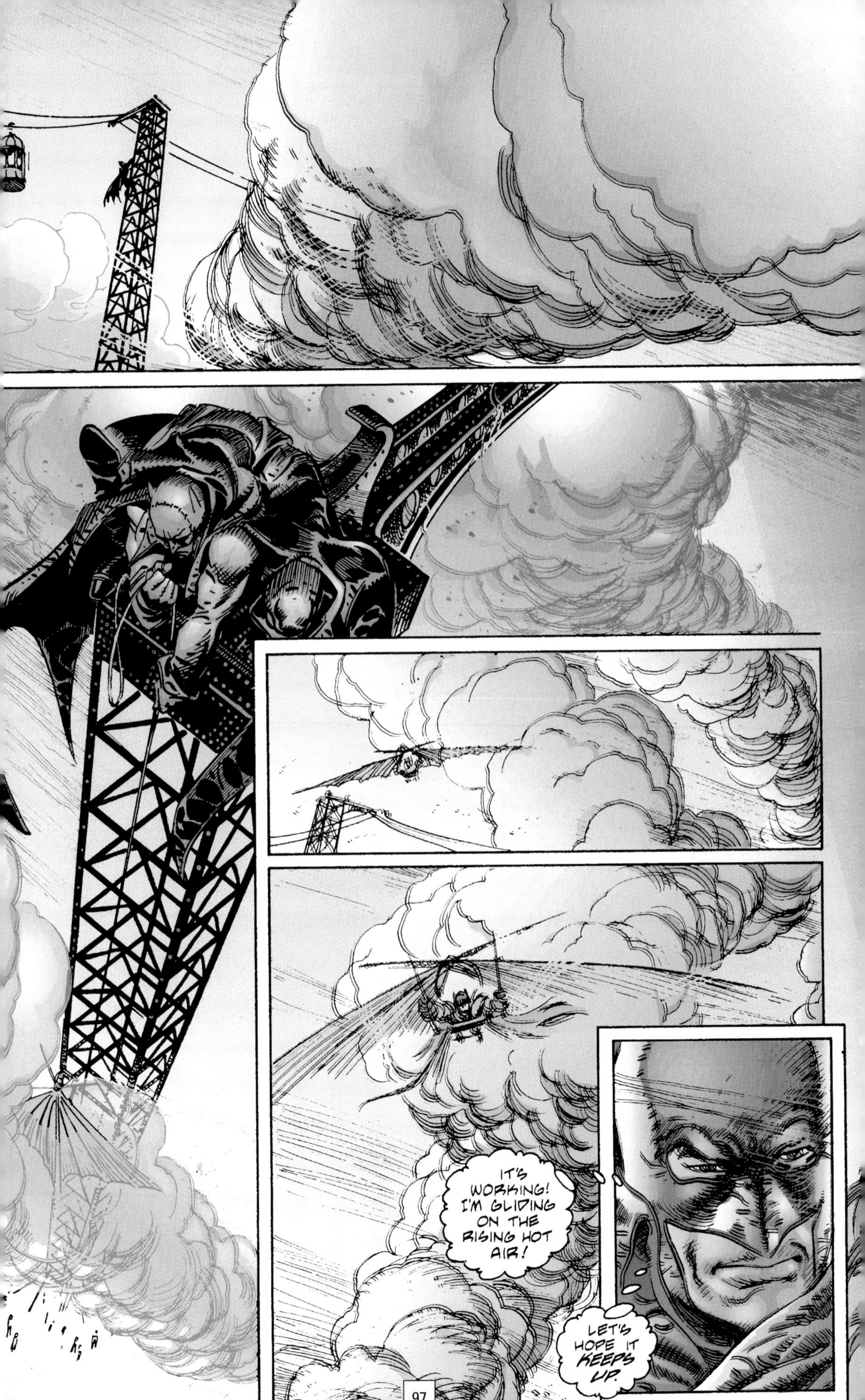

IT'S WORKING! I'M GLIDING ON THE RISING HOT AIR!
LET'S HOPE IT KEEPS UP.

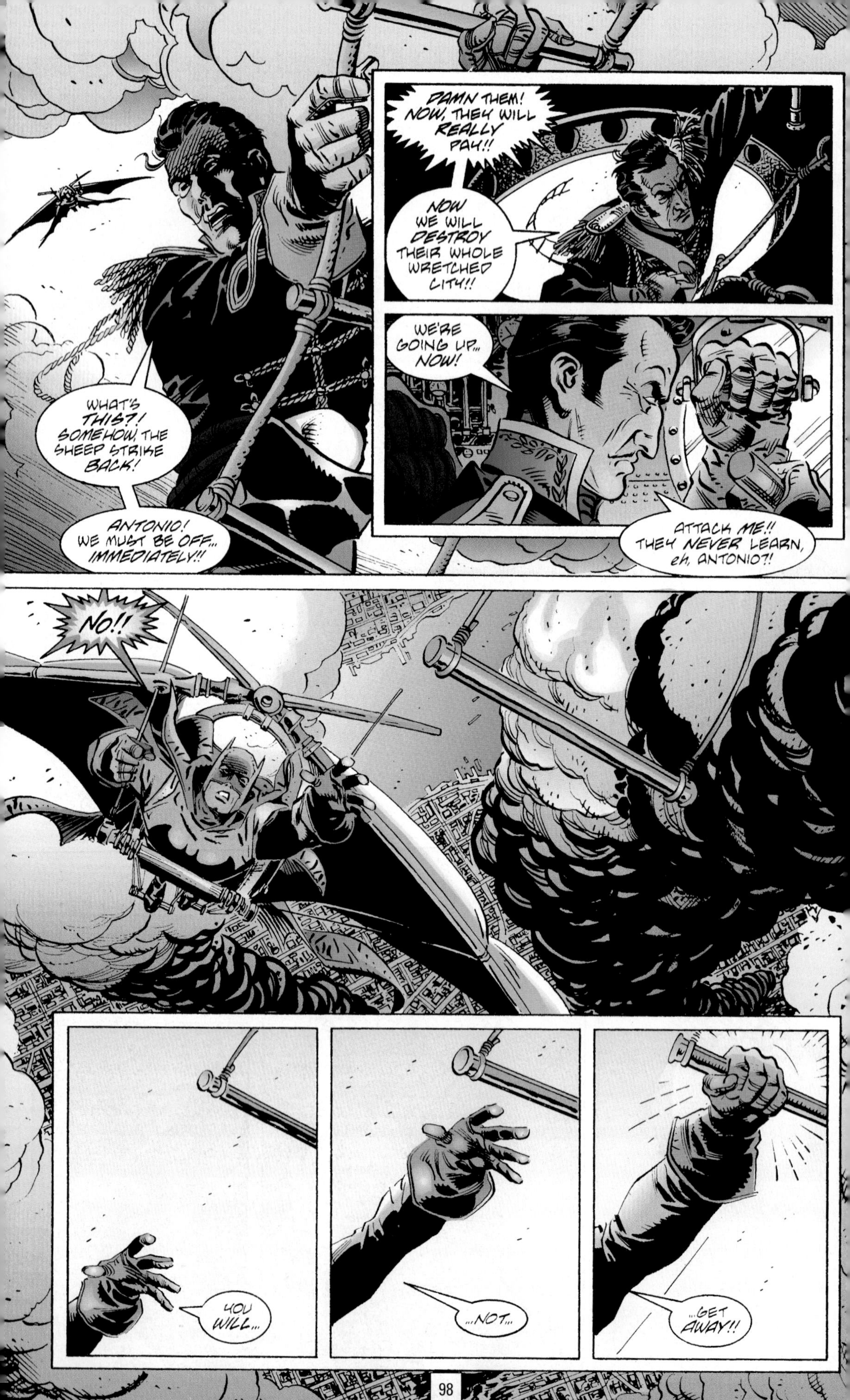
DAMN THEM! NOW, THEY WILL REALLY PAY!!
NOW WE WILL DESTROY THEIR WHOLE WRETCHED CITY!!
WHAT'S THIS?! SOMEHOW, THE SHEEP STRIKE BACK!
ANTONIO! WE MUST BE OFF... IMMEDIATELY!!
WE'RE GOING UP... NOW!
ATTACK ME!! THEY NEVER LEARN, eh, ANTONIO?!
NO!!
YOU WILL...
...NOT...
...GET AWAY!!

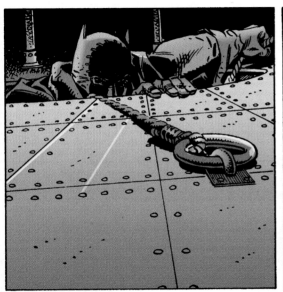

WHATEVER IT WAS, IT *MISSED*.

NO...

...WHAT... HOW?!

IT *ENDS* NOW, MANIAC! AND YOU WILL PAY FOR YOUR CRIMES!!

WH... WHO ARE YOU TO COMMAND ME?

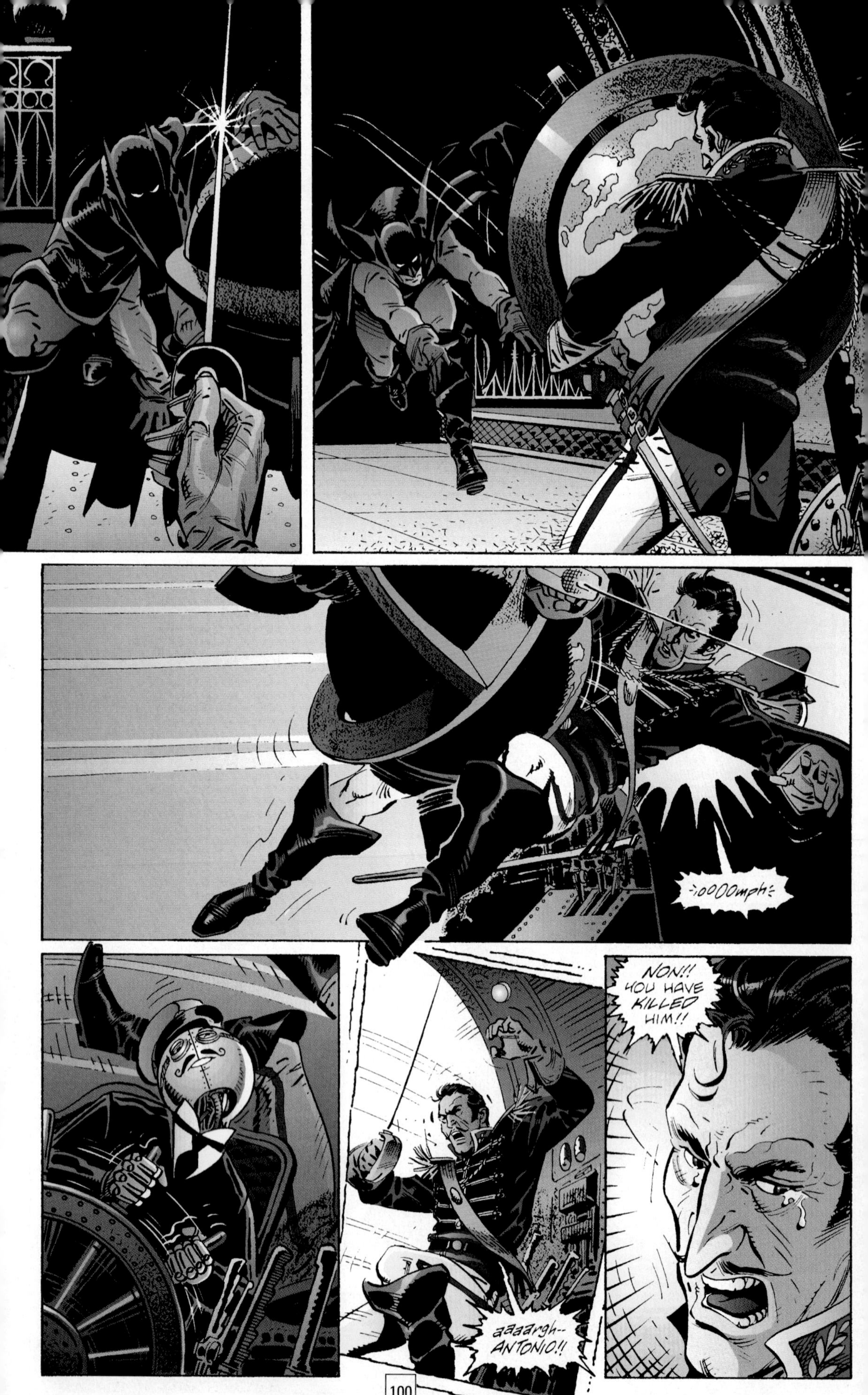
-:00000mph:-
aaaargh--
ANTONIO!!
NON!!
YOU HAVE
KILLED
HIM!!

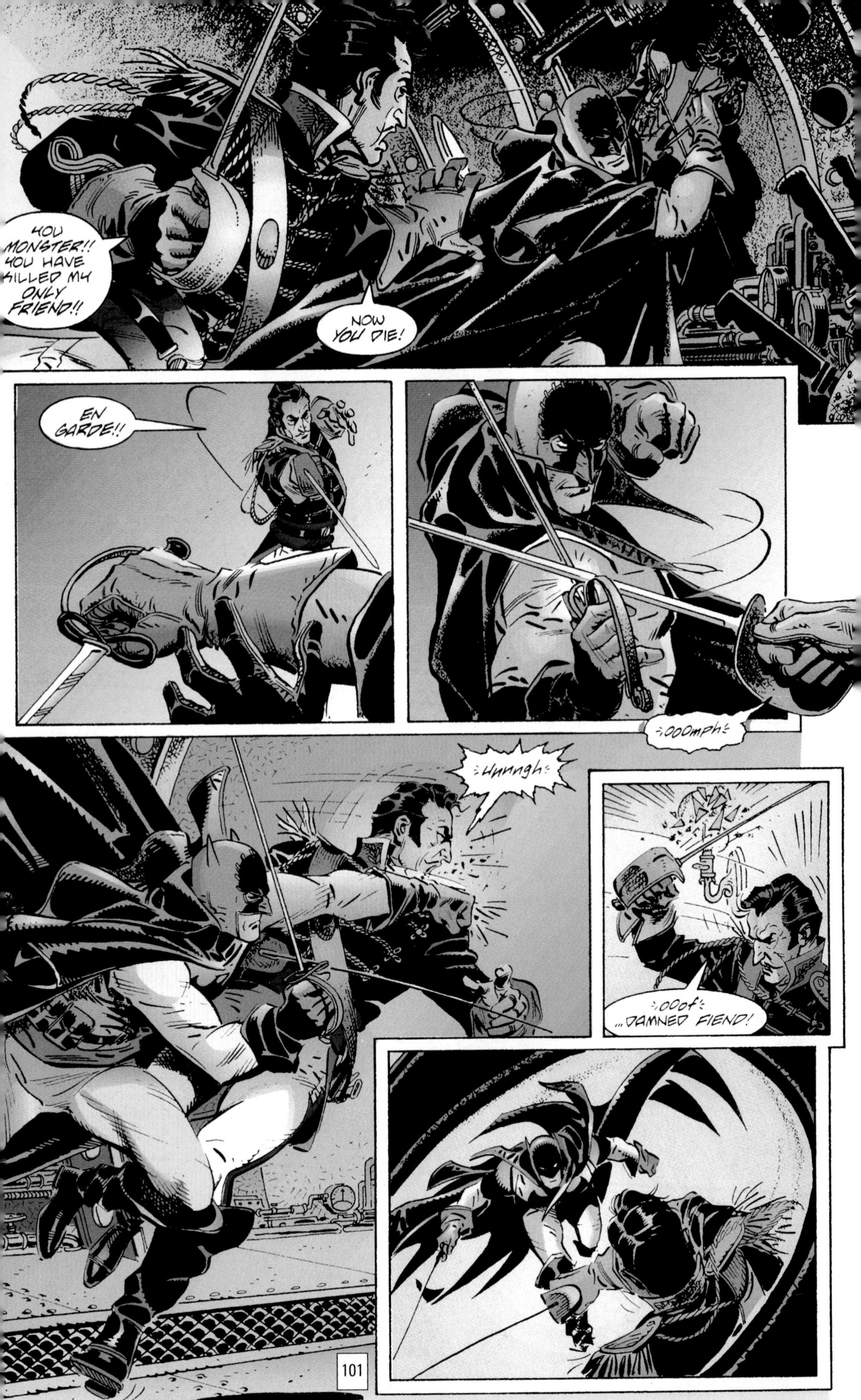
YOU MONSTER!! YOU HAVE KILLED MY ONLY FRIEND!!
NOW YOU DIE!
EN GARDE!!
OOOmph
Unnngh
OOOf ...DAMNED FIEND!

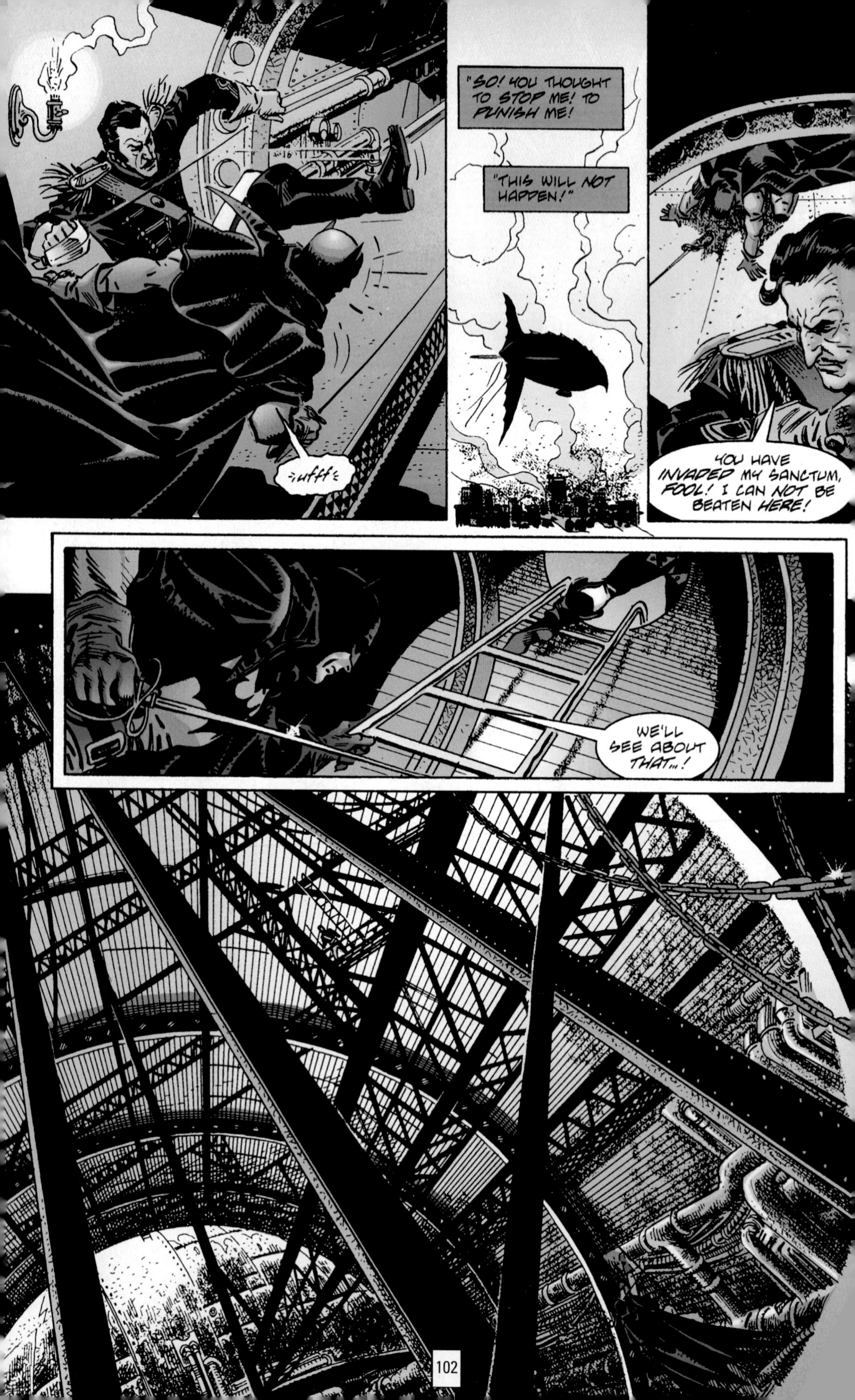

:uffff:
"SO! YOU THOUGHT TO STOP ME! TO PUNISH ME!
"THIS WILL NOT HAPPEN!"
YOU HAVE INVADED MY SANCTUM, FOOL! I CAN NOT BE BEATEN HERE!
WE'LL SEE ABOUT THAT...!

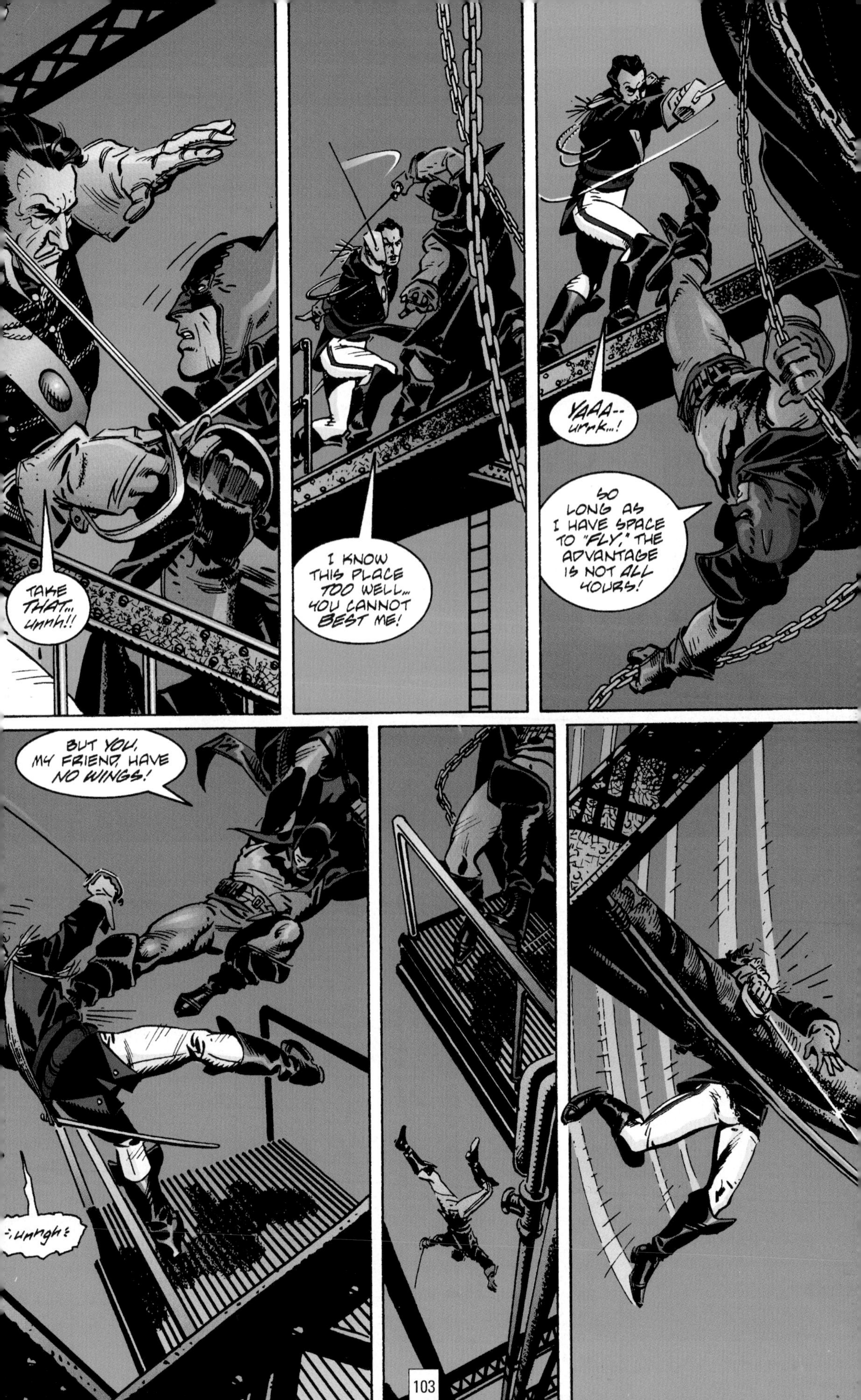
TAKE THAT... unnh!!
I KNOW THIS PLACE TOO WELL... YOU CANNOT BEST ME!
YAAA-- urrk...!
SO LONG AS I HAVE SPACE TO "FLY," THE ADVANTAGE IS NOT ALL YOURS!
BUT YOU, MY FRIEND, HAVE NO WINGS!
unngh

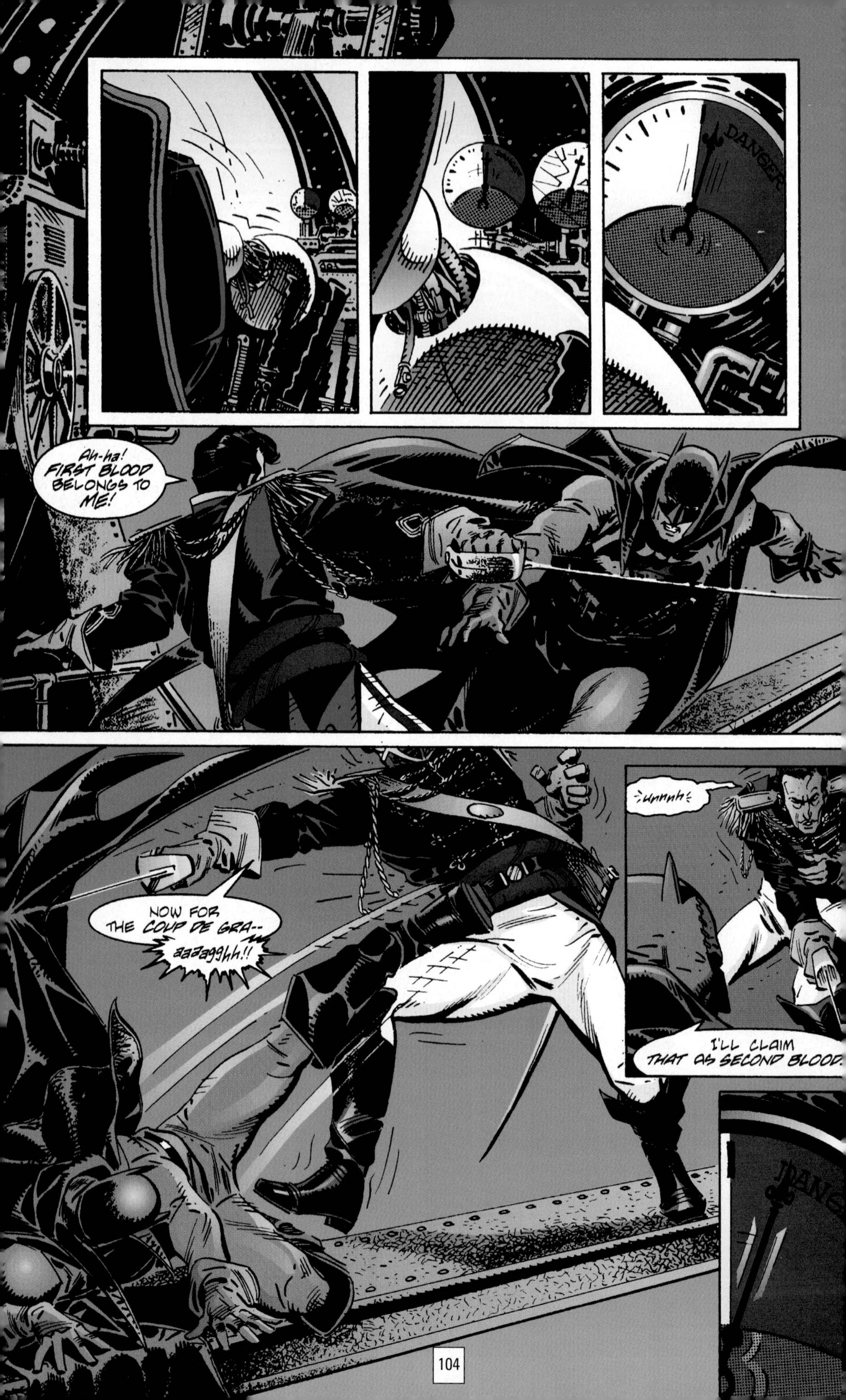

DANGER
DANGER
Ah-ha! FIRST BLOOD BELONGS TO ME!
NOW FOR THE COUP DE GRA--
aaaagghh!!
unnnh
I'LL CLAIM THAT AS SECOND BLOOD.

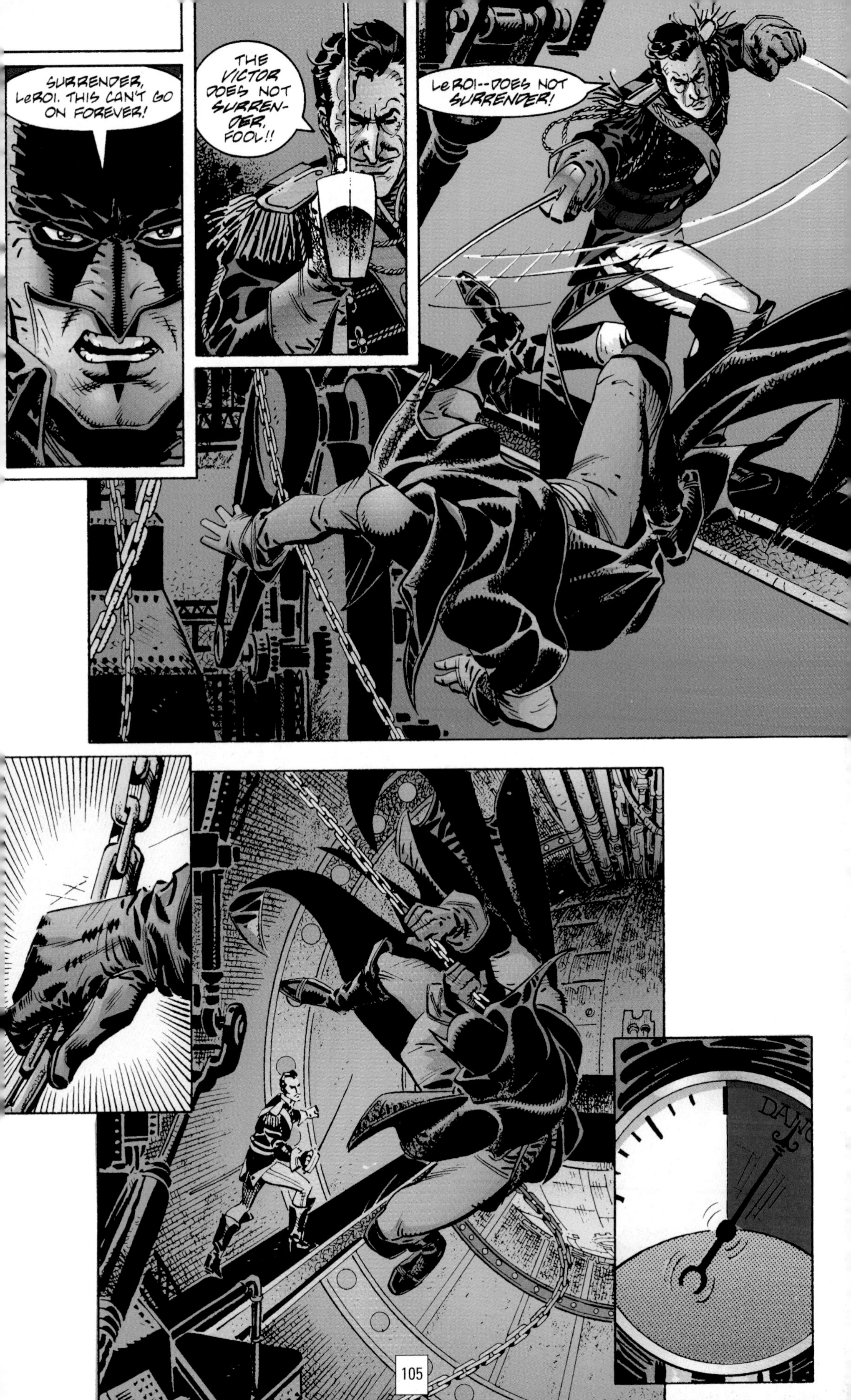
SURRENDER, LeROI. THIS CAN'T GO ON FOREVER!
THE VICTOR DOES NOT SURRENDER, FOOL!!
LeROI--DOES NOT SURRENDER!

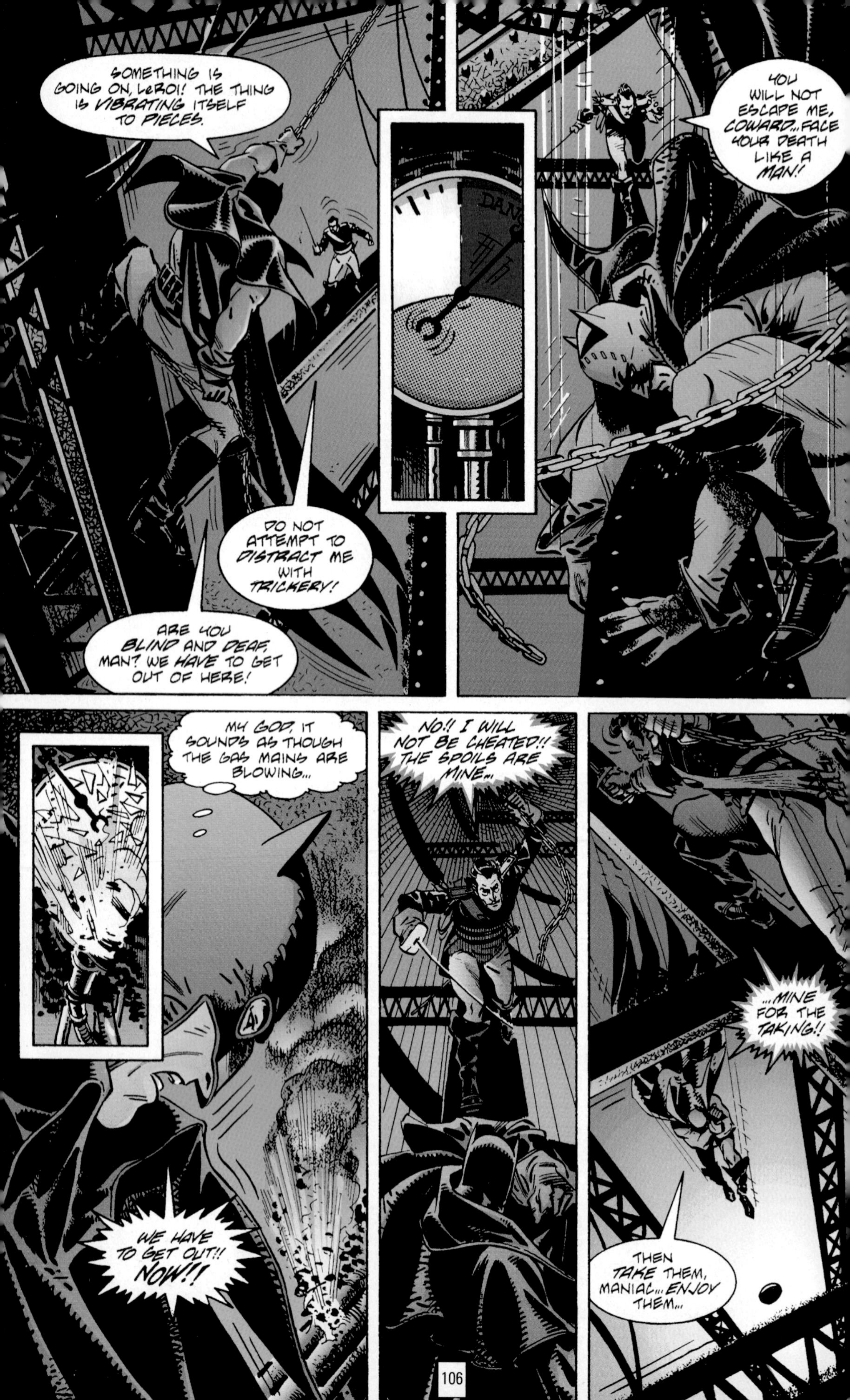
SOMETHING IS GOING ON, LeROI! THE THING IS VIBRATING ITSELF TO PIECES.
DANG
YOU WILL NOT ESCAPE ME, COWARD... FACE YOUR DEATH LIKE A MAN!
DO NOT ATTEMPT TO DISTRACT ME WITH TRICKERY!
ARE YOU BLIND AND DEAF, MAN? WE HAVE TO GET OUT OF HERE!
MY GOD, IT SOUNDS AS THOUGH THE GAS MAINS ARE BLOWING...
WE HAVE TO GET OUT!! NOW!!
NO!! I WILL NOT BE CHEATED!! THE SPOILS ARE MINE...
...MINE FOR THE TAKING!!
THEN TAKE THEM, MANIAC... ENJOY THEM...

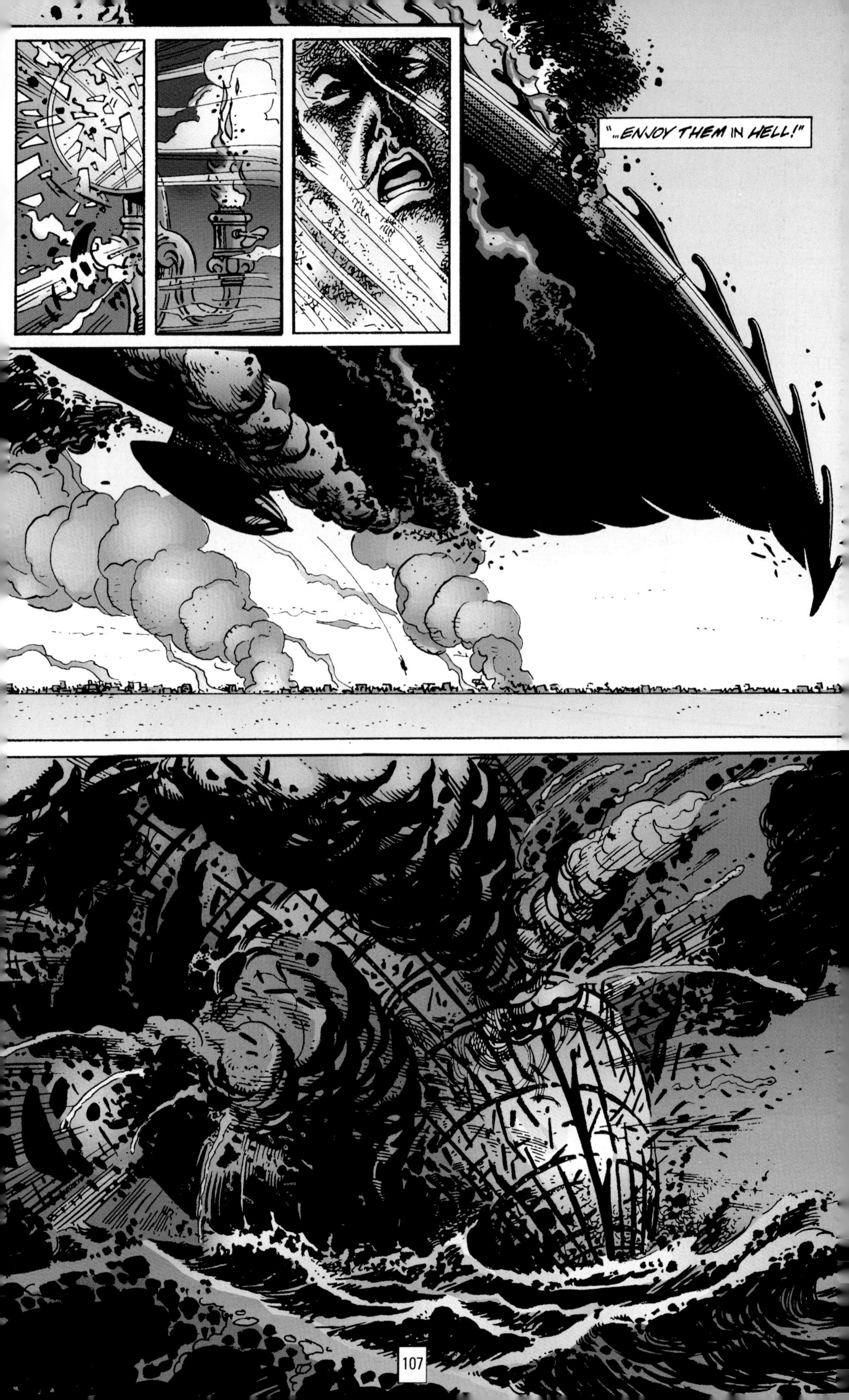
"...ENJOY THEM IN HELL!"

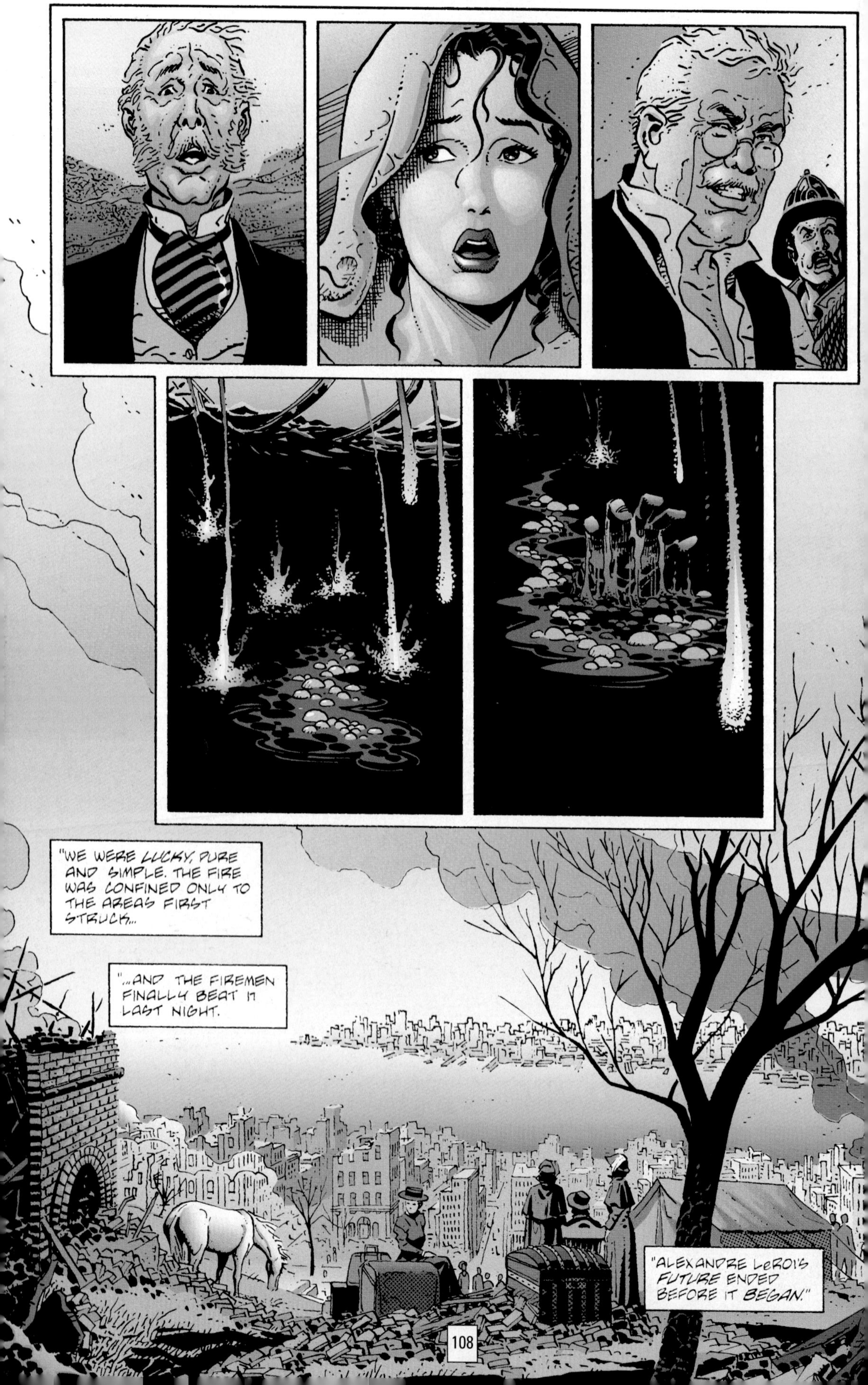
"WE WERE LUCKY, PURE AND SIMPLE. THE FIRE WAS CONFINED ONLY TO THE AREAS FIRST STRUCK...
"...AND THE FIREMEN FINALLY BEAT IT LAST NIGHT.
"ALEXANDRE LeROI'S FUTURE ENDED BEFORE IT BEGAN."

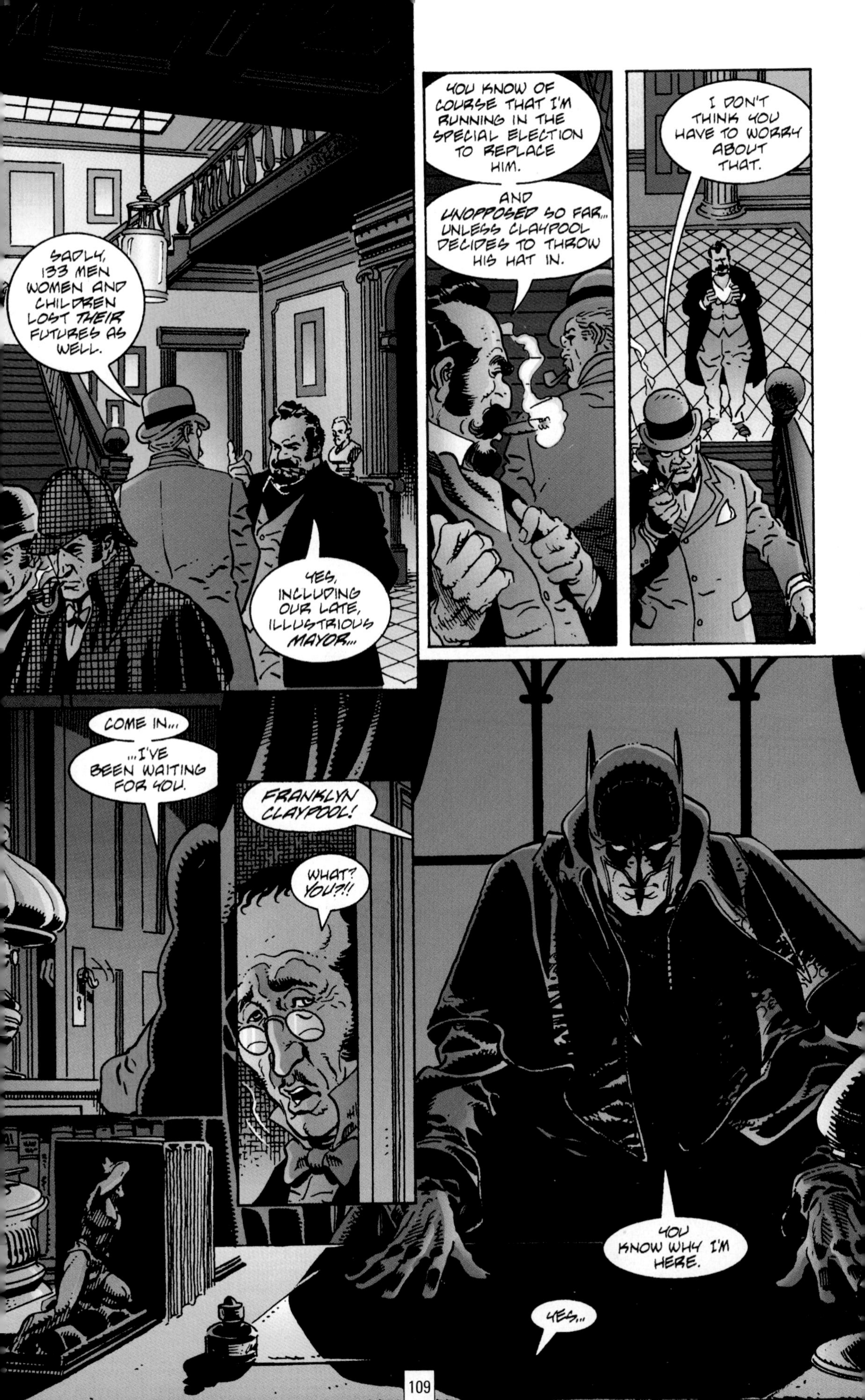
SADLY, 133 MEN WOMEN AND CHILDREN LOST THEIR FUTURES AS WELL.
YES, INCLUDING OUR LATE, ILLUSTRIOUS MAYOR...
YOU KNOW OF COURSE THAT I'M RUNNING IN THE SPECIAL ELECTION TO REPLACE HIM.
AND UNOPPOSED SO FAR... UNLESS CLAYPOOL DECIDES TO THROW HIS HAT IN.
I DON'T THINK YOU HAVE TO WORRY ABOUT THAT.
COME IN...
...I'VE BEEN WAITING FOR YOU.
FRANKLYN CLAYPOOL!
WHAT? YOU?!!
YOU KNOW WHY I'M HERE.
YES...

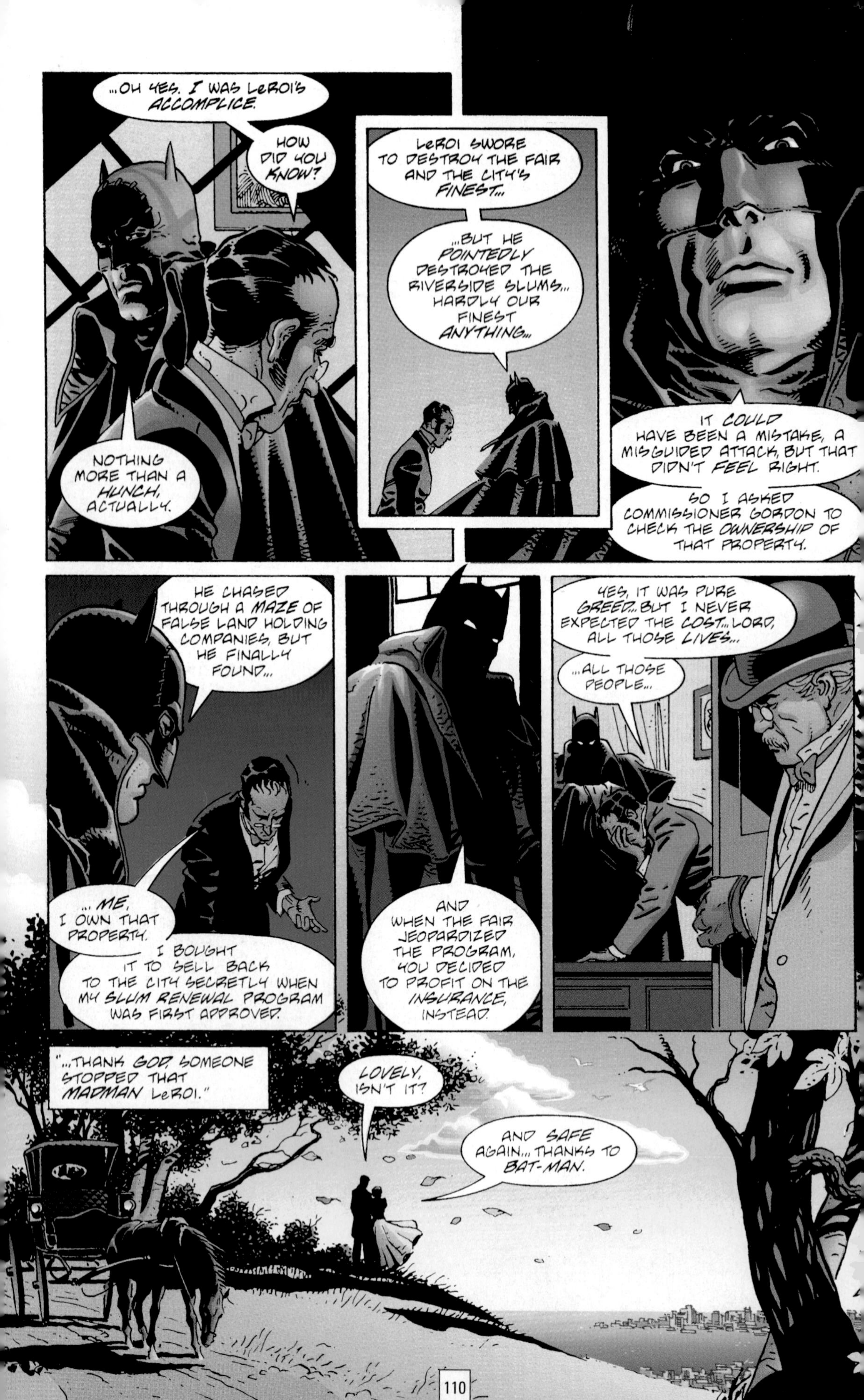
...OH YES. I WAS LeROI'S ACCOMPLICE.
HOW DID YOU KNOW?
NOTHING MORE THAN A HUNCH, ACTUALLY.
LeROI SWORE TO DESTROY THE FAIR AND THE CITY'S FINEST...
...BUT HE POINTEDLY DESTROYED THE RIVERSIDE SLUMS... HARDLY OUR FINEST ANYTHING...
IT COULD HAVE BEEN A MISTAKE, A MISGUIDED ATTACK, BUT THAT DIDN'T FEEL RIGHT.
SO I ASKED COMMISSIONER GORDON TO CHECK THE OWNERSHIP OF THAT PROPERTY.
HE CHASED THROUGH A MAZE OF FALSE LAND HOLDING COMPANIES, BUT HE FINALLY FOUND...
...ME, I OWN THAT PROPERTY.
I BOUGHT IT TO SELL BACK TO THE CITY SECRETLY WHEN MY SLUM RENEWAL PROGRAM WAS FIRST APPROVED.
AND WHEN THE FAIR JEOPARDIZED THE PROGRAM, YOU DECIDED TO PROFIT ON THE INSURANCE, INSTEAD.
YES, IT WAS PURE GREED... BUT I NEVER EXPECTED THE COST... LORD, ALL THOSE LIVES...
...ALL THOSE PEOPLE...
"...THANK GOD SOMEONE STOPPED THAT MADMAN LeROI."
LOVELY, ISN'T IT?
AND SAFE AGAIN... THANKS TO BAT-MAN.

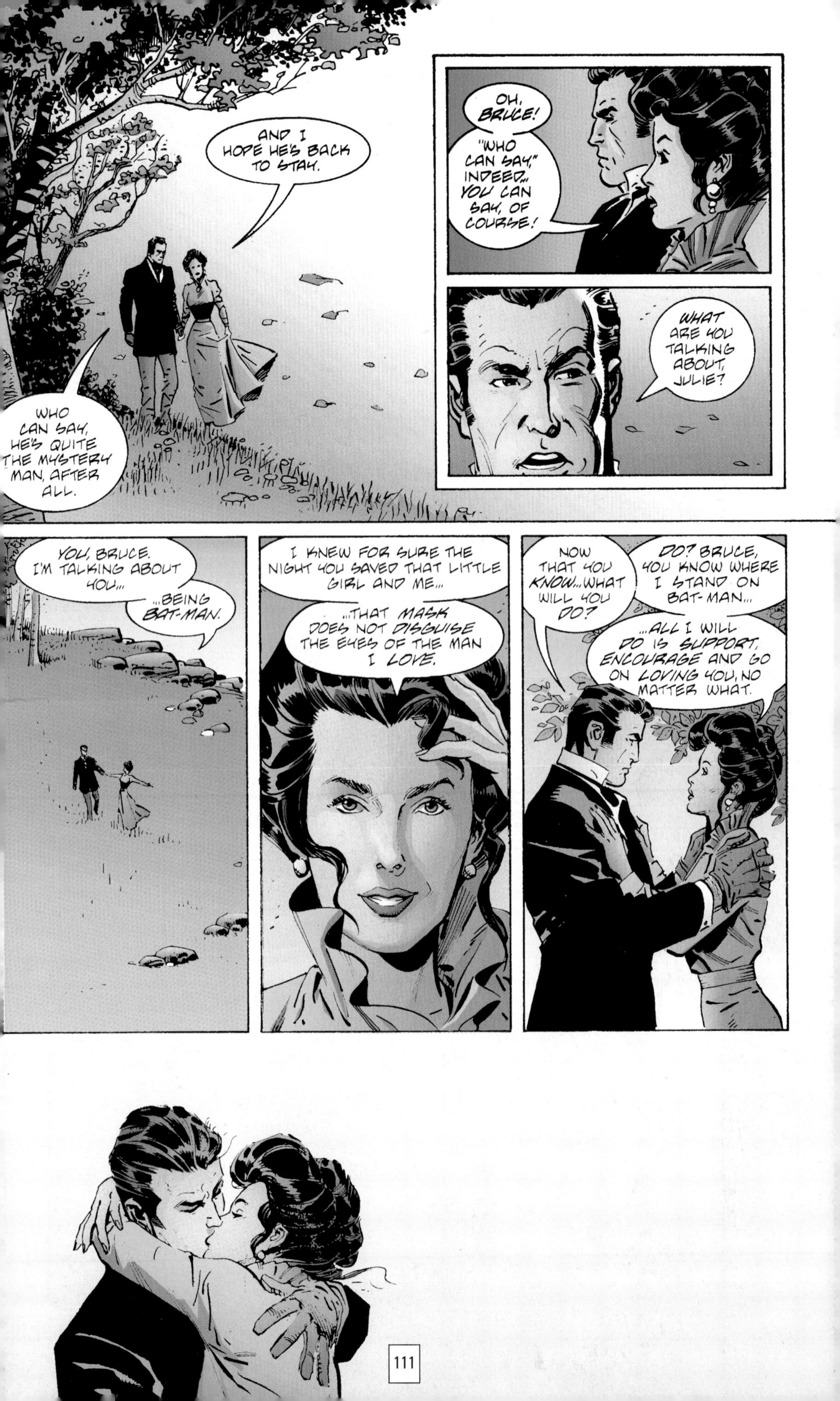
AND I HOPE HE'S BACK TO STAY.
WHO CAN SAY, HE'S QUITE THE MYSTERY MAN, AFTER ALL.
OH, BRUCE!
"WHO CAN SAY," INDEED... YOU CAN SAY, OF COURSE!
WHAT ARE YOU TALKING ABOUT, JULIE?
YOU, BRUCE. I'M TALKING ABOUT YOU...
...BEING BAT-MAN.
I KNEW FOR SURE THE NIGHT YOU SAVED THAT LITTLE GIRL AND ME...
...THAT MASK DOES NOT DISGUISE THE EYES OF THE MAN I LOVE.
NOW THAT YOU KNOW... WHAT WILL YOU DO?
DO? BRUCE, YOU KNOW WHERE I STAND ON BAT-MAN...
...ALL I WILL DO IS SUPPORT, ENCOURAGE AND GO ON LOVING YOU, NO MATTER WHAT.

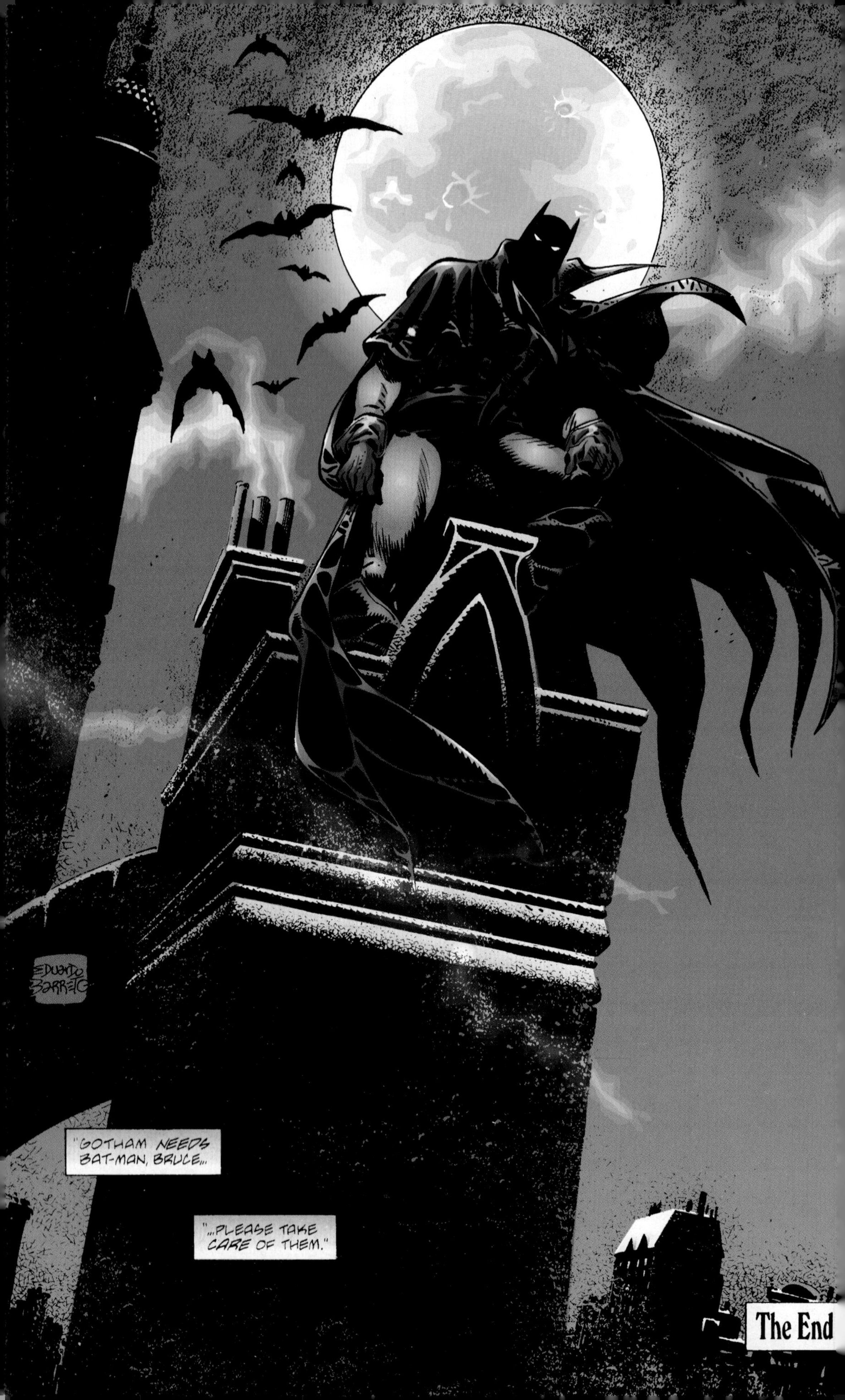
EDUARDO BARRETO
"GOTHAM NEEDS BAT-MAN, BRUCE...
"...PLEASE TAKE CARE OF THEM."
The End